With a decorated journalist's eye, John S. Dickerson has given us not only a realist's analysis of the Post-Truth culture, but also an idealist's sense of hope. Christians who want a sober understanding of the times in which we live and practical ways that will positively impact the culture will get much out of *Hope of Nations*.

ABDU MURRAY, North American director of Ravi Zacharias International Ministries and author of *Saving Truth: Finding Meaning and Clarity in a Post-Truth World*

In my own lifetime, the values of the world have flipped upside down. We have landed not in a wonderland, but in a world of Post-Truth. *Hope of Nations* traces the result and what it means for the church. John S. Dickerson does not stop there, but examines how the church should face this new reality, as hard as it will be. Read this book, and you will be equipped to stand strong, not fearing this new reality but able to face it with a wisdom that comes from what Scripture says about living well in a difficult world.

DR. DARRELL BOCK, *New York Times* bestselling author, Humboldt Scholar, and senior research professor of New Testament studies, Dallas Theological Seminary

John S. Dickerson is forthright about the challenges we are soon to face in a Post-Truth world, but he doesn't simply predict doom and gloom. In *Hope of Nations*, John communicates a practical and powerful path for Christians to be Jesus to our lost world. This is a critical book for every thoughtful Christian.

DR. JULI SLATTERY, cofounder of Authentic Intimacy and author of *Rethinking Sexuality*

John S. Dickerson points to the ultimate solution for today's cultural crisis—the crucified Christ. He correctly concludes that our Christian response to a changing culture should be a return to the teachings of Jesus: to love our enemies, to pray for those who persecute us, to feed the poor and care for the widows, to live knowing that every earthly kingdom will fall, but there is one Kingdom that will never be shaken.

    CAL THOMAS, *USA Today* and nationally syndicated columnist, TV commentator, and author of *What Works*

The foundations are failing beneath us. Much too quickly, Western civilization will find itself frantically looking for a lifeboat as it sinks into a moral and ethical cesspool bearing no similarity to its regal past. Fortunately, there are a few watchmen still seeking to point the way to a profitable and God-honoring future. John S. Dickerson has done it again with *Hope of Nations*. This should be required reading for any follower of Jesus who yearns for our society to escape a nihilistic demise and regain hope.

    J. PAUL NYQUIST, PhD, former president, Moody Bible Institute, and author of *Prepare: Living Your Faith in an Increasingly Hostile Culture*

John S. Dickerson's journalistic research ability and gentle shepherd's heart will take you on an extraordinary journey.

    LINDA PENN, host of Today's Living Hope

I am a believer in John S. Dickerson's ability to hold readers in his thrall, to tell simple, uplifting human stories, to share his eloquent hopes.

    KEN AULETTA, *New Yorker* media critic, bestselling author, and Pulitzer Prize judge

Few writers can gather, process, distill, and apply a host of facts with the precision of John S. Dickerson.

    JOHN MCCANDLISH PHILLIPS, the late *New York Times* star reporter

HOPE

— OF —

NATIONS

HOPE

— OF —

NATIONS

Standing Strong in a Post-Truth,
Post-Christian World

JOHN S. DICKERSON

ZONDERVAN®

ZONDERVAN

Hope of Nations
Copyright © 2018 by John S. Dickerson

Requests for information should be addressed to:
Zondervan, *3900 Sparks Dr. SE, Grand Rapids, Michigan 49546*

ISBN 978-0-310-34193-2 (softcover)

ISBN 978-0-310-35540-3 (audio)

ISBN 978-0-310-34194-9 (ebook)

The author is represented by Ambassador Literary Agency, Nashville, TN.

Cover design: Rob Monacelli | RAM Creative
Cover photo: Pexels
Interior design: Kait Lamphere

First printing April 2018 / Printed in the United States of America

A scared world needs a fearless church.

A. W. TOZER

CONTENTS

PART 3:
HOW WILL WE LIVE?

Introduction

UNDERSTANDING OUR NEW REALITY

When did it become normal and routine for us to daily expect news of another terror attack, shooting, or act of evil?

We are pummeled each day with news of bloody terror attacks, social rioting, deep political hatred, missile launches, global unrest, and moral blindness here at home. Worse than the happenings themselves is the response from many of our neighbors and leaders. Where there was once a civilized pursuit of truth and social cohesion, there is now hatred, division, dishonesty, and destruction.

In the static noise of these cycling conflicts, we sense that we are losing something foundational—an entire way of life. We sense that the world our children and grandchildren inherit may be unrecognizable from the life of peace, stability, freedom, and prosperity that we once knew in America and the West.

The great cataclysm of this era is not merely a catastrophe of disconnected events, but fully the collapse of a culture, a society, a civilization. In moments of perspective, we suspect we're not living through typical shifts in a stable society. No, it seems the tectonic plates are rupturing deep beneath our civilization.

This book explains—definitively, simply, and accurately—just what is happening in our world, our nation, and our society. This book enables you to see where these events are leading and why they are happening. This book combines the research of a decorated journalist with the Bible teaching and guidance of a pastor and bestselling author.

On this eye-opening journey, we will combine cultural reporting, surprising new data, global understanding, Scripture, and history to answer the four pressing questions of our day:

- What in the world is happening?
- Why are these things happening?
- Where will all of this lead?
- And, most importantly, how do we live like Christians now?

As the nations shake in fear, we will gain sure footing by rooting ourselves in Scripture and in timeless truth. So many of our neighbors are confused and increasingly in a panic. But we can know with confidence what is happening, why it's happening, and where it will lead. Ultimately, we can be people who stand strong because our lives are built upon the Hope of Nations.

More than ever, our divided society needs people who model true love, true courage, and true leadership. This book equips you to be such a person.

With an understanding of the times, we can be people of stability. Built on the unshakable Hope of Nations, we can be together a people of stability. We can lead families of stability, churches of stability, and organizations of stability—even within a shaking world.

We can be God's anchored people, full of understanding, compassion, faith, hope, and resolve. We can be the people who shine bright the Light of the world and who declare the Hope of Nations.

In chapter 3, we will examine some unsettling stories and trends that reveal the emerging culture of the United States. One of these stories involves an outdoor "bondage" sex festival on the streets of an American city. The Folsom Street Fair includes naked adults in leather bondage gear, masturbation in public, and outdoor sexual "play places" that emphasize bondage, whips, and chains. All of this happens in broad daylight on the streets of a major American city.

But the real point of the story is that children have frequently been visitors to this annual event. I spoke with a Christian law enforcement officer who has worked security at the event, and he mentioned that he sees multiple minors there every year.

One news report documents a father who brought his two-year-old daughter to the sex festival dressed in leather bondage gear.

When the dad was asked by a newspaper reporter if it was wrong to bring his daughter to such an event, the dad answered, "Every parent has to decide for themselves what is right for them. And I respect that. And we decided that this is right for our children."[1]

Exposing a child to acts of sex would rightly be prosecuted as sexual abuse in many states, but at the Folsom Street Fair in California, it has instead been celebrated.

I mention this disturbing story here in the introduction for one purpose. When you read the term *Post-Truth* in this book, you may be tempted to brush it off as an academic term that doesn't really matter. But a dad dressing his daughter in bondage gear and bringing her to witness enacted sexual abuse is one tangible example of where "Post-Truth" thinking actually leads a culture, its people, and its youth. When a culture has no truth standard, then every family is free to define its own morality.

As we will see in the pages of this book, the Post-Truth shift of American culture is underway, and this shift will bring with it tangible and difficult consequences for our neighbors, our children, and our grandchildren.

Every year the experts at Oxford Dictionaries pick a word of the year. Recently, they chose *Post-Truth* as the single word that best summarizes American and European culture now.[2] They noted that our society now defines truth by *feelings* rather than by *facts*. Western society was once founded on truth, but it has now moved beyond it.

With its "Post-Truth" declaration, the team at Oxford planted a flag, a mile marker between two eras in world history. And it is this shift—from one era of history to another—that underlies the global and social unrest we now see.

In the United States and the West, the previous era was defined by the constant pursuit of truth. That era was an uneven but upward climb toward truth.[3] It lasted more than one thousand years, from the founding of Oxford University and the other early Christian universities until very recently.[4]

Within that era, the pursuit of truth was the light that guided Western scientists, innovators, educators, inventors, and lawmakers to constantly improve the human condition in Europe, the United States, and then the rest of the world. These people were imperfect, but their pursuit of a higher truth beyond themselves produced contributions far beyond their own capacities.

Christian-based Western contributions (the following is a fact, not an opinion) have doubled human life expectancy, created widespread literacy, eradicated open slavery (which had been a global norm previously), and birthed the most prosperous era of human history, thanks to Western democracy, modern medicine, the scientific revolution, and mechanizations that have lifted humanity from darkness to light.

These world-changing innovations sprouted exclusively from one small, focused region of the globe at one focused time in history—Christianized Europe and the nations that exported its Christianized civilization to other parts of the earth, including the United States.

In our lifetime, we have likely witnessed the peak of this Western-Christianized civilization. It is a vast and complex network, and

Western civilization will not collapse overnight. But this much is clear: Western society is now willfully descending back down the mountain of truth—moving willfully away from the very pursuit that produced its wealth and liberty in the first place.

Multiple studies, which we will cite in this book, demonstrate that the tipping point of a Post-Truth shift is upon us. A majority of young Westerners now view reality through a Post-Truth lens, which is creating a predominantly Post-Truth society. The Post-Truth view of reality is set to continue redefining US elections and culture for the next thirty years. It will also play a role in the dramatic reshuffling of global order as the United States recedes from influence and loses its place as the world's largest economy and most powerful military.

What lies ahead we cannot say with certainty. But if human nature plays out as it has in previous eras, then my generation (the millennial generation) will find itself surprised by the brutality and consequences of a society severed from the truth.

This Post-Truth breakage is the fault line underlying the earthquakes presently shaking America, Western Europe, and the world. From this single fault line—a Post-Truth rupture—reverberates shaking in government, media, society, culture, ideals, individuals, economies, and the very global order. We feel the tremors every day as we witness unthinkable acts of public violence and as we realize how divided the United States is becoming.

In the West, a new Post-Truth culture is rejecting the old Truth-Based beliefs. As the older Truth-Based thinkers age out of influence and die, the full shaking of this societal change may exceed what we can imagine or foresee.

Blind groupthink, moral decay, street violence, social unrest, the divisions within Western nations, the reordering of the global superpowers—each of these results from the Post-Truth shift within Western culture's deepest foundation. On a macro scale, global peace and prosperity sway like shifting Jenga-block towers atop the murmurs of this splitting fault line. **When news reports grip us in fear, those events often trace—in one way or another—back to this Post-Truth rupture deep in the tectonic plates of Western civilization.**

In this book, we will discover why Western culture has taken the Post-Truth turn. We will learn where it will likely lead. This analysis will be driven by an aggregation of the best sociological research and cultural surveys available today. It will also be informed by the history of other post-Christian nations that embraced similar post-Christian philosophies in their universities and then in their mainstream cultures. And of course, our response will be shaped by the Word of God.

We will learn the Five Forces shaping world events today and in the next thirty years.

We will prepare ourselves, our families, and our institutions to live for Christ now—and to stand strong for Christ in the social reshaping of the coming decades. With understanding from the Word of God and with empowering from the Spirit of God, we can stand strong for Christ through the coming reshuffling of global order and restructuring of American society.

HOW TO READ THIS BOOK

You will find the practical heart of this journey in part 3: "How Will We Live?" That section includes nine manifestos—positive postures to keep us standing strong while the world reshapes around us.

Each of these manifestos anchors us to an unchanging truth of Scripture specific to a cultural change in our time. These nine manifestos are Christian purpose statements that any family, organization, or individual can adopt as we determine to follow Christ now.

In parts 1 and 2, you will find the analysis, deep thinking, and cultural research of the book. Parts 1 and 2 are the "mind" of the book; part 3 is the "heart."

MY COMMITMENT TO YOU, THE READER

My prayer in these pages is to minister to your head and to your heart, to your mind and to your soul.

As a seminary-trained pastor, a nationally awarded research journalist, and a frequent commentator in news outlets like *USA Today*, it is my calling to aggregate social trends, global events, Christian theology, history, and biblical application. All of these will combine in this book, I pray, to give you new insight into world events, spiritual currents, and the national trajectories shaping the next thirty years.

Together, we will fortify our Christian foundations and our God-honoring response of faith in Christ. In a chaotic world, we will remind ourselves that we are not randomly placed. In fact, the Creator has strategically placed us here so that we can serve our role in the greatest story of justice, goodness, and triumph over evil.

On this journey, we will gain a higher understanding of the world events that continue shocking and shaking our neighbors.

We can understand the great story. We can see our role within this great story. And then, even if the mountains should fall into the sea, even if the nations are in uproar, we will be unshaken.

In this book, we will prepare ourselves to love our neighbors of every race and creed, to show them the Hope of Nations. We are preparing to live as Christians today and in the unpredictable days ahead.

I kneel before God as I write these words, and I ask Him to empower you on this journey. I ask Him to give you divine insight and wisdom, faith and courage.

The thrashing struggle between good and evil will continue in our day. Our choice is not to determine the era in which we live; our choice is to determine the side for which we will fight. And then to become fearless and courageous in joining God's good work in the struggle.

My assignment from God is to prepare you to live fearlessly. Together, we will live for Christ now. We will show and tell the Hope of Nations.

PART 1

WHAT IS HAPPENING, AND WHY?

Chapter 1

MY HOPE FOR THE NATIONS

Charles Gibson, who was the face of *ABC World News Tonight*, set his wineglass on the pressed, white tablecloth. Sophisticated, friendly, and charming, Gibson was everything you'd expect from a world-famous newsman. But he could not hide the confusion in his eyes.

"You're quitting journalism to become a pastor?" He asked me the question a second time.

We were sitting in the Yale Club in Manhattan, and Gibson was about to award me the Livingston Award for Young Journalists. Each year Gibson, Tom Brokaw, and a team of news media A-listers choose three Livingston Award recipients from among the nation's thousands of journalists.

It's a dream honor for any journalist to receive. At age twenty-six, I was among the younger recipients in the award's history. Conversations that night included many of my professional heroes at the time—Christiane Amanpour of CNN, Ken Auletta of the *New Yorker*, editors, majority owners, and powerbrokers from the *New York Times*, the *Chicago Tribune*, NPR, and others.

Seven years since that night, I admit I did not fully understand the prestige and power I was forsaking when I sidelined my journalism career to serve as a Christian pastor.

Had I realized what earthly success I was giving up, it would not have made a difference. God had hold of my heart, you see. **He had convinced me that the greatest change agent in the world is not any media network or government, but the unique and disheveled organism of Christ believers to whom God has entrusted the true Hope of Nations.**

"I'm not abandoning the pursuit of truth," I responded to Gibson. "The same tenacity for truth that drove my news reporting—that tenacity has convinced me that Jesus' message is real. His message is the most powerful force for good in history."

As I said those words, I knew I sounded like a zealot, a weirdo, a fanatic.

No matter. I believed those words to be true.

And I still do.

With all my heart, I believe that Christ's people are the greatest hope for this nation, for all the nations, and for every living, breathing person on the planet.

Sadly, we Christians do not always carry ourselves with the confidence, urgency, or dignity of ambassadors who possess such a powerful hope. We often fumble in carrying this great hope. We get defensive. We lose our perspective. We behave in ways that Christ wouldn't.

Despite those flaws, I have great hope for Christ's followers today. With God's help, when functioning at even half capacity, Christians are the most powerful force for moral good, human rights, equality, social prosperity, and cultural progress in human history.

Many of our neighbors don't know it, but it is Christians who have led the way in creating orphanages, hospitals, universities, literate societies, and women's rights for humanity. The foundation pillars and social structures on which prosperous Western civilization now stands—from democracy and the idea of racial equality to electricity and vaccines—are Christian foundations.[1] In recent decades, this undeniable fact has gone from ignored to denied, despite overwhelming evidence.

We now live during an epoch of great dimming. Fattened by the contributions of previous generations, humanity is now set on improving itself without God's help. As a result, society is getting darker, thunderously dark. Evil is spreading. Hate is reigning. The planet is groaning. Justice and peace are being redefined within once-great institutions.

My generation—the millennial generation—has inherited a complex scaffolding of wealth, prosperity, leisure, and liberty. An interdependent machinery of technology, capability, and ease has been handed down to us. And yet many in my generation do not understand how these prosperous systems were created. We do not understand how truly unique our society is within world history, nor do we understand how to maintain it.

Quite the opposite, most incoming Americans and Europeans have been trained to recoil at any whiff of "exceptionalism" or "imperialism." **We are taught, explicitly, to despise and deconstruct the foundations on which this grand society was built.**[2]

The intentional demolishing of our society's foundation pillars—now being executed by our best and brightest—is but one symptom of the Post-Truth shift. It may take decades to notice the consequences in our refrigerator shelves and living rooms, but we are already beginning to see the consequences in the big cogs of society—national government, media, academia, and popular culture. The *Titanic* did not sink in five minutes, and it will take many years to deconstruct the progress accumulated during the more than four hundred years of Protestant work ethic in the West.

It will take some time to disassemble the gearwork. But what is clear is that the deconstruction has been underway for some time. And it continues today.

Already we're seeing early ramifications of a society that rejects absolute truth. Take, for example, the Post-Truth approach to news and "fake news." **On this point, my most liberal journalist friends and my most conservative Christian friends suddenly agree:**

when it comes to elections—choosing leaders—Post-Truth is not good for American society.

But here is where many fail to connect the dots. **A Post-Truth society is the only logical end of a post-*Christian* society.** Post-Truth is the only possible next step for a culture that once founded itself on Christian truths and ideals but now abhors Christian truth to the extent that it will deny Christianity's role in its history.

New York Times columnist Nicholas Kristof accurately described the anti-Christian sentiment overtaking US culture shapers today, when he wrote, "Today, among urban Americans and Europeans, 'evangelical Christian' is sometimes a synonym for 'rube.' In liberal circles, evangelicals constitute one of the few groups that it's safe to mock openly."[3]

That same disdain that Kristof politely described can be seen more aggressively in other leading edges of American culture—from mainstream news media to entertainment, film, Silicon Valley, Washington, and academia. In less sanitized terms, actress Megan Fox demonstrated this cultural animosity toward Christians in America today. Asked how she would keep an evil robot from destroying the entire world, Fox replied, "I'd barter with him and say, 'Instead of the entire planet, can you just take out all of the white trash, hillbilly, anti-gay, super Bible-beating people in Middle America?'"[4] Fox summarized well the cultural mood as it relates to Christians, especially Bible-believing ones. Her sentiment can be found at every leading edge of American culture today.

University of North Texas sociology professor George Yancey cited Fox's quote when he documented nationwide anti-Christian bias in the United States. In 2015, he released a groundbreaking report in which he used empirical sociological methods to measure what he calls "Christianophobia" in the United States.[5]

Yancey tells the true story of an American high school classroom. When the teacher of the class mentioned that Christians around the world were being killed for their faith, a number of students responded that this was good and that Christians deserved it because they have so frequently been oppressors and slave owners. "To his [the teacher's] amazement, some students approved of these murders. In their minds, it was time for Christians to face the same death that Christians had inflicted on others."[6]

While a majority of Americans surely do not wish death on Christians, Yancey found that an emerging and significant percentage of Americans do believe Christians in the US deserve punishment for their past evils.[7]

Separately, a 2007 survey of American college professors, conducted by a different sociologist, found that more than half of college professors express openly "negative feelings" for evangelical Christians.[8]

In yet another separate study, a significant number of college professors overtly stated they would discriminate against Christian job applicants and not hire a Christian to work in their department.[9] These prevailing student and campus moods are symbolic of the social mood in the new and emerging American culture.

America's post-Christian turn is quickly graduating from apathy about Christians to antagonism toward Christians (at least those Christians who treat the Bible as a serious truth standard). What is lost on many secular observers is that the post-Christian turn inevitably brings with it the Post-Truth turn, because the Truth-Based foundations of this society were intertwined with Christian beliefs.

Anti-Christian indoctrination at the highest levels of culture (the most influential universities) is one cause for the Post-Truth tipping point in this formerly Christianized culture. **We are now beginning to taste a culture in which a majority of influencers have been taught to reject, mock, or disdain the Christian Bible, the Ten Commandments, and the Christ who claims to be the Way, the *Truth*, and the Life.**

Many who mock Christianity today are ignorant of the reality that the institutions, customs, values, and wealth they inherit are, ironically, the fruits of a once-Christianized society. Few of these crit-ics realize that they are literate and educated because of schools, laws, and norms instituted by Christians. They are alive and breathing because of scientific and medical breakthroughs initiated by Chris-tians and Christian-founded institutions such as Harvard, Yale, and Johns Hopkins, but they've never been taught this.

For a while, following the 2016 presidential election, even the most anti-Christian intellectuals became concerned about a society in which a government official's "truth" is internal and subjective. But it is too late to recant sixty years of "relative truth" indoctrination at the nation's prize universities. Since then, it has become evident that the Post-Truth versus Truth-Based war of ideologies is not a Republican versus Democrat war. This is a battle within each party, within fami-lies and communities and institutions. The battle is everywhere, at every level in America and the West. **Simply put, you cannot have a post-Christian society that is not also a Post-Truth society.**

In time, the absurdities of a Post-Truth society—a society where a majority of people set their own standards for moral right and wrong, based on their own feelings and regardless of fact—will pro-duce a tangible, felt impact on American lives and families. Entire industries that we take for granted, from banking and Wall Street to law enforcement and government, will not function as we have assumed they always will, because their Truth-Based foundations are being deconstructed. **People will be confused as the machine of American and Western society stops running.**

As an illustration, consider the person who has never changed the oil on their automobile. They do not understand how an engine works or how to maintain one. They drive around, benefiting from what others built but neglecting its maintenance.

I've heard of some reliable cars continuing to run for tens of thousands of miles beyond their scheduled oil change. But eventually the oil burns out or becomes so slogged with dirt that the engine seizes. And then that car will not be driving anywhere.

In many ways, the American economy and society are so well built and engineered that they have continued operating, even as their fundamentals are neglected and deconstructed. But eventually, the machine will seize.

In the coming years, a populace that does not believe in an objective truth standard will struggle to enforce objective laws and policies. It will also struggle to write laws and policies objectively. In time, courts, neighborhoods, schools, retirement accounts, stock markets, and even grocery store shelves may be affected.

What most of us struggle to understand is how an entire way of life—a society we assume as normal—can change within a generation or two. We should know better, though, as students of the last one hundred years. Consider the immense and rapid societal shifts that overtook average life in Russia in 1917, Germany in the 1930s, China after World War II, or Venezuela just recently.

I believe American and European Christians have a window of opportunity—*right now*—to prepare ourselves. We have a closing window of time during which we can prepare our families and prepare our Christian communities for the forthcoming ramifications of life in a Post-Truth society. I believe we have a historic opportunity before us—to share the hope of Christ as society shakes.

Society may destabilize around us in a gradual, consistent fashion (as Rome's fall was—slow and steady). Or the decline may accelerate at some point into a free-fall collapse. In either scenario, we have great hope because our hope is not in earthly prosperity. Our hope is not in a politician, a party, a nation, or even a civilization. Our Hope dwells on a higher plane. Our Hope is of a higher order and a higher power. We place our Hope in the resurrected Christ, who is the Hope of Nations.

I'm convinced that lights shine brighter in the darkness than in the daylight. And now—during this great dimming—is the time for our light to shine. Americans may face darker days than present generations imagine. An entire way of life, peace, and prosperity that my millennial generation assumes as normal may deteriorate or crumble inward.

We can prepare now to shine Christ's light into this darkness. If we are properly anchored to Christ, then no calamity will unmoor us.

Jesus Christ, the Solid Rock, outlasted the fall of the Roman Empire and the violent dechristianization of France in the late 1700s. He has outlasted the Soviet Union, and He has outlasted brutal attempts to annihilate Christianity in Red China, the Middle East, and North Africa.[10] Jesus Christ has promised that we who believe will also outlast these crumbling and disposable earthly kingdoms. We will rule with Him in a kingdom that will outlast all other human empires.

And so we live out our days on this earth with purpose, knowing Jesus Christ *will* return to set right all that is broken in this world.

Jesus of Nazareth, the Messiah, *will* be exalted as King of kings and Lord of lords.

We *will* be clothed with glory and overcome with ecstasy in His presence.

We *will* inherit and manage a kingdom where justice reigns, where prejudice does not exist, where famine and poverty are no more, and where a tree of life feeds all.

We *will* walk in bodies that feel no pain.

We *will* watch the lion and the lamb lie next to each other in a culture of invincible peace, genuine diversity ("every nation, tribe, people and language"[11]), and infinite abundance. It is His kingdom, and by extension of His love, it is *our* kingdom.

And so, no matter how dark the days get here, we know how the story ends. And because of our confidence in that certain future, we do not weep, we do not grieve, as those who have no hope.[12]

For a time in this world, we may face moments when the throes of ignorance and injustice seem inescapable. We may grieve the unraveling of a stable society. Our hearts may groan at the dimming of righteousness and justice. Our emotions may droop at the injustice and brokenness of the world that our children and grandchildren will inherit. But here, even in the ruins, great hope can burst forth from our heart of faith. For ours is a *resurrection* hope. A living, breathing, muscular hope.

We have believed it, and in our lifetime we will experience it, that the One who is in us is greater than the one who is in the world.[13] The more Satan kills and steals and destroys,[14] the more he buries the nations in mental and moral darkness, all the more brightly will shine the light of Christ, who is the Hope of Nations.

God brought this book into your life to equip you to live well in these times. You can live the adventure of this era with great purpose. You can know with confidence that the Creator of the universe has appointed you, with your gifts, to bring light and life to this moment in human history. You can be secure in understanding God's reason for placing you on this continent, at *this* time, among *your* people, for eternal purposes.

In the following pages, we will explore what is happening in the world, why it is happening, and where it is leading. Most importantly, we will cast a vision for responding to frightening changes with supernatural faith.

Chapter 2

WHAT IS HAPPENING?

In her book *The Hiding Place*, Corrie ten Boom, a Nazi concentration camp survivor and Christian activist, wrote about her older brother Willem. Long before the tanks and bombs of World War II, Willem was able to foresee where German society was heading. He saw this because he understood the power of ideas.

> Willem saw things, I felt. He knew what was going on in the world.
>
> Oftentimes, indeed, I wished that Willem did not see quite so well, for much that he saw was frightening. A full ten years ago, way back in 1927, Willem had written in his doctoral thesis, done in Germany, that a terrible evil was taking root in that land. Right at the university, he said, seeds were being planted of a contempt for human life such as the world had never seen. The few who had read his paper had laughed.
>
> Now, of course, well, people weren't laughing about Germany.[1]

A few pages later, Corrie wrote, "Nobody dreamed that this tiny cloud would grow until it blocked out the sky. And nobody dreamed that in this darkness each of us would be called to play a role."[2]

———————

November 9, 1938—Having festered in the German consciousness for years, the anti-Jewish mood finally erupted into violence. Flames lit the night sky as darkness fell on that Wednesday evening. The first hours of the Kristallnacht ("Night of Crystal," also called "Night of Broken Glass") overtook Germany as a predatory lion overtakes its prey—suddenly, but after much unseen time hiding in ambush.

Previously peaceful members of German society—men, women, and children—burned more than 260 synagogues and destroyed more than 7,000 Jewish-owned businesses. Mobs of printers, architects, professors, schoolteachers, bakers, and bricklayers brutalized and murdered dozens of individual Jews.

The violence was so abrupt and abrasive that other nations assumed it could not get worse. Germany, after all, was a civilized nation. Surely this was an anomaly. A flare-up. A one-time tragedy. But the Kristallnacht was no mere flare-up. It was a violent contraction leading to the annihilation of six million Jews in Nazi-occupied territory.[3]

We must keep in mind that Germany was at that time a post-Christian nation in much the same way that the United States is presently a post-Christian nation. The German landscape was still dotted with Christian cathedrals and churches, and a majority of the population professed to be "Christian."[4] But these self-professed Christians were spiritually no more Christian than the 70 percent of Americans today who identify as "Christian." The culture had moved beyond its old Christian center. And most of its "Christian" population was not following Christ in any practical, theological, or spiritual sense. Most did not read the Bible personally or attend a church that taught biblical understanding.

Germany was post-Christian because the intellectual class had spent the previous century gutting the supernatural out of Christianity. By the early 1900s, the gutting of Christianity's core ideas and truth claims had spread through the cultural leaders and into the society as a whole.

Like so many Americans today, the 1930s generation of Germans merely adopted the name "Christian" because their grandparents had. That generation had a form of godliness but denied its power by denying its truth.[5]

Regarding post-Christianity in the US today, some 70 percent of Americans still identify as Christian, but the best researchers conclude that only 7 to 20 percent of Americans are measurably active in the Christian faith.[6] That a society is post-Christian does not mean the nation has no Christians; it means the society has abandoned Christianity as its stabilizing center. Christian values are no longer a driving influence in shaping the culture.

World War II Germany demonstrates that post-Christian civilizations can be the most dangerous civilizations. They inherit the machinery, institutions, and capability of a Christianized society. They have immense power and organization. But when they forsake the Christian rule book, when they opt to improve humanity by their own definitions rather than by God's, they are bound to veer off course.

We are taught today that Adolf Hitler perpetrated the atrocities of World War II Germany, but that is not the whole truth. The actual perpetrator was an idea, a way of thinking. The most industrious genocide in human history resulted from an *ideology*. The boxcars, the naked prisoners, the gas chambers—these were the logical results of a way of thinking about self, about race, and about reality. That post-Christian way of thinking—sown like a seed into generations of German minds—finally produced its natural fruit.

The early buds of this fruit showed up in the young people of Germany. Nazism was a youth movement.[7] Its seed was planted and watered in the schools, beer halls, and universities and in the budding leaves of violence on the streets—perpetrated not by armed soldiers in the beginning, but by teens and many of the highly educated youth who had attended Germany's best schools and universities.

I am not suggesting that America will foster any carbon copy of the evils perpetrated by Nazi Germany. The post-Christian ideology budding in the United States is markedly different from Nazism.

We cannot predict exactly what a post-Christian, Post-Truth era will produce in the United States, but we can say two things with some certainty: (1) the eventual maturity of the Post-Truth ideology in America will not be good, and (2) it will look different than it did in Germany. It is a different group of people in a very different scenario.

The great German universities, once founded by Christians, had been overtaken less than one hundred years before World War II by various forms of theological liberalism that moved those Christian-founded schools to scoff at Christianity as myth and fable. The truth of Christianity was expelled from the halls of learning.

The German philosopher Friedrich Nietzsche famously marked post-Christian academia for Germany in 1881 when he concluded that "God is dead" in his extensive and popular criticism of Christianity, *The Dawn of Day*. Some fifty-two years later, the German people democratically elected Adolf Hitler, a fan of Nietzsche's work, to lead their national socialist democracy.

From the mid-1800s until World War II, the German universities began teaching a post-Christian, anti-Christian criticism not too different from what American universities teach today about Christianity.[8] It was a condescending view of Christianity as an outdated and dangerous myth for the weak of mind.[9]

This same academic pattern, wearing slightly different clothes, has been in play in the US for more than one hundred years now in every leading university, including Harvard, Yale, and Princeton, as documented by the scholar George Marsden.[10] Princeton's recent revoking of an award that pastor Timothy Keller was scheduled to receive—due to Keller's biblical position on sexual morality—may mark the completion of this Post-Truth turn in the American Ivy League universities.[11]

America's Ivy universities set the tone for America's state universities, and the Ivy graduates largely set the cultural tone for the nation in a trickle-down fashion. Like so many of the German universities, each of the American Ivy universities was founded by Christians, often for the explicit training of Christian ministers and clergy.[12] Many of the Ivies still have their Christian mottos, crests, or cathedrals at the center of campus, but today's Ivy students know little or nothing of their alma maters' Christian heritages. These students largely ignore Christianity, or else they consider it a danger. The curriculum and culture at Yale and other post-Christian Ivies have become as anti-Christian as Germany's universities in the decades between Nietzsche and Hitler.[13]

Much like German students in the 1930s, students in post-Christian American universities today are taught that we have evolved beyond Christianity, that Christianity is mostly myths and fables. They demonstrate a remarkable pride and contempt in their disdain for Christian ideas and truth claims. Our rising young have been taught that we must devise better ways forward for humanity. They are taught that the most dangerous thing about Christianity is to take it seriously.

Cornell professor Allan Bloom summarized the post-Christian, Post-Truth status of American academia in his book *The Closing of the American Mind*. In it, he writes, "The true believer is the real danger."[14]

Back to Germany. We can zoom out from the tanks and roaring bomber planes, from the muddy battlefields and death camps, and we can see one thing with clarity: **It was an *ideology* that infected the German consciousness. It was an ideology birthed in the universities, spread to the leading edges of culture, and then adopted by millions. This is what killed more innocent people than any previous killing campaign in history: *a set of ideas adopted by a majority of a society*, an ideology.**

Nazi fascism is not the only deadly ideology to infect the human mind in the last one hundred years. Lenin's and Stalin's version of Marxism was equally *an idea* for the Russian people. Let us not forget that Stalin also emerged from a post-Christian culture, having studied at a church school in Gori and at Tbilisi Spiritual Seminary before he embraced another post-Christian German thinker, Karl Marx. Stalin wrote *Marxism and the National Question* in a post-Christian vacuum.[15] We will unpack in chapter 5 how Soviet socialist communism also erupted from a post-Christian culture.

Once Russian society adopted Stalin's ideology, it destroyed more lives than Nazi fascism. Mao Tse-tung's Marxist ideology in China also grew out of the post-Christian German academics. The unthinkable genocides and injustices of the last century, the industrial-scale killings and starvations—*all have been the work of ideologies*. Ideas, embraced by millions of people, lead dramatically to death or to life.

IDEOLOGIES ARE WARRING

In our lifetime, we are witnessing a new warring of ideologies. Within the United States, an emerging Post-Truth ideology is at war against the old Truth-Based ideology. Because we live in an ideological civil war, we will focus much of our response (found in part 3: "How Will We Live?") on assuming a Christlike posture within this struggle and its fallout.

In chapter 5, we will further define the Post-Truth and Truth-Based ideologies, as well as explore the conflict between them. In that exploration, we will see evidence that American millennials have recently swung to prefer Soviet-style socialism over traditional American capitalism, according to multiple surveys taken within the last three years.[16] We will also see that 70 percent of American millennials no longer believe that democracy is necessary to accomplish the goal of bettering society.[17]

Combine the new propensity for socialism with the reality that millennials will overtake baby boomers as the largest voting bloc in the next presidential election, 2020.[18] Then add in the trend that each younger generation of Americans (those younger than millennials) values socialism increasingly more, while disdaining capitalism, democracy, and Christianity more, and a clear picture emerges of a nation rapidly changing.[19]

This swing toward socialism is likely to emerge as soon as 2020, with a Bernie Sanders-type candidate. (Note: During the 2016 presidential primaries, Sanders—the first serious socialist candidate for president in American history—earned more votes from young Americans than both Hillary Clinton and Donald Trump *combined*.)[20] This shift will occur when the number of voting Post-Truth millennials and younger Americans overwhelms the number of Truth-Based Americans (mostly older and aging out), likely either in 2020 or 2024.

This gravitation toward socialism is just one result of the Post-Truth shift in ideology, which, again, we will examine in chapter 5. These and other trends do not mean all millennials are Post-Truth thinkers or all boomers are Truth-Based thinkers, but research indicates that the switch from Truth-Based to Post-Truth thinking falls along generational lines.

We will continue witnessing this civil war of ideologies within the US for the next fifteen to twenty-five years.[21] Today's news media reports do not explain this ideological civil war. That is because many reporters now fail to see the world through the lens of ideologies. This is a result of their Post-Truth education, which teaches them to believe that all ideologies are equal and harmless. And so most news reports today provide only myopic updates on small events. What is missing is that most of the conflict in the world today results from ideological struggles.

Beyond the US, other muscular ideologies are also shaping global events. And by sheer number of believers, the ideologies outside the US are far larger than the entire US population.

A new hybrid communist ideology remains ignored by Americans but is incredibly strong in China,[22] affecting a massive and influential chunk of the world population. In the next ten years, as China overtakes the United States to become the world's wealthiest economy,[23] China's larger population may also show itself to be more unified in ideology than the US, giving China a practical advantage over a divided and squabbling US.[24]

As a preview of these trends, here's an interesting note. PricewaterhouseCoopers projects that thirty years from now, the world economies will rank as follows:

1. China
2. India
3. United States
4. Indonesia.[25]

If other factors remain stable, that's the world our children and grandchildren will navigate in their prime.[26]

Harvard professor Graham Allison recently studied the history of global empires reshuffling like this. He concluded that in the last five hundred years, when a #2 world power has overtaken the #1 power, it has led to war twelve out of sixteen times.[27]

Consider that as recently as 2000, the top four economies were the United States, Japan, the United Kingdom, and France, and you can see the global power center moving in our lifetime. The widespread global implications of such a shift are difficult to comprehend. In time, this shift will affect every nation, the global order, the global power center, military balance, dominant currencies, and cultural trade expectations.

The gravitational center of the globe is on course to shift east—both geographically and ideologically—with India being predominantly Hindu and Indonesia being fundamentalist Muslim. In 2017, a Christian governor in Indonesia was sentenced to two years in prison for blaspheming Islam.[28] The world's #2 economy, India, will have larger populations of Muslims and Hindus than any other country in the world. Meanwhile, China still bans nonregistered Christian gatherings, censors Christian expression on the internet, and demolishes Christian church buildings routinely. These will be three of the four most powerful nations in the world.

Simultaneously and unlimited by national boundaries, the ideology of Islam is marching forward to tie Christianity as the most dominant ideology on the globe. **In 2015, the Pew Research Center concluded that Islam is growing faster than any other major religion and is on course to grasp the minds of one in three people during the next decades.**[29] In 2017, they wrote, "Muslims are projected to be the world's fastest-growing major religious group in the decades ahead, as Pew Research Center has explained, and signs of this rapid growth already are visible. In the period between 2010 and 2015, births to Muslims made up an estimated 31% of all babies born around the world."[30]

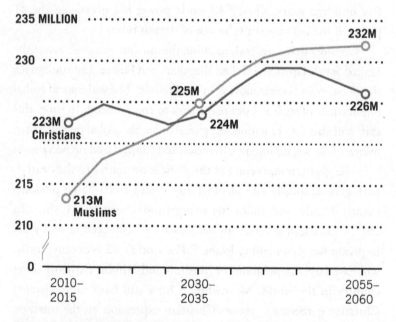

Babies Born to Muslims Will Begin to Outnumber Christian Births by 2035

Estimated number of babies born, by mother's religion, during each five-year period

Source: Pew Research Center demographic projections (see Methodology for details): "The Changing Global Religious Landscape"

PEW RESEARCH CENTER

Figure 2.1

About 220 million new babies are born into Muslim families every five years. That's far greater than the total population of Russia (143 million). Every five years! The same is true of babies born to Christian families every five years, about 230 million.[31] Combined, the total of new Muslim and Christian babies born every five years (about 450 million together) nearly equals the combined standing populations of Russia and the United States. In contrast, China only adds about 90 million births per year, even following the elimination of its one-child policy in 2016.[32]

Islam will continue to grow in influence—not only because of its muscular ideology and momentum, but also because of its sheer size, birth rate, and young population. For these reasons, Islam is set to become the fastest-growing ideology in the world during our lifetime. This will bring dramatic shifts in the global order. Projecting into the next thirty years, Pew researchers concluded:

> Muslims—a comparatively youthful population with high fertility rates—are projected to increase by 73%. The number of Christians also is projected to rise, but more slowly, at about the same rate (35%) as the global population overall.
>
> As a result, according to the Pew Research projections, by 2050 there will be near parity between Muslims (2.8 billion, or 30% of the population) and Christians (2.9 billion, or 31%), possibly for the first time in history.[33]

By 2050, there will be 6.7 Muslims in the world for every one American. There will be five Muslims in the world for every one European in the combined EU territories.[34] In 2050, the five most populous Muslim nations will be home to 1.2 billion people, or roughly the population of China today and about four times the current US population.[35]

Note that the year 2050 is not fifty years from now; it's more like thirty years from now. I'm thirty-five years old as I write this.

Islam Growing Fastest

Muslims are the only major religious group projected to increase faster than the world's population as a whole.

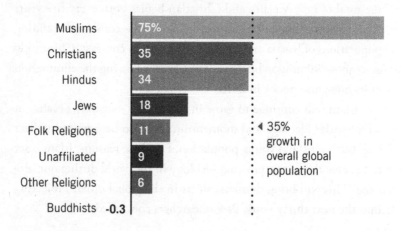

Source: "The Future of World Religions: Population Growth Projections, 2010–2015"
PEW RESEARCH CENTER

Figure 2.2

These footnoted experts are projecting that when I'm sixty-seven years old, Islam will have nearly equaled Christianity as a percent of global population and also that America's economy will be playing third chair globally.

Islam will be the formal religion in dozens of wealthy nations with increasingly sophisticated militaries, which each have 80 percent-plus Muslim populations and theocratic Muslim law. Christianity, on the other hand, will remain loose—a non-state entity in comparison and a waning percentage within the US and Europe. The Christian growth of the next decades is projected beyond the West into the poorest parts of the world.

As a sociological note, where Islam expands, it is much more formal than Christianity and much more likely to overtake national government and laws (a doctrinal requirement in many Islamic inter-pretations). While militarized nations formally adopt Islam as their ruling law and required ideology (see Turkey, Iran, Indonesia), there is no indication of any such militarized Christian nations emerging on the global scene in the next thirty years.[36]

SIMPLIFYING THE DATA

Christianity will be the second-fastest-growing ideology during the next thirty years. At today's trends, Christianity's future growth will be the result of births within existing Christian families, not due to conversions. And these Christian births will occur in the poorest and least developed parts of the world.

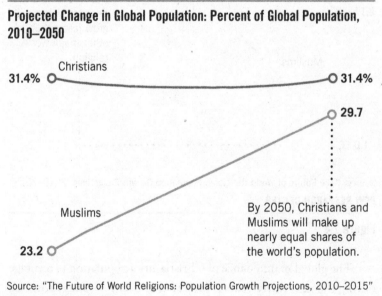

Projected Change in Global Population: Percent of Global Population, 2010–2050

Christians
31.4%   31.4%

29.7

Muslims

23.2

By 2050, Christians and Muslims will make up nearly equal shares of the world's population.

Source: "The Future of World Religions: Population Growth Projections, 2010–2015"
PEW RESEARCH CENTER

Figure 2.3

This same figure can be visualized as the change in the actual number of Christians and Muslims in the world.

Projected Change in Global Population: Number of People, 2010–2050

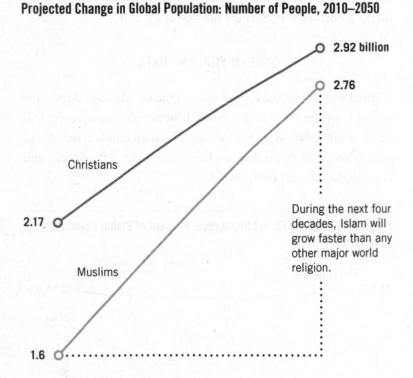

During the next four decades, Islam will grow faster than any other major world religion.

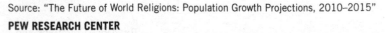

Source: "The Future of World Religions: Population Growth Projections, 2010–2015"
PEW RESEARCH CENTER

Figure 2.4

The global maintenance of Christianity's population percentage during the next thirty years is projected to occur *in spite of* America and the West, not because of it. In fact, Pew projections show the continued dramatic exodus of Americans and Westerners away from Christianity and into agnosticism and spiritual nonbelief. In all, Pew projects another 106 million American and European Christians will quit the faith between now and 2050, with most "switching" to become nonreligious or "unaffiliated."[37]

Projected Cumulative Change Due to Religious Switching, 2010–2015

Source: "The Future of World Religions: Population Growth Projections, 2010–2015"

	Switching in	Switching out	Net change
Unaffiliated	97,080,000	35,590,000	+61,490,000
Muslims	12,620,000	9,400,000	+3,220,000
Folk Religions	5,460,000	2,850,000	+2,610,000
Other Religions	3,040,000	1,160,000	+1,880,000
Hindus	260,000	250,000	+10,000
Jews	320,000	360,000	-310,000
Buddhists	3,370,000	6,210,000	-2,850,000
Christians	40,060,000	106,110,000	-66,050,000

PEW RESEARCH CENTER

Figure 2.5

Note the exodus of 106 million "switching out" or *away from Christianity* in the bottom row (under the bold heading "Switching out" and then trace down to the bottom row). Most of these ex-Christians switch to become nonreligious or "Unaffiliated" (see the top row, where 97 million will be "switching in" to become religiously "unaffiliated").[38] This trend is almost entirely due to the Post-Truth shift in America, Europe, and the formerly Christian Western nations.

In short, America and the West will continue bleeding Christians out spiritually, while sub-Saharan Africa, Latin America, and other developing regions will make up the loss with their own gains in Christians—so that Christianity holds even as a percentage of the world population.[39] As a result, the global hub of Christianity will migrate from the wealthiest, most influential nations to the poorest, most dependent nations. Thirty years from now, two in five Christians globally will live in sub-Saharan Africa.[40]

These thirty-year trends from Pew, as well as a look back at thirty years in Gallup data (see chapter 6), expose the ignorance of the argument that "Christianity is actually doing fine in America." This glib optimism is myopic and sadly ill-informed. Christianity has undeniably failed to retain its own and has lost its influence on American culture. The percentage of young Americans abandoning the faith continues to increase dramatically with each new generation since the 1980s, and the blood loss is on course to continue.

Unaffiliated/agnostic Americans (those leading the Post-Truth cultural turn in America) will continue to dominate American culture and increase rapidly as a percentage within America.[41]

Projected Change in Global Population: Number of People, 2010–2050

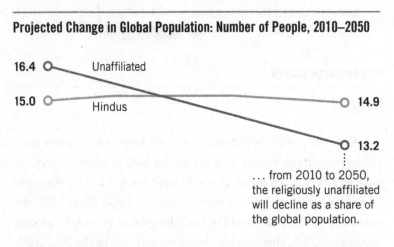

16.4 Unaffiliated

15.0 Hindus   14.9

13.2

... from 2010 to 2050, the religiously unaffiliated will decline as a share of the global population.

Source: "The Future of World Religions: Population Growth Projections, 2010–2015"
PEW RESEARCH CENTER

Figure 2.6

In summary, then, the projections and sociology findings I consulted lead to the following conclusions. Each represents a simple thesis of this book:

1. The Post-Truth era will dominate US culture for some decades, dramatically reshaping society in the United States for the next thirty years.
2. Outside of the United States, Islam, Chinese communism, Hinduism, and other muscular ideologies will continue to grow rapidly and powerfully, likely leading to conflicts between competing ideologies.
3. The future Post-Truth culture in the United States, declining in economic clout and cultural cohesion, will eventually find itself vulnerable to some other, more muscular outside ideology that may subvert America from within or without.

To summarize in paragraph form: **In the next three decades, Post-Truth thinking will overtake Truth-Based thinking in the United States, resulting in massive societal implications for all Americans. Meanwhile, massive global conflicts of ideology will be playing out beyond the US, and eventually these globally dominant ideologies will affect a less globally dominant US, which will rank about third in global economic power.**

We cannot predict which ideology may overtake Post-Truth America in those future decades or when such a conquering could occur or what specifically will happen in global events, but we will suggest some theories in part 2: Where Will It Lead?

As ideologies go, communism and Islam are muscular ones. The consequences of communist and Islamic societies have been well documented in their impacts on human rights, life expectancy, economic activity, personal liberty, women's rights, and other measurable outcomes. But few Americans under age forty are interested in these objective facts.

Young Americans are not interested in the end results of ideologies because they have been conditioned to believe that all cultures are equally good. Even more significant, most young Americans have been conditioned to believe it is a moral evil to critique any culture or religion other than Christianity.[42] As a result, it would be "wrong" in the view of most incoming Americans to factually critique the consequences of communist or Islamic cultures. To do so—even if the facts are obvious—would be bigoted, prejudiced, "white," racist, or imperialistic. In chapter 6, we will further document research suggesting this social climate among young Americans.

Islam has proven its resilience as an ideology for about 1,400 years. As powerful as Islam and China's hybrid communism will show themselves to be in the coming decades, their rise will largely be the result of Western civilization's decline at home and then globally.

A great vacuum of world power will result as the West continues to abandon its old Truth-Based values (and, as a result, its Truth-Based prosperity, liberty, and influence). Simply put, because the West no longer believes its way of life is any better than any other culture, it will not make any effort to propagate, spread, or protect its culture. This is a consequence of the Post-Truth view of Western civilization.

This apathetic self-posture will concur with the rapid global rise of muscular ideologies in China (hybrid communism), India (Hindu), Indonesia (Muslim), and other nations with large populations, like Turkey (Muslim). The West will also decline economically, globally, and militarily, which comes after more than forty years of abortion policies and a shrinking population in the West.[43]

As a result of these abortion policies, academic researchers recently found that "in Europe today there is virtually no overall population growth from natural increase."[44] And so the Western nations have shrinking natural-born populations, even as Muslim, Hindu, and developing nations are exploding in population growth because they have not institutionalized abortion to the extent that Western nations have.[45]

Note that the future ranking of world economies is simply today's ranking of the nations with the largest populations: China, India, US, Indonesia. As one writer notes, with technology equalized, economic production is simply the result of population size.[46] Until recently, the West held such technological advantage that its smaller populations could produce more wealth than larger populations, but exported technology has changed that equation so that the largest populations with modern technology will become the largest economies.

This population shrinkage within the West is an unstated aggravator in the present struggle over "globalism." Europe's shrinking natural population is a factor in its bipolar, love-hate struggle with immigrants from nonassimilating cultures.

The reality is that Europeans have killed so many of their own youth through abortion and population control that aging Europeans *must* have North African and Middle Eastern immigrants to do their physical labor, work in their nursing homes, and power their working economy. Yet, a percentage of these immigrants do not wish to assimilate into the values of their European host cultures. Thus, we see conflict.

We will likely witness in our lifetime a struggle between hybrid communism (China), Islam (globally the fastest-growing ideology), New Nationalism (Russia and others), Hinduism (India), and other ideologies to wrest control of the power vacuum that is emerging as a result of the West's decline.

That struggle will be unpredictable and will include internal conflicts within large ideologies and regions. These internal conflicts include the coming violent Sunni versus Shia power struggle within global Islam;[47] the underreported but deadly struggle between Hinduism and Islam in India; and in our neck of the woods, the Post-Truth versus Truth-Based ideological struggle now dividing the US—a struggle that will likely continue splintering our culture for as long as the baby boomers are with us.

The warring of ideologies in our lives will include open battles among some of these dominant ideologies, such as hard-line Islam's present conflicts in India, Europe, and around the world. Other ideologies will rise globally as the West forsakes its Truth-Based ideology and assumes its passive Post-Truth ideology.

In the end, it may turn out that the most dangerous ideology in the coming century is not some villainous, obviously violent ideology, but rather the chaos that will result from the absurd Post-Truth ideology now overtaking America and Europe. That is, the Post-Truth ideology, once it fully overtakes Western nations, will open the door for the most forceful and muscular ideology at that moment to prevail. And as imperfect as the Christianized, Western Truth-Based culture was, future Westerners may learn the hard way that it was an exceptionally noble, free, prosperous, and dignifying culture compared to most cultures in history (and compared to whatever may supplant it). In the meantime, while Westerners argue with each other on social media, each of these dominant muscular ideologies is arming itself with nuclear weapons, building armies, and raising rigid, ideologically unified populations.

The struggle I've described in this chapter—this warring among ideologies—is one force among the Five Forces shaping world events today. And this force interplays with four other equally powerful forces.

FIVE FORCES SHAPING WORLD EVENTS TODAY

More than seven billion people are alive today. In a precise sense, there may be as many factors in global change as there are people, religions, and cultures. However, we will see that five dominant forces underlie most world events.

If we can understand these Five Forces, we will be less surprised and shaken by the changes set to erupt during the next thirty years. Let's consider them in summary:

1. Humans Are Sinning
2. Satan Is Scheming

3. Ideologies Are Warring
4. Western Civilization Is Unraveling
5. Christ and His People Are Prevailing

These Five Forces are swirling currents that contradict and complement each other in various ways. Our reality each day is the by-product of these Five Forces competing, advancing, and struggling with each other. Just as our universe is constantly moving at the atomic, planetary, and cellular levels, in the same way, global humanity is constantly moving under these Five Forces. It is not a stagnant system.

Four of these forces (1, 2, 3, and 5) are true in every generation, and I do not write them as journalistic observations but as scriptural truths. These are outlined in the Word of God, and they will remain true in every generation from Eden until Christ's return. Understanding them allows us to make sense of reality in ways nonbelievers cannot.

The fourth force, Western civilization's decline, is unique to our era. In the simplest sense, you might think of Western civilization today as North America and Western Europe. By *Western civilization*, I refer to the once-Christianized cultures of the United States and Western European nations such as the United Kingdom, Norway, Sweden, Germany, and so forth;[48] my use of the term *Western civilization* includes "Western" offshoot nations such as Canada, Australia, New Zealand, and other societies where foundational laws, norms, and values were heavily influenced by Christian values and ideas.

Fragments and remains of Western ideas can now be found worldwide, but we will use *Western civilization* to refer to those Christianized populations that were largely Western/Christian in their lawmaking and culture in the last five hundred years. This includes both Protestant and Catholic Christianized societies.

What we are witnessing is the unraveling, the descent, of Western civilization. This decline may drag on for two hundred years, during which the standards of living, personal freedom, and prosperity slowly deteriorate in America and other Western nations. Or the decline could become more sudden if accelerated by other factors (internal or external). Only God knows that future. I do not pretend to know if the decline of the West will be sudden or gradual, but I aim to prepare myself and you to thrive for Christ in either scenario.[49]

For now, if you'd like a simple demonstration of the reality that Western civilization has peaked, ask five Americans under the age of thirty what "the West" or "Western civilization" is. Then note how many of them give answers about rattlesnakes, cowboys, Arizona, or the Wild West.

Their ignorance is not incidental. The National Association of Scholars has found that "Western Civilization"—for generations a required freshman college course—is no longer a required course at America's leading universities.[50] In fact, many of the leading universities in the US today do not allow Western Civilization as a course in the curriculum. More often, the very concept of Western civilization as an ideal is something to be mocked.

Many in my generation do not know what Western civilization is. They do not know how the West has lifted humanity from darkness or that we have inherited Western civilization.

Separately, those incoming young Americans who *do* have a historical understanding of Western civilization are likely to view the West as dangerous, imperialistic, colonialist, white, nationalist, or populist.

For the most part, Americans under age forty have not been taught to see the West as the society that produced widespread literacy, doubled life expectancy, established modern medicine, abolished slavery, and created the women's rights movement and Western democracy.

Rather, they've been taught to see the West in Marxist terms—as a monopolizing, colonizing, imperialistic group of rich white people who have taken advantage of everyone else in the world. The West is only rich, they've been taught, because it exploited the rest of the world, not because of its ideas, work ethic, values, or truth beliefs.

Contrast the West's self-ignorance and self-loathing with the ideological education of young people in China or in any Muslim nation. In those societies, any young person can tell you with clarity what communism or Islam is, respectively.

And those young people can also tell you why communism or Islam is vastly superior to Christianity, the West, and any other ideology. They far outnumber Westerners, and they are far more unified and clear in their ideologies.

We will further define and explore the West's unraveling (both its ideological unraveling and the practical consequences) in chapter 6.

When we understand all five of these forces together, world events will begin to make more sense to us. Again, the Five Forces are, in summary:

1. Humans Are Sinning
2. Satan Is Scheming
3. Ideologies Are Warring
4. Western Civilization Is Unraveling
5. Christ and His People Are Prevailing

Our exploration of Forces 3 and 4 (Ideologies Are Warring and Western Civilization Is Unraveling) will be our deepest dives; they'll be the most thorough chapters in this book. In them I will aggregate the best sociological research, demographic data, global statistics, historical trend lines, and expert opinions to shed light on these two unique forces today.

The Five Forces may appear theoretical or distant, but I assure you, they affect the food in our refrigerators, the balances in our retirement accounts (even the fact that we have retirement accounts), global war and peace, and the way of life for our children and grandchildren.

It is because of these Five Forces that our society is now a post-Christian society. And it is because our society is post-Christian that it is also a Post-Truth society. And it is because we are a Post-Truth society that we are witnessing massive and frightening shifts in American culture, the European Union, and the global order—shifts that will have an impact on governments, the global economy, and our entire way of life in ways we cannot fully predict.

While many close their eyes and hope these global and societal shifts will resolve themselves, the reality is that these shifts are likely small pre-tremors preceding far more dramatic tectonic shifts.

Chapter 3

PRE-TREMORS

To demonstrate that the Post-Truth shift is not mere theory, here are five present-day examples of the Post-Truth shift and its consequences in American culture today. These examples are pre-tremors or foreshocks compared to the future ruptures that may result from the Post-Truth shift as it saturates US courts, classrooms, neighborhoods, laws, and global policies.

Example 1: American parents are taking children to watch sexualized public nudity in city-sanctioned events. Some of my Christian friends in the San Francisco Bay area have struggled with what to do about the annual gay pride parade. The event now attracts more than one million spectators and has become a sort of local holiday. The city removes the American flags so that the flag holders on many downtown streets are occupied by gay pride rainbow flags.

Some of the large tech companies whose logos you would recognize and whose products you use require their employees to attend the gay pride parade. This is an annual point of difficulty for some Christians who work at these companies.

At the parades, the ultimate driver of the movement can't help but slip out—sometimes literally, in the form of public nudity. *SFGate*,

which is the online website of the *San Francisco Chronicle*, compiled
a guide to encourage families who want to take their children to the
celebration. The reporter writes, "To help families going to Sunday's
Gay Pride Parade have a smooth experience, *SFGate* gathered some
words of wisdom and practical tips from parents who've taken their
children over the years." Here is the first tip:

> **Don't worry.** "We have been bringing our daughter (now 7)
> annually since she was a baby," shares S.F. mom Beth Winegar-
> ner. "Yes, there is some nudity and leather but there's little to
> no overt sexual stuff as there is at, say, Folsom Street Fair. Kids
> in general aren't at all fazed by seeing nudity—after all they
> like to run around and play with as little on as possible too."[1]

So, yes, your child will see public nudity, lots of phallic imagery, and
possibly a "little . . . overt sexual stuff" from naked people, but—the article
continues—don't let that stop you from taking them to the celebration.

Minors have been exposed to sexualized nudity and even public
masturbation at parades and events on the streets of San Francisco.
The *East Bay Times* documented children who were wearing bondage
leather at the annual Folsom Street Fair in San Francisco, where
there is public sex, hundreds of naked adults in bondage gear, and
"masturbating in public."[2]

Without going into graphic detail, the Folsom Street Fair includes
hundreds of nude people arousing each other, public orgasm, and
demonstrations of sex toys—along with public "play places" for using
those toys on others—and most of this carries with it the themes of
bondage, whips, chains, and S&M.[3]

This quote from a dad who brought his two-year-old daughters
dressed in bondage-style leather summarizes a culture severed from
any objective definition of truth. Answering the question of whether
it's appropriate to dress his young daughters in bondage leather and
let them witness public sex acts, the dad replied, "Every parent has

to decide for themselves what is right for them. And I respect that. And we decided that this is right for our children."[4]

Note the values of the statement that "every parent has to decide for themselves what is right for them." This is a model display of the Post-Truth ideology. Some Post-Truth thinkers will have more reservations than this dad (because of the families they were raised in), but most likely their children will end up believing exactly what this dad believes—that "every parent has to decide for themselves what is right for them."

Note the lack of any moral standard outside of felt opinion. The dad believes it is a good thing to dress his two-year-olds in leather bondage gear and expose them to public masturbation. "We decided that this is right for our children."

Disgusting, perverse, and immoral as this approach is, this man is merely practicing with purity the ideology that millions of American children have been taught to believe for decades—that there is no truth standard and that the only real evil is to judge another person as wrong.

The Post-Truth ideal is in *not judging others* and in others *not judging him*. There is no objective truth standard of right and wrong apart from this. We'll see in chapter 5 that, while it does not always surface so dramatically, this is the prevailing ideology of Americans under the age of thirty-five.

The same *East Bay Times* article quoted a ten-year-old boy who has attended the Folsom Street Fair for six years in a row, walking between nude adults, abusive arousal, and public acts of sex. Of kids attending the festival, the executive director is quoted as saying, "I've seen a thousand doting aunts and uncles, and a kid having the time of his life."[5]

The story again demonstrates the Post-Truth absurdity when it quotes event volunteer Adam Hawkins as saying it is up to the parents to decide what is best for their kids, and he isn't going to stop them at the gates.

This *East Bay Times* story incited a public backlash, and the Folsom Street Fair has since changed its official policy. Technically, it now claims to bar children from entering the gates. However, parents who live in the area warn that the fair takes over entire neighborhoods of San Francisco and is held on the streets in the daytime, so it's difficult to leave the house and not have your children see the naked festival-goers or observe what they're doing with their bodies.

An acquaintance of mine serves in law enforcement in San Francisco. He is routinely assigned to patrol the Folsom Street Fair. He stated that he still sees children there every year and that his every impulse is to confront their parents. But to do so, he said, would probably lead to him getting sued. "It'll come out that I'm a conservative Christian," he said, "and I would probably lose my job on grounds of prejudice and discrimination."

The scene of naked adults arousing each other in the city streets—occurring openly in the daylight and with no regard for children—conjures images of some well-known Bible stories.

The Folsom Street Fair is not the only public festival of this nature in the daylit streets of San Francisco. The annual Nude Valentine's Day Parade has featured at least one naked prepubescent minor marching alongside groups of naked men.[6]

That some of my millennial peers would call me a prude or closed-minded for critiquing an invitation for children to view sexualized nudity or to walk naked with a group of naked men who are celebrating complete sexual freedom, well, that is in itself a demonstration of the Post-Truth culture.

Others will argue that events like these only represent the fringe of the culture. But the corporate sponsors for the headline Gay Pride parade are anything but fringe. Recent corporate sponsors include Bud Light, Alaska Airlines, Blue Shield of California, Xfinity, Amazon, Apple, Disney, Facebook, McDonald's, BMW, Uber, T-Mobile, AT&T, Bank of America, Gap, Levi's, Nordstrom, Macy's, Safeway, Wells Fargo, State Farm, and US Bank, among many others.[7]

The reality is that every year on the streets of San Francisco, multiple events expose children to graphic sexualized nudity in ways that would be rightly deemed sexual abuse if they were ever done in a church or school. But out in the street, with thousands of other adults cheering and waving flags, this is deemed acceptable and literally applauded. Such are the liquid morals of a Post-Truth society. Welcome to a leading edge of American culture. The overt exchange of societal values is perhaps best summarized by the 2011 annual theme for the Gay Pride parade: "In Pride We Trust."

Example 2: A convicted murderer is given hundreds of thousands of dollars to get sex-change surgery for free, while law-abiding, tax-paying citizens don't get the same or life-saving procedures for free. A legal ramification of the Post-Truth culture shift is that words like *rights* and *justice* become subjective in their meaning. Because truth is no longer based on an external standard, words like *fascist*, *bigot*, or even *constitutional right* become expressions that anyone can apply to their opinion rather than words actually defined by an objective dictionary or the Constitution.

Demonstrating this, a California court recently ruled that it was the "constitutional right" of a convicted murderer serving a life sentence to receive hundreds of thousands of dollars' worth of sex-change surgery—paid for by the state. The Associated Press filed this report:

> A 57-year-old convicted killer serving a life sentence has become the first U.S. inmate to receive state-funded sex-reassignment surgery, the prisoner's attorneys confirmed Friday.
>
> California prison officials agreed in August 2015 to pay for the surgery for Shiloh Heavenly Quine, who was convicted of first-degree murder, kidnapping and robbery for ransom and has no possibility of parole.[8]

Quine, who was to be relocated to a women's prison after the surgery, shot and killed a thirty-three-year-old father of three in 1980 while robbing him of $80 and his car. The ruling that Quine deserves government-funded transgender sex surgery now requires the state to provide the same surgery for other inmates. In the process, California officials have agreed to provide male inmates who identify as female with scarves, necklaces, nightgowns, and similar items.

The Associated Press reported that the daughter of the man murdered by Quine "objects to inmates getting taxpayer-funded surgery that is not readily available to non-criminals, regardless of the cost."

> "My dad begged for his life," said Farida Baig, who tried unsuccessfully to block Quine's surgery through the courts. "It just made me dizzy and sick. I'm helping pay for his surgery; I live in California. It's kind of like a slap in the face."[9]

This $100,000-plus award of "justice" and "rights" for the murderer—at the literal expense of the victims—symbolizes well the absurdities that take place in a Post-Truth culture's courtroom.

Capturing well the Post-Truth impact on law and justice, California Department of Corrections spokeswoman Terry Thornton explained why the state had no choice but to pay for the sexual-reassignment surgery: "The 8th Amendment of the U.S. Constitution requires that prisons provide inmates with medically necessary treatment for medical and mental health conditions."[10]

Now, my point here is not to disparage in any way those individuals who identify as transgendered; God loves these individuals, and God wants the best for them. The point here has nothing to do with sexual orientation. The reality for the larger culture is that a very costly surgery is not freely provided to law-abiding citizens but is now guaranteed for all law-breaking citizens. Furthermore, biologically life-and-death surgeries (such as organ transplants or open-heart surgery) are not given freely by the state to law-abiding, tax-paying citizens.

And so the Post-Truth impact on law is this: convicted murderers are awarded hundreds of thousands of dollars in surgical procedures that are not awarded to tax-paying, law-abiding citizens.

A Post-Truth culture will become saturated with such incongruences. Let's be intentionally clear again that God loves all people, including those who identify as transgendered, and we as Christians have the joy of demonstrating God's love for all people, including those who self-identify as LGBTQ. The point of this example is that convicted murderers now have more rights than law-abiding, tax-paying citizens because the definitions of "constitutional rights" and "medically necessary" have been changed to fit the Post-Truth cultural mood rather than to correlate to the actual Constitution or to physiology.

Some who read this may say "Well, that's just California." But it's not that simple. This ruling affects all fifty states, and more significantly, this way of thinking is the fruit of Post-Truth thinking. We'll see in coming chapters that such Post-Truth thinking is becoming the dominant way of thinking in all fifty states.

And so in fighting for the "rights" and "justice" of one group (convicted criminals who identify as transgendered), the basic "rights" and "justice" of another group (law-abiding taxpayers and victims of crimes) have been eclipsed and ignored. We will continue to see this trend in Post-Truth society. The vigorous fight for one group's rights will come at the expense of another group's rights because the foundational standards of justness and fairness have been removed.[11]

I use the word *absurd* to describe this scenario—not as pejorative to any individual or party, but as a literal descriptor for any government that would treat its citizenry with such basic unfairness—rewarding law-breaking murderers with benefits not afforded to law-abiding taxpayers. It's a socially absurd position.

We'll see this same miscarriage of justice carried out in a thousand variations during the next thirty years—often benefiting people from the classes that the Post-Truth moral scaffolding deems as deserving of special protection and often at the expense of those classes of people that the Post-Truth moral scaffolding deems as deserving of being put in their place because they were the majority or the oppressors in past decades.

Example 3: Dis-integration is taking place in Western nations and the European Union. While the European Union never explicitly stated that Christian values or Christianized society held it together, it is a fact of history and sociology that the vestiges of Christian values bound the nations in the European Union together.

The nations of the European Union had vastly different languages, currencies, and cultures, along with a bloody history of disputes. The one thing they had in common was a trajectory—over the course of nearly one thousand years—of Christian influence. This resulted in shared Christian values and a shared somewhat Christian vision for a cohesive culture, even if those values weren't explicitly stated.

The dissolving of the European Union (beginning with the United Kingdom's exit, Brexit) is a clear example of what happens when older generations assume some of their inherited Christian values, even while the truth foundation erodes beneath. In time, younger generations inherit the structure, and—having no foundational reason for some of the Christianized policies and values—the new generations adjust the structure to fit their new foundation.

Without unifying values, there can be no European Union as it was envisioned. There can only be a corrupt union or no union. And with Christianity largely removed from the popular cultures in the European Union nations, we can expect to continue to see the individual national cultures deteriorate and infight socially.

Example 4: Western leaders—with far superior military technology— are unable to contain or defeat terrorism. Western leaders, equipped with the best military technology in history, are unable to uproot violent Islamic terrorism from regions of the world that were recently centuries behind in weaponry and technological innovation. Why?

Because many Western leaders are impotent to combat the *ideology* that drives Islamic strains of terrorism.

During World War II, President Franklin Delano Roosevelt (FDR) accurately identified that the bloody conflict was, in fact, a conflict of ideologies. He stated that the unconditional surrender by Germany, Italy, and Japan "does not mean the destruction of the population of Germany, Italy, or Japan, but it does mean the destruction of the philosophies in those countries which are based on conquest and the subjugation of other people."[12]

Note the final sentence. FDR recognized what World War II was actually about: "*the destruction of the philosophies in those countries which are based on conquest and the subjugation of other people.*" FDR wisely saw that an ideological struggle was at the heart of World War II. The ideology of the peaceful Western nations was in combat against the ideology of the Axis powers that sought "the conquest and the subjugation" of others.[13]

FDR understood that the enemy in World War II was not Germany or Japan, but the ideologies that motivated their populations and armies. And so FDR and Western leaders (who had been trained by American universities to understand ideology at that time) declared war on a way of thinking.

A reality of world history is that most ideologies aspire to conquest and subjugation. And yet some Western leaders today have been educated to believe that all ideas and cultures are equal and can all be embraced simultaneously.[14] Leaders who have been indoctrinated into this Post-Truth view are ill-equipped to operate in the real world, where muscular ideologies seek to conquer, defeat, and subjugate *any* other ideology, including the American way of life.

This book is not a call for nativism or nationalism, nor is this book a call to stop globalism. Rather, this book calls Christians to our highest citizenship, which is in heaven, and then to operate globally with an understanding of our neighbors' ideologies rather than with blind ignorance of other world cultures, values, and aspirations.

Christianity applies to "every nation, tribe, people and language."[15] It is the first and largest multiethnic, global movement in which people of all races and nations are viewed as equally valuable and made in the image of God. In this way, Christians seek a spiritual globalization, but culturally we do well to operate with an awareness of what others believe. While we will always pursue peaceful coexistence, we will not fall under the blind assertion that all cultures seek peaceful coexistence.

Today, global terrorism continues advancing because of the rigid ideology underneath it. But many Post-Truth European and US leaders do not have the vocabulary or tools to identify the ideology that continues recruiting terrorists from a massive population. And so, even if the ideology is beheading children, stoning women, and attacking innocent people, many Western leaders lack the moral vocabulary, the understanding, or the basic education to identify that *ideas* are what is driving ISIS, al-Qaeda, Boko Haram, and hundreds of other violent expressions of the same ideology. They also fail to understand the scope and size of that ideological movement.

It is too politically incorrect to declare the reality that many millions of people in the world are being indoctrinated toward variations of this violent ideology every day. Additionally, because of the failure to understand ideology, Western nations are routinely arming, weaponizing, and training the very people and nations who share that violent ideology but have not acted it out yet.

As a result, we will continue to see the fight against terrorism drag along in its bloody, impotent cycle. Like the frog in the kettle, the frequency and bloodiness of terrorist attacks in the US and Europe have increased every few months during the last decade.

Fighting terrorism in only the physical realm when the opponent is an ideology is akin to following a toddler around a house. Every time the toddler throws a vase or picture frame on the floor, you pick it back up, but you never teach the toddler that it's a bad idea to throw things down.

Until the West acknowledges in a unified fashion that *ideas are driving violent terrorism*, the West will constantly be cleaning up bloody messes, with no slowing of the destruction. And those bloody messes will continue to spill deeper into American and European cities.

Barring a radical change in Western posture, we can expect to see violent, ideologically driven terrorism continue to spread around the world during the next thirty years. Many billions of dollars in weaponry and training may slow its progress, but they will not stop it.

And all too often, because of a failure to understand ideology, those weapons and training end up in the hands of future terrorists. Consider, for example, the number of ISIS leaders in Syria and Iraq who were previously trained and armed by the US military or the CIA simply because the Western leaders organizing those programs failed to understand ideology.

Example 5: There is a trend toward taxing churches and Christian ministries. Spend some time with influential Post-Truth thinkers in New York, Los Angeles, leading news outlets, or higher education, and you may hear this theme: It makes no sense that American churches are not taxed, especially those churches that discriminate against the LGBTQ community by not hiring LGBTQ individuals on their staffs or by declining to perform same-sex weddings.

Consider just two examples of this kind of thinking. First, the *Washington Post*'s online magazine *Slate* recently published an article declaring, "Let's tax churches! All of them, in a non-discriminatory way that doesn't consider faith or creed or level of political engagement. There's simply no good reason to be giving large tax subsidies to the Church of Scientology or the Diocese of San Diego or Temple Rodef Shalom in Virginia or the John Wesley African Methodist Episcopal Zion church around the corner from me."[16]

As Bill Maher voiced, "Almost a quarter of us are being forced to subsidize a myth that we're not buying into."[17]

The most symbolic argument for this emerging position came in *Time* magazine when a columnist declared, "Now's the time to end tax exemptions for religious institutions."[18] This essay embodies two Post-Truth views held by many young Americans: (1) Any church that holds a traditional view on sexual morality is discriminating against LGBTQ individuals. As such, these churches and religious institutions should be penalized for their bigotry rather than rewarded for it. The *Time* article puts it this way: "So yes, the logic of gay-marriage rights could lead to a reexamination of conservative churches' tax exemptions . . . When that day comes, it will be long overdue."[19] (2) The article demonstrates the erroneous but prevailing view that if all the church's money was in the hands of the government, the government would be more effective at using the funds to help the poor.

> Defenders of tax exemptions and deductions argue that if we got rid of them charitable giving would drop. It surely would, although how much, we can't say. But of course, government revenue would go up, and that money could be used to, say, house the homeless and feed the hungry. We'd have fewer church soup kitchens—but countries that truly care about poverty don't rely on churches to run soup kitchens.[20]

Of course, those of us who are Truth-Based thinkers and Christians would challenge the author to identify one country in world history where the poor and homeless have better care than in the Christianized nations. But as we'll see in upcoming chapters, presenting facts does not often sway an argument in a Post-Truth setting. And as the writer above demonstrates, today's cultural leaders have zero historical understanding of the Christian influence in the land they inherit.

I'm not suggesting that conservative churches may lose their tax exemptions because of one *Time* magazine essay. Rather, I'm suggesting that this essay embodies beliefs that will be held by a majority of

Americans at some point in the coming decades. These two views are inevitable by-products of the Post-Truth and post-Christian culture shifts. As Post-Truth thinking overtakes Truth-Based thinking, this sort of reasoning is on track to become the majority view among the Americans who select lawmakers and shape policy.

I'm not confidently predicting that churches and Christian colleges will lose their tax-deductible status within fifteen years, but I will say—based on the body of research in the following chapters—that such a change would not surprise me at any point after 2020, particularly in regions like California and New York where a majority of the populations are Post-Truth thinkers.

Of course, the ramifications for churches and religious schools are massive. For many, the loss of tax-exempt status would force them to shut their doors.

As Post-Truth thinkers become the largest voting bloc, we can expect trends like these—which seem sporadic now—to surface more frequently and more consistently across the national social fabric. For Americans under the age of thirty-five, the social peer pressures away from the old traditional values are incredibly strong—perhaps stronger than I can summarize in the written word.

These pre-tremors are brief examples of the blindness that Post-Truth thinking produces. We will witness many more Post-Truth consequences in our lifetime. In time, there may be social pushback on conservative Christians, perhaps including the eventual loss of state and federal loans for students who attend Christian universities. In some regions, basic licenses to operate religious schools, colleges, or churches could also be denied to those organizations that hold to "discriminatory" or "prejudiced" beliefs about morality, according to the Post-Truth definitions.

I hope I'm wrong.

Chapter 4

FORCES 1 AND 2: HUMANS ARE SINNING AND SATAN IS SCHEMING

We have seen that ideologies are warring for control of the population in the United States, in Europe, and in the world. This warring among ideologies is one of the Five Forces shaping world events today.

Before we go any further, let's gain an elementary understanding of the Five Forces. We will consider Forces 1 and 2 together in this chapter. Then we will dedicate an entire chapter to Force 3 and an entire chapter to Force 4. Together, Forces 3 and 4 capture the heart of our unique analysis. We will then conclude this part of the book positively with an overview of Force 5.

In summary:

- Force 1: Humans Are Sinning
- Force 2: Satan Is Scheming
- Force 3: Ideologies Are Warring
- Force 4: Western Civilization Is Unraveling
- Force 5: Christ and His People Are Prevailing

FORCE 1: HUMANS ARE SINNING

But mark this: There will be terrible times in the last days.
People will be lovers of themselves, lovers of money, boastful,
proud, abusive, disobedient to their parents, ungrateful, unholy,
without love, unforgiving, slanderous, without self-control, brutal,
not lovers of the good, treacherous, rash, conceited, lovers of
pleasure rather than lovers of God—having a form of godliness
but denying its power.

2 TIMOTHY 3:1–5

God begins His love letter to us, the Bible, with an important
statement about human nature. Humans are not presently the way
God originally created them to be. There has been a great corruption
of human nature. Because of that, humans, who are made in the
image of God and capable of great nobility and virtue, are inherently
broken.[1]

We are broken physically—no longer safe from sickness and
physical mortality, as Adam and Eve had been before evil. And we
are broken morally. Theologians refer to this moral brokenness as
depravity. It is a Christian understanding of depravity that prompted
Western democracy to have checks and balances in government.
These are necessary because "all have sinned and fall short of the
glory of God."[2]

Human nature is both glorious and ruined.[3] Humans are not irre-
deemable. The sin nature does not mean every human being *always*
does the wrong thing. Fallen humans are capable of great nobility
and self-sacrifice. But depravity does mean that all humans do the
wrong thing *some of the time*.[4] And enough of us do enough wrong
that we undermine our own progress. Our brokenness also makes us
more susceptible to manipulation by clever and evil people among
us—as Joseph Stalin, Adolf Hitler, and Mao Tse-tung demonstrate.

Place human beings into an inherited, stable, and prosperous system like the United States, and on the surface, it can appear that people aren't all that bad. Perhaps this is why the teaching on depravity has been ignored for many American generations. But much of this seeming good nature is the fruit of the old Christian values and laws still lingering in the society.

Even fallen humans are capable of great good, nobility, and creativity. However, separated from God by sin, humans inevitably drift back toward the destruction of sin. This is true both of human individuals and human societies. Much of the warfare, murder, and political battling in the world today results from this human brokenness of depravity.

Apart from Christ, we are unable to conquer this brokenness entirely. Apart from Christ, we are blinded from the truth. Our thinking becomes futile, and our foolish hearts and minds become darkened.[5] This is why people behave unreasonably. This is why people do not "just get along." This is why a world with more than enough water, food, and resources still contains millions who lack clean water, sufficient food, and basic freedoms. This blindness limits the human capacity for peace and production. This blindness also keeps humanity enslaved spiritually to our adversary, Satan.

So much of the injustice that happens in national politics, in cultures, and in our own workplaces and families traces back to this foundational brokenness in human nature. God intentionally described the fall of humanity at the very beginning of the Bible because it is a foundational truth. If we forget this reality about human nature, the world will not make sense. Indeed, our Post-Truth neighbors, having been taught that all people are basically good, struggle to make sense of realities like ISIS and drunk drivers.

This concept—"the depravity of man"—used to be a basic understanding in Western civilization. Generations in the old Truth-Based America were taught that all humans are "endowed by their Creator with certain unalienable Rights,"[6] but they were also taught that the human heart "is deceitful above all things and beyond cure."[7]

This dual understanding was unique in world cultures and gave generations of Westerners an ability to love the deplorable even while holding the powerful accountable. A sturdy belief in depravity led to the checks and balances on power that made Western democracy unique and uniquely effective. A grasp of human depravity gave Western democracy the moral compass to begin navigating toward justice. After World War II, the same view enabled the West to be noble in rehabilitating and restoring Germany and Japan, as has happened from 1945 onward.

Post-Truth Americans have not been taught to understand human depravity. Quite the opposite, they've been taught that people are generally good. As a result, this new generation is struggling to understand why when we give aid, internet capabilities, or military technology to people of other ideologies, these people sometimes use it for evil. That these people would ever use the money and military technology against us still seems unthinkable to many.

Ironically, the lie that humans are inherently good will lead to great evil—because it creates a society that does not restrain evil in oneself or in others. History and Scripture teach that all people are significantly bent toward evil, in need of a Savior, in need of a moral makeover, and able to be redeemed only after they acknowledge their bent toward evil.

The same human nature that undermined humanity in Lot's day, in Noah's day, in Jesus' day, and in the Middle Ages—the very same depravity that undermined Germany, Japan, and Russia in our grandparents' lifetime—that same depravity continues to undermine humanity in our day. Sadly, even many *Christians* in our day have not been taught this basic reality about human nature as Scripture defines it.

Because humans continually sin, many peace accords will continue to fail. Many international treaties will be forsaken. Many wrongly motivated leaders will muscle their way into positions of power. Many nations will inflict war on other nations, and many people groups will commit evil against others.

Understanding that humans are infected by sin does not require us to be pessimistic, but it does force us to accept the fact that the only true Hope for humanity is Christ, who can change the human heart and heal the ultimate human sickness. As biblical Christians, we will be sad when we see the painful consequences of sinners acting like sinners, but we need not be surprised.

FORCE 2: SATAN IS SCHEMING

"The thief comes only to steal and kill and destroy."

JOHN 10:10

In addition to humanity's own blindness and brokenness, an unseen cosmic battle is being fought daily in the spiritual realm. The tangible object of competition between heaven and hell is humanity, the crown jewel of God's creation.

Satan, a fallen angel, operates in the realm of ideas and information, exercising his primary weapons of lies and deception.[8] He is a master at mixing nine parts truth with one part error, so that his victims imbibe just enough deception to bring about death and destruction. He did this first with Eve and Adam.[9] Today his unseen supernatural allies, the demons, are at work, deceiving people on every continent in order to cause pain, death, and destruction globally.[10]

Jesus summarized this force by saying that Satan came into this world "to steal and kill and destroy."[11] Satan is weaker than God, of course, but he is also described as having significant power at this time.[12] We must never underestimate our God. It's also wise not to underestimate our opponent. In Christ, Satan is defeated, but we cannot defeat Satan in our own power, apart from Christ.

As Christians, we know that Satan was defeated at the cross. But it's important to note too that Satan has not yet been bound and thrown into the lake of fire. The day is coming, the book of Revelation tells us, when Satan and his forces will be forever chained.[13]

At present, though, Satan still "prowls around like a roaring lion looking for someone to devour."[14]

Scripture describes Satan as having intellectual power on a higher order than the smartest humans.[15] He presently "has blinded the minds of unbelievers, so that they cannot see the light of the gospel that displays the glory of Christ, who is the image of God."[16] Scripture also describes Satan presently as the "ruler of the kingdom of the air, the spirit who is now at work in those who are disobedient."[17]

Satan was judged and defeated at the cross, but he is still on the prowl. He is still a force to be reckoned with. He is like a criminal who has been judged guilty in court but hasn't yet been sentenced to serve his prison time. When Christ returns, He will sentence Satan and his allies so that they can no longer steal, kill, and destroy. Until then, Satan—the enemy of our souls—is on the loose, wreaking as much destruction on earth as he can.[18]

When world events or life events seem evil beyond what can be explained by the depravity of human nature or the fall of creation (Force 1), it is usually because Satan and his hosts are at work in the unseen spiritual realm. From Hitler's Germany to ISIS today, we can be sure that Satan is at work, longing to carry out a supernatural evil more destructive than what fallen humans alone could conjure.

Further evidence of Satan's scheming can be seen in the historical record of persecution against the Jewish people and against Christians. No group has been more systematically targeted than God's chosen people, the Jews, in generation after generation, for thousands of years. In every century, Satan is attacking God's people, and in every century, God is preserving a remnant for His glory on earth.

On this note, it is shocking, not even one hundred years since the Holocaust, to see anti-Semitism resurfacing in strains of academia here in the US, even while violent ideologies that promote the killing of Jews, Christians, and homosexuals are defended or ignored.

How can such ignorance exist in "the hallowed halls of learning"? Forces 1 and 2 explain why: Fallen humans are blinded by a scheming adversary who deceives continually in his mission to steal, kill, and destroy. With the truth standard eradicated from education, our finest institutions become nothing more than brick-and-ivy expressions of fallen human nature.

God's other chosen people, the Christians, also have an astonishing record of being oppressed under tyranny in every century since Christ. Like the Jewish people, a remnant of Christ's church is always miraculously delivered. Much more, it is promised that Christ's church will prevail (Force 5).[19]

Why are Jews and Christians so targeted by governments, dictators, people of power, and people of other religions across every boundary of century and continent? It is too consistent a pattern to be a coincidence. We are targeted because we are, in fact, under attack by the enemy of our souls. We are targeted because we are the chief tangible object over which heaven and hell are warring.

Scripture clearly teaches that Satan employs the people of this world as wartime slaves in his quest to destroy God's remnant on earth. We should not be surprised if we see satanic, supernatural persecution during our journey through earth.[20] Nor, as we'll see in chapter 20, should we be afraid.

———————————

We have just covered the first two of the Five Forces. Because the exploration of Forces 3 and 4 will be much lengthier, let's review all of the Five Forces before we explore Force 3.

- Force 1: Humans Are Sinning
- Force 2: Satan Is Scheming
- Force 3: Ideologies Are Warring
- Force 4: Western Civilization Is Unraveling
- Force 5: Christ and His People Are Prevailing

Chapter 5

FORCE 3:
IDEOLOGIES ARE WARRING

> For the weapons of our warfare are not of the flesh but have
> divine power to destroy strongholds. We destroy arguments and
> every lofty opinion raised against the knowledge of God, and
> take every thought captive to obey Christ.

2 CORINTHIANS 10:4–5 ESV

An ideology is a set of ideas combined into a way of thinking.
Popular ideologies are adopted by groups of people, who then
move in unison because they see the world through the same set of
ideas. A common ideology enables a group to work in unison, even
if they don't realize it or agree on every point outside the ideology.[1]

Ideology can also be referred to loosely as a belief system or worldview. From ancient Greece and Rome to Muhammad's conquests to
the founding of the United States and the USSR, it is ideologies that
have moved tribes, nations, and civilizations in every century toward
their actions—whether noble, evil, or harmless.

We began chapter 2 ("What Is Happening?") with the true story
of the ideology that took hold of the German people and led to World
War II. Not all Germans adopted the ideas of Nazi fascism, but a
majority did. And in the struggle for the heart of Germany during

the 1930s, that majority was enough to wreak havoc, destruction, death, genocide, and pain on a scale the world had never seen.

Germany isn't the only post-Christian nation to lurch into violence and blood in the streets as it completed its turn away from Christianity. Before the Bolshevik Revolution in 1917, Russia was "known as 'Holy Russia,' a land blossoming with the multi-domed church buildings so associated with the Eastern Slavs' Orthodoxy [Christianity], a land pregnant with spiritual heritage and strongly in touch with the oldest traditions of the [Christian] faith. But around the turn of the 20th century, something drastic happened."[2]

As post-Christian Marxist ideas gripped the Russian mind, Christianity was quickly and violently uprooted. Keep in mind that Orthodox Christianity had been part of Russian culture for about one thousand years—much longer than Christianity has been in North America, to the extent that Joseph Stalin's education, where he first learned of Karl Marx, was in a "church school" and "seminary."[3] Like the United States today and Germany in the early 1900s, the best learning institutions in Russia during Stalin's childhood were Christian-founded institutions.

And yet in the first year of Russia's revolution, "all church organizations lost the powers of legal entity and the right to own property. To have the decree put into effect, a special liquidation committee was set up to evict the monks from their monasteries, many of which were destroyed, not without acts of vandalism, in which church utensils and bells were melted down and shrines containing relics were broken open."[4]

Of course, Christianized Russia looked far different from Christianized America, and one could argue that the final version of Christianity in Russia was corrupted on many levels. However, the principle from post-Christian France and post-Christian Russia is this: the more politically involved the church becomes, the more overt and violent will be the eventual backlash against the church when the culture completes its post-Christian turn.

In the first decade of the Soviet Union's social revolution, more than 1,200 Christian priests were murdered.[5] Thousands more were sent to Gulag forced labor camps in Siberia. We know that this was just the beginning of millions of Christians being tortured, frozen, or killed in Soviet Gulags. As with post-Christian Germany, the ideas that drove post-Christian Russia to such insane violence began in universities as claims of peace and equality, not as violence. Then those ideas moved to the intellectual ruling class and spread through the leading edges of culture to the populace.

Two paintings from Russian artist Mikhail Nesterov symbolize this transition well. Nesterov's *Holy Rus* (*Holy Russia*), which he completed about ten years before the October Revolution, shows Russians gathered at the feet of Christ, with steeples and Christian cathedrals dotting the sky in the distance. This represents well the once-Christianized culture of Russia prior to socialism.

Holy Rus

Figure 5.1

In 1916, as the revolution was beginning to overtake the Russian mind, Nesterov painted *The Soul of the People*. It was his last Christian painting, because religious art was banned after 1917. *The Soul of the People* depicts representatives of all classes of Russian people, including the clergy, joining together to follow a new ideal. At the center, a darkened face of Christ is held by grieving clergy. Between the people and the new ideal, a hysterical, nearly naked prophet attempts to warn the nation about the dangers of their new ideal.

The Soul of the People

Figure 5.2

Nobel Prize winner Aleksandr Solzhenitsyn summarized the atrocities of the socialist Soviet Union best. He spoke from experience, having nearly died in the Gulag prisons himself: "If I were asked today to formulate as concisely as possible the main cause of the ruinous Revolution that swallowed up some sixty million of our people, I could not put it more accurately than to repeat: 'Men have forgotten God; that's why all this has happened.'"[6]

Some older Truth-Based Americans today were educated in classrooms that reported the atrocities of the USSR as a warning against communism, tyranny, socialism, and deadly ideologies. In contrast, younger Post-Truth Americans are now being raised in classrooms that ignore the consequences of Marxist ideas. More often today, young Americans are challenged to identify any bias they might have against communists.

Young Americans are so unaware of Marxism's record that a majority prefer Marxist "socialism" over "capitalism." As with Christianity and other American traditions, the incoming generations have been overexposed to the "errors" of capitalism. But they have not been taught the basic merits of traditional American beliefs. Incoming generations of Americans believe in a new ideal, and the new ideal—as we will see from the data—largely detests the traditional and Christian values that produced Western prosperity as we've known and inherited it.

IDEOLOGIES ARE WARRING FOR THE SOULS OF AMERICA AND OF HUMANITY

Every day as we go about our lives, ideologies are warring for the souls of nations and individuals. The war of ideas did not stop on D-Day or when the Berlin Wall fell. The present prosperity in America has distracted many of us from the reality that a war of ideologies is taking place daily in our lives, families, and society.

The story of the next thirty years in global humanity will not be the story of global warming or American party politics; it will be the story of ideologies. It will be the sad consequences of an American populace never trained to understand how ideologies are a more powerful force in human history than technology, progress, "acceptance," or the material world.

Today, when it comes to the remaining once-Christianized societies (like the United States, Canada, and portions of Europe), Satan probably doesn't care which ideas replace Truth-Based Christianity as long as some ideas replace Christianity.

On the surface, today's Post-Truth ideology can seem harmless enough, with its spineless "acceptance of all" and resulting emphasis on "tolerance."[7] Satan delights as post-Christian Americans adopt this Post-Truth ideology, which seems harmless and peaceful on the surface.[8] Satan delights because he knows that the Post-Truth ideology is flimsy. It will not be sustainable, but will quickly give way to something else, just as post-Christianity led to revolutions in France (1789–1799), Germany (1920–1945), and Russia (1917–1989).

It is a theme of world history that whenever Christianity is uprooted from a civilization, women and children suffer. Individual freedom, prosperity, and life expectancy all decrease when Christianity is uprooted.[9] Satan knows that Christianity is the only ideology that leads to ultimate freedom, peace, and eternal life. He knows this better than most Christians know it.

Today's Post-Truth ideology advertises itself as advocating for global human improvement and equality. Post-Truth thinkers genuinely believe the Post-Truth system will deliver this equality. Of course, Mao, Lenin, Stalin, and Mussolini[10] utilized similar language about equality, fairness, bettering humanity, and achieving justice for the poor. And their millions of followers genuinely believed them. Sadly, the blindness of the Post-Truth ideology will produce consequences that are far different from its noble-sounding intentions.[11]

We will cover a lot of important material in this chapter, so let's outline our journey into the Warring of Ideologies:

I. Global Ideologies: The Four Ideologies Claiming 86 Percent of Humanity Today

It is not that they [young, educated Americans] know very much about other nations, or about their own. The purpose of their education is not to make them scholars but to provide them with a moral virtue—openness.

Allan Bloom, *The Closing of the American Mind*

We may not learn it from our social media feeds, CNN, or the *New York Times*, but a handful of non-American ideologies dominate the thinking of 7.4 billion people alive today.

Thanks to the good work of the Pew Research Center, we can know with clarity what is actually happening in the world ideologically. We can know which ideologies dominate humanity today and which ones are on a trajectory to shape world events in our lifetime.

Surprisingly, some 86 percent of people in the world today view reality through one of just four basic ideologies, each of which is nearly absent in mainstream news reporting today.

Of the 7.4 billion people in the world today:

- Hinduism has about 1.1 billion adherents.[12]
- Atheistic communism has about 1.2 billion adherents.[13]
- Islam has about 1.8 billion adherents.[14]
- Christianity has about 2.3 billion adherents.[15]

Those four ideologies account for six out of every seven people alive today. And yet in my anecdotal experience, many educated Americans and Europeans today know little about these four most common ideologies. Nearly 86 percent of people alive today are motivated by one of these four ideologies. A vast majority of people in the world wake up in the morning, eat their breakfast, plan their day, and shape their entire life around one of these dominant ideologies. And yet many formally educated Americans who hold post-college degrees cannot recite the essential beliefs of any one of them.[16]

The remainder of the world population (those who are not Hindu, communist, Muslim, or Christian) is about one billion people, or less than one-seventh of the 7.4 billion people alive today.[17] The emerging Post-Truth generations in Europe and the United States are a subgroup of this one billion, accounting for about half of it.[18]

In the US and other Western nations, there is a mass exodus from Christianity. The result is the growing group of agnostics called the "nones"—presently the fastest-growing religious classification in America. These Post-Truth thinkers control most cultural posts in the US and Europe and are poised to shape Western cultures for the next thirty years. However, on a global scale, these Post-Truth thinkers are only a small fraction of the world population.

Note that these four dominant ideologies are underrepresented in our mainstream American media because mainstream news content is largely produced by writers, editors, and producers who see reality through the lens of America's Post-Truth agnosticism. Incidentally, less than 10 percent of the world shares the ideological lens and beliefs of mainstream American news.

The reason that humans—rather than, say, whales or elephants—shape world history is not the physical strength of the human body. The reason for human superiority is *reason*—that is, the power of ideas. When a group of humans adopts an idea and decides to act on it, social change and historical change happen.

Dominant World Ideologies Today

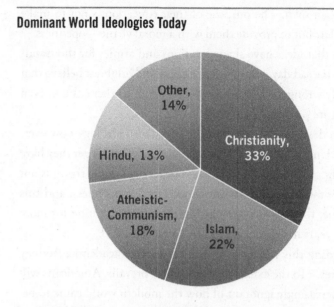

Source: Created by author as an aggregation of multiple data sources, including those mentioned on pp. 83–84 and 39–46.

Figure 5.3

It is a tragic moment for American society when many of our most educated are indoctrinated to believe that all ideas are more or less equal and harmless. This is a fallacy that will have severe consequences and lead not only to ignorance in world affairs but also eventually to subjugation by some conquering ideology.

Of the educated young Americans who prefer socialism to capitalism, one wonders how many know that Nazi is an abbreviation of *Nationalsozialistische*—the German word for "National Socialist." Hitler belonged to the National Socialist German Workers' Party, commonly referred to as the Nazi Party.

This ignorance regarding ideologies has been overtaking American universities for decades, according to such academics as Allan Bloom. Of America's brightest university students, Professor Bloom wrote, "It is not that they know very much about other nations, or about their own. The purpose of their education is not to make them scholars but to provide them with a moral virtue—openness."[19]

Given that ideas have shaped nations and armies for thousands of years, it is a sad day when America's best and brightest believe that it is morally wrong to critique the ideology of any other culture, even if that culture perpetuates unjust violence.

Bloom described the spirit of the Post-Truth ideology now overtaking the United States and Western culture: "The danger they have been taught to fear from absolutism [a belief in absolute truth] is not error but intolerance. Relativism is necessary to openness; and this is the virtue, the only virtue, which all primary education for more than fifty years has dedicated itself to inculcating."[20]

Regarding this educated ignorance, another academic, Rodney Stark, writes, "To the extent that this policy prevails, Americans will become increasingly ignorant of how the modern world came to be. Worse yet, they are in danger of being badly misled by a flood of absurd, politically correct fabrications, all of them popular on college campuses."[21]

Stanford scholar Thomas Sowell, who has held professorships at both Cornell and UCLA, summarized this: "Decades of dumbed-down education have produced people with no sense of the importance of a moral framework within which freedom and civil discourse can flourish. Without a moral framework, there is nothing left but immediate self-indulgence by some and the path of least resistance by others. Neither can sustain a free society."[22]

Even though we have more access to information and education than any other people in history, Americans are presently insulated from the brutality of other world ideologies. Contrary to the Post-Truth ideology, it is a fact that not all ideas are equal. Some ideas prevail. Some ideas fail. Some ideas lead to life, and some ideas lead to death. The same goes for cultures. Perhaps no century of world history has demonstrated this more clearly than the last one hundred years, with the hundreds of millions of people killed under Mao,

Stalin, and Hitler—each of which was propelled by an ideological revolution that seized control of a culture.

Here we sit, not even one hundred years removed from the three greatest mass killings in world history.

- World War II killed about 60 million people, driven by the Nazi ideology.
- Stalin's famines, Gulags, and firing squads killed between 20 and 60 million, driven by his socialist ideology.[23]
- Mao's "Great Leap Forward" was "responsible for the deaths of at least 45 million people between 1958 and 1962."[24]

It is a fact that all of these atrocities were driven by ideologies.[25] Each had a book (Hitler's *Mein Kampf*, Stalin's *Marxism and the National Question*, and Mao's *Little Red Book*) because each was a set of ideas, a lens for viewing all of reality, an ideology.

Here we sit, not one hundred years removed from the bloodiest genocides in history, and incoming generations of Western thinkers and cultural leaders have been trained to believe that all ideas are equal and equally harmless. With two notable exceptions:

- Traditional American/Christian ideas can be assaulted and demeaned.
- Any person who disagrees with the Post-Truth moral scaffolding can be labeled a "fascist," regardless of whether the person is an actual fascist.[26]

II. Ideologies in the US: The Civil War between Post-Truth and Truth-Based Ideologies

As the four dominant ideologies (Hinduism, communism, Islam, and Christianity) wrestle for control of the global population, two other ideologies are wrestling for control of the American mind, soul, and society.

The older *Truth-Based ideology* has been integral to society in the United States since the 1600s. However, the truth claims that produced this prosperous and free society have been under attack by America's most influential thinkers for about sixty years. As a result, a deadly moral relativism and self-loathing have resulted in the emerging dominant ideology, namely, the *Post-Truth ideology.*

Within our lifetime, we are witnessing the early consequences of a Post-Truth society (that is, a society in which more than half of the people are Post-Truth thinkers). This great sea change has just begun at the popular level, and it is on a trajectory to continue, according to generational data we will examine.

This shift in thinking leaves Americans self-ignorant and with a sense of self-loathing about the exceptional wealth and freedom they have inherited. It leaves incoming Americans ignorant about how the broader world works, and incapable of sustaining or protecting the massive inheritance bestowed on them.

A. Defining the Post-Truth and Truth-Based Ideologies

How do we define *Post-Truth* and *Truth-Based*? The Oxford Dictionary defines *Post-Truth* as "relating to or denoting circumstances in which objective facts are less influential in shaping public opinion than appeals to emotion and personal belief."[27] In other words, Post-Truth thinking defines reality by feelings more than by facts. In the simplest sense, a Post-Truth ideology is a view of the world in which reality and morality are defined by a person's emotions, feelings, local culture, or subjective personal criteria rather than by objective facts or fixed standards, such as written law or immutable principles.

Here is a simple litmus test. How would you answer this question: Are right and wrong defined by a fixed standard outside of my personal feelings and experiences? Truth-Based thinkers will answer yes; Post-Truth thinkers will answer no.

- Truth-Based thinkers look to an outside, fixed, unchanging written standard to define right and wrong.[28]
- Post-Truth thinkers look to their feelings, intuitions, cultural norms, and peers to define right and wrong.

A Truth-Based view of reality was the predominant ideology for hundreds of years in the United States. Right and wrong were defined by an objective, outside standard. Historically in the US, the outside standard included Christian values, the Bible, the Ten Commandments, and the written laws of the government, especially the Constitution.

Truth-Based thinkers today still view all of morality and reality through the lenses of these unchanging outside standards. The objective standards (the Bible, the Constitution, etc.) define good and bad, right and wrong, up and down. If a person or culture contradicts these standards, then that person or culture is "wrong." In the Truth-Based ideology, it is not bigoted, prejudiced, or mean-spirited to tell someone they are wrong when they contradict the truth. It is a simple statement of fact, as simple as telling someone they are "wrong" to believe that "5" is the correct answer to "2 + 2."

Conversely, at its simplest, the Post-Truth ideology trusts feelings, experience, or moral peer pressure as the decider of what is right or wrong for each person. As a result, the Post-Truth thinker is not concerned with the writings of history, Christianity, religion, or even the Constitution. Those writings are not the standard of right and wrong today or for all people. Post-Truth thinkers define what is right or wrong based on their feelings or opinion at any given moment.

For Post-Truth thinkers, the social pressure of a group or culture can also define what is right or wrong—separate from any written, objective, or historical standard. And so for a Post-Truth thinker, it is immoral and condescending to tell people from other cultures that their morality or behavior is wrong. As we see in the struggle against terrorism, and as we'll continue to see in the next thirty years, Post-Truth thinkers will not even label a terrorist who beheads children as "wrong" in his thinking or motivation.

To use some older academic terms, the Post-Truth ideology operates from a "relativistic" view of morality. However, Post-Truth is much more than just "relative truth" as theory; it is the maturing of that theory as it breaks into actual society. Of course, most Post-Truth thinkers would not use words like *relative truth, morality*, or *Post-Truth* to describe themselves.[29] They would also be appalled at the beheading of a child, but would not be able to give any concrete reason why it is wrong other than to state, "It's just wrong."

What Post-Truth thinkers are doing is defending a floating set of moral imperatives that they have been conditioned, in classrooms and in popular culture, to believe. Thomas Sowell summarized this moral peer pressure when he wrote, "If facts, logic, and scientific procedures are all just arbitrary 'socially constructed' notions, then all that is left is consensus—more specifically peer consensus, the kind of consensus that matters to adolescents or to many among the intelligentsia."[30] That this floating set of imperatives is rife with self-contradiction and historical contradiction does not occur to them or matter to them.

Professor Sowell added this about what I define as Post-Truth thinking: "[The problem in American universities today] is not merely that Johnny can't read, or even that Johnny can't think. *Johnny doesn't know what thinking is*, because thinking is so often confused with feeling in many public schools."[31]

In *The Closing of the American Mind*, Professor Allan Bloom writes that when confronted with the inconsistencies of the Post-Truth framework, young Americans in his classrooms recoil with concern that he would even dare to question the Post-Truth view of reality.[32] Describing college students of varying races, classes, and regions across the US, Bloom writes, "They are unified only in their relativism and in their allegiance to equality . . . The point is not to correct the mistakes [of history] and really be right; rather it is not to think you are right at all."[33]

Then Bloom describes how Post-Truth thinkers respond when their system is challenged. He offers a scenario in which he asks Post-Truth students if they would stop the burning of a widow in India (where, prior to Western intervention, widows were traditionally burned at their husbands' funerals). But the students respond that it was wrong to be in India in the first place. In so doing, they completely ignore the widow who is being burned on the funeral pyre.

> The students, of course, cannot defend their opinion. It is something with which they have been indoctrinated. The best they can do is point out all the opinions and cultures there are and have been. What right, they ask, do I or anyone else have to say one is better than the others? If I pose the routine questions designed to confute them and make them think, such as, "If you had been a British administrator in India, would you have let the natives under your governance burn the widow at the funeral of a man who had died?," they either remain silent or reply that the British should never have been there in the first place.[34]

Believe it or not, Bloom wrote these words in 1987. Yet how incisively they describe our society today. We are witnessing today this view of the world—the Post-Truth ideology—as it graduates from university lecture halls to Main Street and to middle school classrooms. The Post-Truth ideology is evolving from a minority "progressive" ideology to a majority "society" position.

Bloom describes the conflict between Post-Truth and Truth-Based thinking in these paragraphs:

> The palpable difference between these two can easily be found in the changed understanding of what it means to be an American. The old view was that, by recognizing and accepting

man's natural rights [an objective truth standard outside of oneself], men found a fundamental basis of unity and saneness. Class, race, religion, national origin or culture all disappear or become dim when bathed in the light of natural rights, which give men common interests and make them truly brothers . . .

The recent education of "openness" has rejected all that. It pays no attention to natural rights or the historical origins of our regime, which are now thought to have been essentially flawed and regressive. [The new Post-Truth ideology is instead] progressive and forward-looking . . . It is open to all kinds of men, all kinds of life-styles, all ideologies. There is no enemy other than the man who is not open to everything.[35]

And then Bloom asks this prophetic question: "But when there are no shared goals or vision of the public good, is the social contract [Western democracy as we've known it] any longer possible?"

The disastrous implications of a truly Post-Truth America cannot be fully imagined. The most central institutions, cultural norms, and facets of American prosperity have been built on Truth-Based foundations. Take basic law and justice, for example. The US Supreme Court has engraved over its pillared entrance these words, referring to the 14th Amendment: "Equal Justice Under Law."

The law has been, until now, an objective third party, an outside truth standard, that can fairly provide equal justice to all because it is not partial or biased, as human beings are. In a Post-Truth culture, that will no longer be the case—even in a building that states so, because each of these words is being redefined by cultural moods rather than by an objective definition.

Ask a Post-Truth American what *justice* and *equal* mean, and you'll likely hear a moral opinion in response, not a factual definition. When such thinkers graduate with a law degree or become judges, they do not cease to view the world through their Post-Truth lens.

Post-Truth thinkers are not consciously aware that they see reality through a "Post-Truth ideology." The Post-Truth ideology does not have formal doctrine in the sense that communism, Islam, and Christianity have formal doctrinal statements. While this ideology lacks an official doctrinal statement, it is nonetheless being indoctrinated into Americans through a number of approaches, both direct and indirect. Despite the lack of formal doctrine, Alan Bloom suggests that this ideology has been indoctrinated through the best American universities for more than seventy years now.

George Marsden has done some of the best work documenting this post-Christian shift in the elite universities and the resulting Post-Truth shift. He documents the most noticeable shift in this direction around 1900 and growing consistently since—"from Protestant establishment to established nonbelief."[36]

B. America's Post-Truth Turn and Its Tipping Point

A slight majority of American adults are already Post-Truth thinkers, according to a 2016 Barna Survey. It found that 57 percent of American adults agree that "knowing what is right or wrong is a matter of personal experience."[37] In many ways, this near fifty-fifty split underlies the deep cultural division presently tearing the United States in two. However, the future belongs to the Post-Truth ideology, according to generational trends.

Like other trends traced in this book, the Post-Truth view grows rapidly among younger generations of Americans. As the Barna Group reports, "This [Post-Truth] view is much more prevalent among younger generations than among older adults. Three-quarters of Millennials (74%) agree strongly or somewhat with the statement, 'Whatever is right for your life or works best for you is the only truth you can know,' compared to only 38 percent of Elders."[38]

Notice the increase in the Post-Truth posture among each younger generation of Americans. Combine the "agree somewhat" and "agree strongly" categories in the figure on the next page to get the total percentage of those who agree in each generation.

Morality and Truth

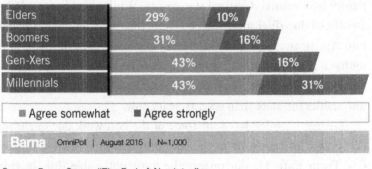

	Agree somewhat	Agree strongly
Elders	29%	10%
Boomers	31%	16%
Gen-Xers	43%	16%
Millennials	43%	31%

Barna OmniPoll | August 2015 | N=1,000

Source: Barna Group, "The End of Absolutes"
Barna OmniPoll | July 3–9, 2015

Figure 5.4

As you can see, the percentage of people who hold to a Post-Truth ideology increases consistently with each younger generation of Americans: from 39 percent in the elder generation to 47 percent in the baby boomer generation, to 59 percent in Generation X (those between boomers and millennials) to 74 percent in the millennials.

We can surmise that—barring a change of course in the social trajectory—the generation younger than millennials (sometimes known as Generation Z) will almost entirely hold to the Post-Truth view of morality. At the rate of increase above (about 15 percent increase per generation), some 89 percent of the incoming Generation Z will be Post-Truth thinkers. The subsequent generation then would be at 100 percent agreement at today's rate of cultural change. The result will be, of course, an entirely different society.

A different question in the same Barna survey reveals, again, that a slight majority of American adults already hold to a Post-Truth view of what is right or wrong when truth is defined by a group's host culture: "A sizable number of Americans see morality as a matter of cultural consensus. About two-thirds of all American adults (65%) agree either strongly or somewhat (18% and 47% respectively) that 'every culture must determine what is acceptable morality for its people.'"[39]

Summarizing the results, Barna Group president David Kinnaman states that this subjective morality "has all but replaced Christianity as the culture's moral norm." His researchers found that "the morality of self-fulfillment can be summed up in six guiding principles, as seen in the table below."[40]

The Morality of Self-Fulfillment

% "completely" + "somewhat" agree	% all U.S. adults
The best way to find yourself is by looking within yourself	91
People should not criticize someone else's life choices	89
To be fulfilled in life, you should pursue the things you desire most	86
The highest goal of life is to enjoy it as much as possible	84
People can believe whatever they want, as long as those beliefs don't affect society	79
Any kind of sexual expression between two consenting adults is acceptable	69

Barna   OmniPoll | August 2015 | N=1,000

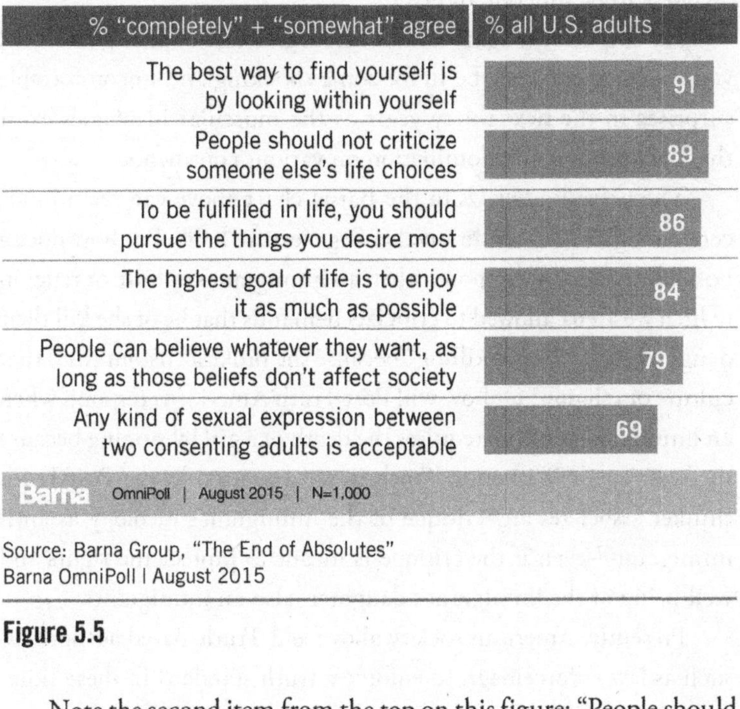

Source: Barna Group, "The End of Absolutes"
Barna OmniPoll I August 2015

Figure 5.5

Note the second item from the top on this figure: "People should not criticize someone else's life choices." It is this trait of Post-Truth thinking that is impairing the West's ability to understand world events. Post-Truth Westerners are failing to understand the competition of world ideologies because they have been conditioned to never criticize another culture.

Increasingly, Americans are so frightened to criticize anyone else's choices that they refuse to critique the ideology of Islam or the consequences of communism or much else. But whether Americans acknowledge it or not, communism, Islam, and other muscular ideologies are advancing around the globe, and almost all dominant ideologies claim to be exclusively superior.

Furthermore, ideologies like communism and Islam often require their devout adherents to force the ideology on the rest of society (for the good of society, they say) because they believe their ideology to be superior and true.

Having been taught that all ideologies can coexist peacefully, young Americans may be in for some shocking and uncomfortable surprises in the next thirty years as the muscular ideologies exert their subjugation and domination on various continents.

The prevailing views in the Barna chart above can seem innocent enough in air-conditioned college lecture halls. But how does a Post-Truth ideology respond when an immigrant's culture or religion (which we aren't allowed to criticize) demands that he or she kill their daughter in an "honor killing" because she broke a custom from that culture or religion? Or how will Post-Truth Americans respond when an immigrant's culture requires the death of a girl by stoning because she was raped? Without a Truth-Based framework, the Post-Truth thinker associates any critique of the immigrant's ideology as anti-immigrant—even if the critique is meant to protect the rights and well-being of the immigrant's daughter (also an immigrant).

Presently, American society allows old Truth-Based authorities, such as law enforcement, to enforce a truth standard in these situations. But it will become an obvious inconsistency with the emerging culture, and at times Post-Truth thinkers will protest, revolt, riot, or eventually rewrite the laws.

How will a Post-Truth culture respond if a person, being "true to himself," feels he must express his love sexually to children? How about when a brother and sister are sexually attracted and must either be sexually active together or else "deny their true identity" and not "be who they really are"? How will a Post-Truth culture respond when an emerging socially popular group's rights require the silencing, firing, or property seizure of a socially unpopular group? These are the sorts of conflicts that Post-Truth Americans will be ill-equipped to handle or understand as they reshape cities, workplaces, and society into the Post-Truth image.

Modern Westerners remain confused and impotent when the ideas of other cultures—which they have been conditioned to respect, no matter what—turn out to be dangerous or even murderous.

Beyond the US and Europe, the believers of most muscular ideologies accept that the best way to serve humanity is to force their ideology on the rest of humanity. We see a good example in the words of a British Muslim cleric who advocates violence against the West. He explains that Islam will be better for Westerners, and so it should be forced on them, by violence if necessary, even if they do not want it. Following the murder of French journalists who had dishonored Muhammad, Anjem Choudary explained that it was the religious duty of all Muslims to violently enforce their "peace" on the ignorant masses in England and the United States. Writing in *USA Today*, Choudary clarified:

> Contrary to popular misconception, Islam does not mean peace but rather means submission to the commands of Allah alone. Therefore, Muslims do not believe in the concept of freedom of expression, as their speech and actions are determined by divine revelation and not based on people's desires.[41]

A lecturer in sharia, Anjem Choudary concluded with these words:

> Muslims consider the honor of the Prophet Muhammad to be dearer to them than that of their parents or even themselves.

To defend it is considered to be an obligation upon them. The strict punishment if found guilty of this crime [dishonoring the prophet] under sharia (Islamic law) is capital punishment implementable by an Islamic State. This is because the Messenger Muhammad said, "Whoever insults a Prophet kill him" . . .

It is time that the sanctity of a Prophet revered by up to one-quarter of the world's population was protected.[42]

It was brave of *USA Today* to print this. In today's climate, many of our most educated would call it Islamophobic to print the opinion of a Muslim—if that opinion calls for violent interpretations of Islam.

In my experience with intellectuals in America today, opinions like Anjem Choudary's get explained away with a flip of the wrist: "Oh, he doesn't know what he's talking about." But do these intellectuals realize the condescending superiority of such a statement? An "educated" American who cannot recite a single pillar of Islam believes he or she knows more about Islam than a Muslim scholar who lectures on sharia. Why? Because that Muslim scholar stated a call to violence. The American intellectual has been indoctrinated to believe that exotic foreign cultures would never call for violence in our modern era.

Sadly, ideas have consequences. **As the impotent West continues to ignore the muscular ideologies that overtly seek its destruction, those ideologies march ahead violently.** Between 2015 and 2017, Islamic terror seemed to randomly explode in France, Germany, England, and across Europe. Multiple incidents involved bombings, the beheading of a priest during a Mass in a Catholic church, mass shootings, and the mowing down of civilians with cars or trucks. These terror events have become so routine that many Americans now skip past the headlines, numb to the reality that this was not always normal in Europe or the United States.

In the spring of 2017, an Islamic terrorist bombed the Manchester Arena in England, killing twenty-two concertgoers.[43] Just one month earlier, another Islamic terrorist mowed down pedestrians on the Westminster Bridge and then stabbed police, injuring fifty people and killing four.[44]

I cite these two attacks in 2017 because it was a full two years earlier that the British Muslim Anjem Choudary wrote in his *USA Today* opinion piece, "Muslims do not believe in the concept of freedom of expression, as their speech and actions are determined by divine revelation and not based on people's desires . . . It is time that the sanctity of a Prophet revered by up to one-quarter of the world's population was protected."

What Does Post-Truth Look Like?

Here are some common *assumptions and traits of Post-Truth thinkers.*[45] Post-Truth thinkers are

- **hesitant** to critique any outside culture, religion, or way of life
- **repulsed** by traditional American claims of morality or absolute truth
- **eager** to promote exotic ideologies without examining the impact on human rights
- **prejudiced** against any truth claim that originates in the Christianized West, including the Bible, Judeo-Christian ethics, Christian morals, or patriotism
- **conditioned** to be suspicious of or even prejudiced against certain classes that they've been trained to view as oppressors (for example, rich white males, Christians, etc.).

Here are some *characteristics that are true of Post-Truth ideology* itself:

- A Post-Truth ideology is less a logical system and more a **floating set of moral imperatives** or societal assumptions that often contradict each other.

- In contradiction with its basic premise, a Post-Truth ideology **views itself as superior** to the old Truth-Based view of reality. It will rarely claim supremacy over ideologies that are foreign or exotic.

- Facts that support the Post-Truth constellation of right and wrong will be utilized with bravado, whereas **facts that contradict** the Post-Truth constellation of right and wrong **will be ignored**.

- A Post-Truth ideology will **adopt old Truth-Based language** or schema when doing so serves its own purposes. For example, anything a Post-Truth thinker feels people should be able to do is "a constitutional right," regardless of whether that behavior is factually mentioned in the Constitution—or whether the person resides in the US.

  "Constitutional right" becomes the tool for justifying a position rather than the standard for defining if the position is justifiable. The same becomes true of words like *justice, equality,* and *morally right*. These words become adjectives describing how we feel about what should be done.

  A Post-Truth thinker might say, **"Jesus would never condemn _____."** They say this not because they've read the words of Jesus or have attempted to conform their life to Jesus' statements. Instead, they wish to co-opt the vestiges of power in the old Truth-Based language (words like *Jesus, rights, justice, moral imperative*) to validate their predetermined point of view.

Some of the common *behaviors of Post-Truth thinkers* are as follows:

- When challenged, Post-Truth thinkers will **respond with a sense of disgust**, shock, contempt, or moral superiority. They will respond that you have no right to judge them or anyone else. Since only a racist or bigot would challenge the Post-Truth view, you have proved yourself to be a racist or bigot by challenging their view. The facts, evidence, or logic of your argument are irrelevant and will not be considered on their own merits.

- They **label their critics** as racist, xenophobic, Islamophobic, bigoted, or prejudiced, even when the questioning is logical and delivered as inoffensively as possible.

- Conversely, the Post-Truth thinker has the right (nay, the responsibility) to **use any amount of foul language and even inaccuracy** to demean those bigots who would question today's arrangement of the Post-Truth constellation of right and wrong.

- The most devout Post-Truth thinkers also **use violence to silence conservatives and others who disagree** with them. A good example is an antifascist protester who vows to push Republicans to the ground because all conservatives "espouse hatred toward LGBT, immigrants, people of color or others."[46] The fact that prejudging all Republicans and threatening to "drag and push" them is itself a form of hatred is lost on the Post-Truth protesters.

- For a Post-Truth thinker, **arguments about society or morality based on objective facts are largely irrelevant**. The exception is any evidence that already fits the Post-Truth narrative at the moment—for example, truths such as Thomas Jefferson having had slaves or white people having committed genocide against Native Americans. Evidence is considered or not considered based on its alignment with the floating constellation of what is actually right and wrong in the Post-Truth framework.

- The Post-Truth view will **have contradictions with hard science** and within storied journalistic institutions such as the *New York Times* and the *Washington Post*. These institutions are the sworn defenders of truth. They hold this calling with great pride (rightly so). And yet, in a self-contradiction, a majority of the minds in their newsrooms no longer believe that truth is objective.[47]

- Post-Truth thinkers **do not necessarily know they see the world through this specific ideology**. Nor do they understand, for the most part, the power of ideologies in general.

- Post-Truth thinkers **do not know that most people outside of the West despise the idea that all ideas are equal** and hold their competing ideologies (Islam, Hinduism, communism, etc.) to be exclusively true and worthy of subjugating weaker ideologies.

- The Post-Truth **constellation of right and wrong** is floating and unanchored. It **can change and will change**. In this sense, peer pressure and cultural influencers will increasingly define what is right and wrong for the next thirty years. Incidentally, if it ever became culturally popular to deride "Post-Truth," the Post-Truth thinkers would be among the first to do so, not because of any facts, but because of the social pressure to do so. Post-Truth morality is **a bandwagon severed from facts**.

- Post-Truth thinkers **will not critique foreign or minority views**, even if these views produce violence.

- Post-Truth thinkers **will largely fail to understand the role of ideologies** in the world beyond the United States.

- Post-Truth thinkers will **fail to understand that devout adherents of any religion or ideology see their view as exclusively superior** to the degree that many devout people are willing to give their lives to protect their ideologies.

- Post-Truth thinkers **will be quick to defend** Islam, communism, or any non-American (such as Fidel Castro), citing that Truth-Based Westerners told a "skewed narrative" that "villainized" those other ideologies through an "imperialistic" perspective.

- Post-Truth thinkers **will go so far as to blame the West** for violence perpetrated by other ideologies beyond the West (for example, "ISIS would not be killing people if the US hadn't invaded the Middle East"); any opponent who produces facts about violence in Islam before the United States even existed will only be proving themselves to be "Islamophobic."

- Post-Truth thinkers **will not be persuaded by arguments** from history or fact.
- Post-Truth thinkers **will rally in protest** against any traditional American-made truth claim, particularly those put forth by the groups they've been conditioned to view as imperialistic or oppressors, including white people, the rich, conservatives, Christians, and, most recently in some settings, Jews.
- Post-Truth thinkers **will quickly turn against a true minority individual** (such as an African-American woman) if that individual sides with a Truth-Based ideology.[48]
- Post-Truth thinkers **will largely disagree** that Islam, communism, Hinduism, or other foreign/exotic ideologies would ever **claim to be superior** to others—even in the presence of a Muslim, communist, or Hindu who is overtly stating that their opinion is exclusive and superior to others.

Ironically, the same Post-Truth thinker who accuses a Truth-Based thinker of being demeaning and condescending toward minority views is, in fact, the party being demeaning and condescending to a Muslim, communist, or Hindu. The Post-Truth thinker refuses to believe what a Muslim says about Islam if that Muslim's statement of fact contradicts the Post-Truth view of other ideologies as harmless.

A Truth-Based thinker, while labeled closed-minded, is actually in a position to take foreign believers seriously because a Truth-Based thinker can comprehend that all muscular ideologies claim exclusivity and reason to validate their superiority.

A Post-Truth ideology has the effect of banning certain classes. It likely does so with the highest of motives—to protect the little people and the oppressed. This banning of classes is not intended to be overt hatred toward certain groups, but it is the result of constant coursework emphasizing the historical flaws of these groups. These classes can include traditional Americans, patriotic Americans, rich white males, Christians, and sometimes Jews.

Because truth is not an objective reality but an expression of oneself, people from the classes banned by Post-Truth do not have any meaningful truth within themselves—nothing that really bears considering. And so they do not deserve the stage or even the opportunity to express themselves. They have controlled the world long enough, and now it's time for them to take a back seat.

Because of the relativistic mood of our times, many Americans hold contradicting pieces of both the Post-Truth and Truth-Based ideologies simultaneously. Determining if someone is a Post-Truth thinker is not always clear-cut. And it may change from day to day. Indeed, many Americans probably do change from a Truth-Based to a Post-Truth view gradually, including the two in three evangelical Christian youth who abandon the Christian faith between the ages of eighteen and twenty-nine.[49]

The shift to a Post-Truth ideology has vast implications for society. Because Truth-Based language and values have been embedded into US culture since its inception, the remains of Truth-Based language and values will be seen in institutions and individuals for many years, even while a Post-Truth ideology gradually becomes the majority view in the US.

The lingering of Truth-Based laws will eventually result in obvious contradictions. For example, Post-Truth society says it is wrong to criticize anyone's sexual expression. And yet the US still has Truth-Based laws about polygamy, incest, and sex with minors. These laws, once their truth foundation is removed, will remain for some time, but eventually they will be exposed as contradicting the Post-Truth mood.

Similarly, because the Truth-Based society in the US once valued Christianity, churches, clergy, and the Bible, specific tax advantages for churches and clergy have been part of US law for centuries. However, as Post-Truth values take hold of the mood of culture, many of these clergy and churches may be relabeled as "hate groups" because of their absolute beliefs about sexual morality or other matters.

And so there will come a time when Post-Truth Americans begin to question why "these bigots" receive tax advantages. That will be step one. Eventually, the Christian and church groups that remain "bigoted" may not only lose any tax advantages, but also someday lose the right to function as open organizations at all, being denied zoning permits or other city, county, state, or federal licenses. I don't suggest this will happen overnight, but steps toward it have already been considered in the California legislature.[50]

Presently, most of the contradictions between Truth-Based societal foundations and the Post-Truth mood have gone unexamined—which may be, in part, because the first generations that are majority Post-Truth (beginning with millennials) are just now taking the helm of society. Also, as the first majority Post-Truth generation, millennials still have some lingering Truth-Based foundation in their values and institutional memory. The more severe turning will be when the children raised in a fully Post-Truth society take the helm of US society in 2025 and beyond.

Further Defining a Truth-Based Ideology

If you've made it to this point in this book, there is a good chance you are a Truth-Based thinker. But let's not take this for granted. And let's force ourselves to be clear in our thinking.

For our purposes, a Truth-Based ideology holds truth to be an objective standard distinct and separate from one's feelings, experiences, culture, or background. Cultures, moods, and opinions change, but truth remains fixed and absolute.

Technically speaking, all serious religions are Truth-Based in that they claim their truth to be exclusive. Technically, Marxism and many other social theories are also Truth-Based in that they claim exclusive models for humanity.

However, for our purposes, the term *Truth-Based* in this book refers to the ideology that prevailed in the US until very recently. And so we're speaking specifically of the Judeo-Christian Truth-Based ideology—that set of values and thinking that clearly influenced the writers of the US Constitution, resulted in churches often being built before homes in early American cities, and shaped US culture in ways that sociologists such as Rodney Stark have clearly documented.

Since this book primarily assesses the US and the West—where the truth standard for hundreds of years was the Bible and Christian values—I'll use the term *Truth-Based* to refer to the uniquely Christian Truth-Based ideology that imperfectly but pervasively saturated Western Europe and the United States from the Protestant Reformation until very recently.

Here are some *assumptions and traits that are typically true of Truth-Based thinkers*:

- They **hold objective standards of truth** to be more authoritative than personal experience. Pervasively, those standards in the US have been the Bible, Christian values, and the US Constitution.
- They **are eager to critique** and weigh truth claims because they have been taught to pursue the truth.
- They **can disagree with a person about "the truth"** without hating the person—because truth is a separate party from the disagreement. **Truth is a third party.**
- They **value factual accuracy**.
- They **can be condescending or closed-minded** toward ideologies they deem to be false.
- They **can lack grace** when defending the truth.

Just as Post-Truth thinkers live with many unexamined contradictions, it is a reality that many Truth-Based Christians have not fully aligned their lives with the truth claims of the Bible.

Here are some *characteristics that are true of the Christian Truth-Based ideology* itself:

- The Christian Truth-Based ideology **is the ideological seed in the founding of most American universities**. Evidence of this remains to this day in many university crests—like Harvard's, which includes the word *truth* written in Latin on a Bible: *Veritas*. Almost all of the Ivy crests have images of open Bibles or the word *light*—a reference to God's Word being a lamp for our feet and a light on our path.[51]

- The Truth-Based ideology **is the philosophy that revolutionized the study of science and the natural world**, because facts about the natural world were believed to be orderly and consistent. Thus, Christians who held this ideology led the way in unlocking the scientific revolution and moving humanity away from mystery and superstition about "spirits" causing all sickness.[52]

C. What Is at Stake? Evidence that America's Old Truth-Based Ideology Created Unprecedented Wealth and Freedom

When the supernatural beings behold planet Earth, they see God's people spiritually, perhaps as lights shining in the darkness—Christ's people spread like constellations around the globe, shining like stars in the night sky. During the last few hundred years, a concentrated cluster of light, a beacon, has shined from the Christianized nations, including the United States and portions of Europe.[53] This beacon of light has exported hospitals, women's rights, vaccines, the abolition of slavery, life-giving medicine, and humane laws to the entire globe, benefiting all of humanity (not perfectly, but consistently).

God loves all people of all races and religious creeds, and He desires to benefit all of humanity through the fruit of His people on earth, imperfect as His people are. The ideology of Christianity as adopted by Western nations in recent centuries has undeniably benefited humanity, almost beyond measure.

An Increase in Global Literacy

Since the Protestant Reformation, **global literacy has rocketed from nearly 12 percent to nearly 85 percent, driven by the Christianized regions.**[54] With literacy came Christian-founded universities, which in turn produced medicine, hospitals, innovation, invention, the abolition of slavery, the Protestant work ethic, and prosperous society as we know it. None of these were the work of any one race or nation, but rather, all were the fruit of an ideology.

Literate and Illiterate World Population

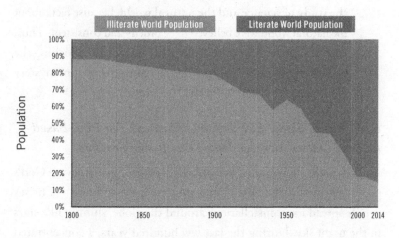

Source: Our World in Data based on OECD and UNESCO (2016),
https://ourworldindata.org/literacy/#historical-perspective

Figure 5.6

Born into prosperity and education, we struggle to comprehend that just two hundred years ago, nine out of ten people globally could not read. This explosion of literacy was driven by the Christianized Western nations following the Protestant Reformation (1517–1648). If we traced the line backward for thousands of years, it would remain below 10 percent for most of history prior to the Protestant Reformation.

No serious historian would deny that **the burst toward world literacy originated in the Christianized West.**[55] Italy, Sweden, Great Britain, Germany, and other Christianized nations launched it, and it then spread to the rest of the world.[56] It is an undeniable fact of history that the Protestant Reformation drove literacy as an obvious result of Protestant Christianity's invention of the printing press and the coinciding emphasis on reading the Bible for oneself.

An Increase in Life Expectancy and a Decrease in Child Mortality

A national and regional look at the dramatic increase in life expectancy during the last 150 years reveals that **the doubling of human life expectancy also originated in the Christianized West.**[57] In a similar fashion to the scientific revolution and its effect on medicine, the Christianized nations led the world in this dramatic increase in life expectancy and better health. Europe, the Americas, and Oceania (which largely tracks with the Americas) led the world in doubling life expectancy as a global norm.

Throughout human history, almost four in ten children died by age five. This was because the world did not have advanced medicine or a scientific understanding of germ theory. Infant deaths, childhood disease, malnutrition, and poor living conditions were common. From 1730 until now, child mortality (the percentage of children who die) has dropped from about four in ten children dying by age five to far less than one in ten.

Even as recently as the year 1800, about four hundred out of every thousand children born would die by age five. Now that number is less than one in every thousand. Studies have again shown us that this worldwide benefit originated in the Christianized Western nations.

———————————

Literacy and life expectancy more than doubled, thanks to the science and innovations that originated in Christianized nations, led largely by the universities that Christians founded, such as Oxford and Cambridge in the early years and then Harvard, Yale, Princeton, and Johns Hopkins, all founded to further the Christian ideology. Child mortality has dropped dramatically, also led by Christian- ized nations. These are neglected and unpopular facts in today's curriculum.

An Increase in Acts of Service to Those Needing Justice

Similarly, **women's rights and the uprooting of slavery also link up with Christianized regions**. In many settings, pointing out these facts is no longer allowed because it can be perceived as ethnocentric. But these facts aren't about ethnicity; they're not even about nations or nationalism. These facts are about *ideology*. The reality is that the Truth-Based ideology of Christianity benefits the societies that embrace it.

In fact, the benefits of Christianity tend to spread far beyond Christian societies to benefit the rest of the world too. For example, slavery was not banned in some Muslim-majority countries until the last fifty years. Why did these societies finally ban slavery? Because Western nations required them to do so if they wished to sell oil or do business. In our day, Christian "missionaries" continue to export hospitals, orphanages, medical clinics, job training centers, and clean water to the world.

New York Times columnist Nicholas Kristof, a humanitarian who travels the world, has written openly about how he routinely finds Christians doing the behind-the-scenes good works of the world, operating hospitals and orphanages and addressing social issues in the most disadvantaged and repressive parts of the world today.[58]

It is a fact that the most anti-Christian activists of our day ignorantly enjoy the benefits of Christianity in their life expectancy, their freedom to speak, their standard of living, and even in their basic ability to read and write their arguments against Christianity. These all result from the works and beliefs of Christians in our recent ancestry. It is no wonder, then, given Satan's aim to keep humanity as slaves in the darkness, that he has strategically attacked the foundation of Truth-Based Christianity within the lighthouse beacons of the United States and Western Europe.

Again, these benefits are not the results of races or nationalism, but of the Christian Truth-Based ideology. Nor is it to say that these Western societies were ever perfect or ever perfectly implemented the Christian ideals. Christianized civilizations have blood and injustice in their history—just as does every other civilization in human history. However, inasmuch as the Western nations did implement the Christian ideals, albeit imperfectly, Western society improved more than any other society in history. **To the extent that the West practiced the Christian ideals, its society rose above the global averages in health, freedom, rights, wealth, and well-being.**

While the regions and their populations have never been perfect or perfectly Christian, the Western nations are (1) the regions where New Testament Christian beliefs have most affected society, government, and culture by the willful choice of the people and (2) the regions where the same beliefs' contributions to medicine and human rights are an undeniable matter of record.

Take, for example, the invention of the university, the vaccine, the airplane, the automobile, germ theory, and social literacy—and the list goes on of innovations that sprouted exclusively from these Christianized regions. The concentrated origin of these innovations is a disregarded mystery to those who profess that ideology does not affect society. Some will credit raw materials, imperialism, or even better weather for producing these advances, but a simple analysis of historical conditions reveals other societies with superior materials, conquests, or weather that didn't produce these advances.

The facts are clear. What is sad is that so many refuse to consider them.

Today, Satan is using the same strategy he employed in post-Christian Germany that led to World War II. It is the same strategy he used to an extent in post-Christian Russia that led to the Stalin years. For decades, the deceiver has been attacking Christianity's Truth-Based view of reality, dismantling it from the ground up, beginning at its foundations.[59]

The deconstruction began with intellectual arguments against Christianity in the leading universities. Now graduates of these universities have carried the anti-Christian ideology into every leading edge of culture. Sadly, many of these anti-Christian thinkers are kind people who mean well, but who have been deceived about the role of Christianity in society. Nicholas Kristof summarized this well when he wrote, "In these polarized times, few words conjure as much distaste in liberal circles as 'evangelical Christian' . . . It reflects a kind of reverse intolerance, sometimes a reverse bigotry."[60]

At the leading edges of American culture today, there is a sincere belief that Christianity is a dangerous ideology. There is a curious hunger to promote Islamic thinkers, old forms of communism in new clothes, and any passionate thinker who argues against Christianity. There is little interest in or even fairness toward sincere Christian ideas or the people who carry them. We are witnessing the graduation of America's anti-Christian, Post-Truth ideology as it moves from the university to positions of cultural dominance. It has progressed from academia to now occupy most of the leading edges of culture.

The final vestiges of belief in the old Truth-Based ideology are concentrated in the baby boomer and older population. These Truth-Based Americans are not surrendering quietly, but they are gradually aging out of influence in most industries. The deep division in the United States is largely the struggle between the remnant of Truth-Based American thinkers in conflict with the new Post-Truth American thinkers. The divide may be close to fifty-fifty at present, but we will see that the younger age of Post-Truth Americans, on average, makes Post-Truth's victory nearly inevitable in the coming decades.

D. Socialism Surging among Post-Truth Americans

As a result of the shift toward Post-Truth thinking, eighteen- to twenty-nine-year-old Americans are more likely to have a positive view of socialism than of capitalism, according to Pew researchers.[61]

Consider the generational change in this Pew Research chart on views of capitalism versus socialism.[62]

REACTION TO . . .	CAPITALISM		SOCIALISM		Diff in % Positive (for Capitalism)
	Positive	Negative	Positive	Negative	
	%	%	%	%	
Total	50	40	31	60	+19
Age 18–29	46	47	49	43	-3
Age 30–49	50	40	34	58	+16
Age 50–64	53	39	25	68	+28
age 65+	52	32	13	72	+39

Source: Pew Research Center December 7–11, 2011

Figure 5.7

Note the "age 18–29" row, in which 47 percent have a negative view of capitalism, but only 46 percent have a positive view of capitalism—that is, more have a negative view of capitalism than a positive one. Then note in the same "age 18–29" row that 49 percent have a positive view of socialism, and only 43 percent have a negative view of socialism.

This is the first generation of Americans ever polled in which more Americans prefer socialism to capitalism. This shift is not likely due to a pure understanding of capitalism and socialism. I suggest the shift is one repercussion of the Post-Truth education in which Western traditions are constantly deconstructed and critiqued, while other world ideologies are praised as equally good or better.

This is the first American generation in which nearly half

hold a positive view of socialism. Approval of socialism jumped 15 percentage points from the previous generation, and the favorable view of socialism nearly doubled from the next older generation. In 1989, as the Berlin Wall fell, defining the failure of socialism in Russia, could anyone have imagined that less than thirty years later, a majority of Americans under the age of thirty-five would prefer socialism to capitalism?

As we will see throughout this book, the rapid change of these views (compared to previous generations, indicated in the rows "age 30–49" and "age 50–64") is a primary factor in forthcoming social changes already beginning to divide the United States and soon to reshape the social fabric entirely.

In short, each younger generation of Americans thinks less of capitalism and more of socialism. We can begin projecting the next generation moving in below "age 18–29." If they continue the trend line, a majority will have a negative view of capitalism, and 64 percent will have a positive view of socialism.

One wonders how many of the younger "educated" Americans know that the second "S" in USSR stands for "Socialist." One also wonders how many are aware of the atrocities of the USSR after it formed in 1922 as the "Union of Soviet Socialist Republics." Now, after its documented atrocities, genocide, and economic collapse— far exceeding the destruction of Nazism—we have a generation of Americans who would prefer life in a socialist republic than in a capitalist democracy (continue reading for statistics on the declining importance of democracy to young Americans).

How many young educated Americans know that Germany was a socialist democracy in the 1930s when Adolf Hitler was elected? Or that Benito Mussolini and Joseph Stalin were both socialists? This is an astounding break in the generational transfer of "American" values, and it is part of the reason that differing groups today hold entirely contradictory views of what "American" is (another Post-Truth symptom).

Incidentally, young Americans' embrace of socialism continues strengthening, even as Venezuela, a newer model of socialism, unravels into starvation and anarchy in South America. It is a fitting example of the Post-Truth era that many who praise Hugo Chavez or wear Che Guevara T-shirts remain ignorant of the fallout happening in Venezuela, where government seizure of farms and factories has produced uncontrollable hyperinflation that has wiped out the savings of hardworking families, emptied store shelves, and led to societal breakdown and the starvation of many.[63]

Stanford scholar Thomas Sowell has personally observed this shift toward socialism among his students. In a recent column, he lamented how the Bernie Sanders generation of American youth is embracing socialism:

> Many people of mature years are amazed at how many young people have voted for Senator Bernie Sanders, and are enthusiastic about the socialism he preaches.
>
> Many of those older people have lived long enough to have seen socialism fail, time and again, in countries around the world. Venezuela, with all its rich oil resources, is currently on the verge of economic collapse, after its heady fling with socialism.
>
> But, most of the young have missed all that, and their dumbed-down education is far more likely to present the inspiring rhetoric of socialism than to present its dismal track record.[64]

Where previous generations of Americans revered Abraham Lincoln, Thomas Jefferson, George Washington, and John Adams, a flood of history classes critiquing these Americans and focusing only on their flaws has led young Americans to elevate other heroes, such as Che Guevara. Of course, those wearing Che Guevara T-shirts are likely ignorant that he oversaw firing squads or founded Cuba's labor camps, which eventually exterminated gays alongside political dissidents.[65]

This quote from Guevara, an overt Marxist-Leninist, sounds eerily similar to the popular opinion held by many Post-Truth Americans today:

> The struggle against imperialism [America and the West], for liberation from colonial or neocolonial shackles . . . is not separate from the struggle against backwardness and poverty. Both are stages on the same road leading *toward the creation of a new society of justice and plenty . . .*
>
> Ever since monopoly capital took over the world, it has kept the greater part of humanity in poverty, dividing all the profits among the group of the most powerful countries. *The standard of living in those countries is based on the extreme poverty of our countries. To raise the living standards of the underdeveloped nations, therefore, we must fight against imperialism . . .* The practice of proletarian internationalism is not only a duty for the peoples struggling for a better future, it is also an inescapable necessity.[66]

The Marxist assumption that Western wealth is only the result of exploitation has become an assumption among a new majority of Americans. And this, historically, has been the tipping point toward an eventual socialist society, which often leads to an authoritarian society.

In addition to their affinity for socialism, most millennials and younger Americans have been taught to abhor and fear capitalism, for various reasons—typically, that capitalism is "imperialistic," a vestige of slave owning, a system through which white men control others, and so forth.[67] It doesn't help capitalism's reputation that, in recent decades, unrestrained greed has overtaken the old Protestant capitalism of hard work with responsibility, charity, humility, and prudence.

These indoctrinated preferences will eventually impact US laws and leaders. Pew researchers project that millennials will overtake baby boomers to become the largest and most influential generation of voters, and so the 2020 election may be the beginning of this generational turning point.[68] In addition to influencing voters, the Post-Truth view will increasingly be the view of lawmakers, prosecutors, judges, law enforcement officials, news media producers and editors, and federal and state officials.

These generational beliefs will reshape which ideologies influence national elections and which policies are enacted nationally. After a conservative Republican White House, this likely snap toward socialism in 2020 or 2024 may be unexpected and severe to those who haven't considered the generational data.

In time, the electorate will determine whether judges and elected officials use the old Truth-Based objective standard to interpret the Constitution by its literal words, or whether they'll simply reinterpret "constitutional" to justify the popular mood of the age, derived from their felt-truth, as has already happened occasionally—for example, in *Roe v. Wade* and in other rulings.

As economist Thomas Sowell predicts from the historical record of every nation that has embraced socialism, "Worst of all, government giveaways polarize society into segments, each trying to get what it wants at somebody else's expense, creating mutual bitterness that can tear a society apart."[69]

Reporting their findings in the *Journal of Democracy* in 2016, two sociologists caution that young Westerners have become shockingly detached from democracy and are increasingly open to authoritarian government structures if those structures will enable the social causes in which they believe. To the historically informed, this sounds a lot like we're reading from Stalin's book *Marxism and the National Question*.

The researchers warn that young Americans and Western Europeans have "become more cynical about the value of democracy . . . and more willing to express support for authoritarian alternatives. The crisis of democratic legitimacy extends across a much wider set of indicators than previously appreciated." Researchers Roberto Stefan Foa and Yascha Mounk added, "On the whole, support for political radicalism in North America and Western Europe is higher among the young, and support for freedom of speech lower."[70]

Clarifying their methodologies, the researchers wrote, "Support for radicalism is measured by responses to a left-right political scale, with '1' as radical left and '10' as radical right. In both Europe and North America, self-reported political radicalism is higher among the youngest age cohort (born since 1980) than any previous generation in any previous survey."[71]

In October 2016, the Victims of Communism Memorial Foundation commissioned a similar survey. It also found a dramatic rise among young Americans who said they would vote for a socialist candidate for president. Marion Smith, the director who commissioned that study, drew this conclusion:

"The millennials are sadly unaware of the history of communism in the last century and of the crimes committed by the Communist Party in the last 100 years," said Smith.

"As a result, the younger generation is not looking for ways to improve the existing system of free enterprise, the rule of law, democratic government, and respect for human rights, but want to try a completely different system. They are interested in the socialist system, which we think is dangerous."[72]

All of that data was confirmed in real life by the overwhelming support of millennials for America's first overtly socialist candidate, Bernie Sanders, during the 2016 presidential primaries. As the *Washington Post* reported, "More young people voted for Bernie Sanders than for Trump and Clinton combined—by a lot."[73] Hillary Clinton and Donald Trump together earned about 1.5 million votes from Americans under the age of thirty. Compare that to 2 million votes for Bernie Sanders.[74]

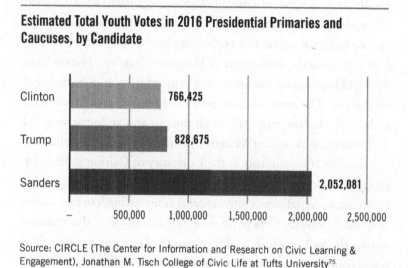

Estimated Total Youth Votes in 2016 Presidential Primaries and Caucuses, by Candidate

Candidate	Votes
Clinton	766,425
Trump	828,675
Sanders	2,052,081

Source: CIRCLE (The Center for Information and Research on Civic Learning & Engagement), Jonathan M. Tisch College of Civic Life at Tufts University[75]

Figure 5.8

Clinton's win over Sanders in the Democratic primary (accusations of cheating or collusion aside) is a good example of the baby boomer vote overpowering the millennial vote in 2016, perhaps for the last time. That scenario will almost certainly flip in 2020, with the millennial vote overpowering the boomer vote for the first time.[76]

The point here is that basic "American" ideas and values that have been long assumed and shared are no longer valued by young generations of Americans. This is a consequence of the Post-Truth shift in ideology; its ramifications will become tangible in time.

In fact, America's incoming generations increasingly believe the direct opposite of the "traditional" Western view on matters such as capitalism, Christianity, Islam, communism, and even free speech, with many believing that speech should be limited when it is perceived as hateful or bigoted. The reversal on these issues is another result of the removal of the Truth-Based standard.

In 2016, students at London's City College voted to ban conservative newspapers and other right-wing publications from their campus, accusing the publications of inciting hatred, racism, and fascism. City College is the alma mater of Margaret Thatcher. The voices of those publications on the list are now banned from even being heard on campus. The same student council session included funding for additional Muslim prayer spaces on campus and an initiative to rid the curriculum of white (Western Christian) perspective authors.[77]

In early 2017, students at the University of California-Berkeley protested violently, causing more than $100,000 in damage, to prevent a controversial conservative speaker from setting foot on campus to speak.[78] Berkeley College Student Republicans were also attacked during the violent protests. Three months later, conservative firebrand Ann Coulter also saw her speaking event officially cancelled.[79]

Those who lived through the 1960s will remember when Berkeley was known for its radical free speech. That's what *far left* used to mean. But now with the Truth-Based foundation removed, *free speech* is redefined as speech that "should" be protected based on the floating moral whims of the incoming generations. Anything contradicting those whims may be shut down and labeled as fascism or racism, regardless of facts, logic, or evidence.

These specific instances and broader trends are all, very simply, symptoms of the Post-Truth ideological shift that is now underway. In coming decades, this shift will continue to reshape society in America and Western Europe in ways we cannot predict.

E. Spiritual Success in a Post-Truth United States

In every generation, the war of ideologies plays out at two levels: the human level and the spiritual and supernatural level.

Ideological Warring at the Human Level. Humans, competing for power and well-being, leverage ideologies to strive for their own well-being. Many humans adopt whatever ideology they are taught in their childhood, regardless of its validity. Human history demonstrates a remarkable flair for fighting to the death for childhood ideologies, regardless of correlation to reality or fact.

Presently, Americans are in conflict with each other because some were raised in the Truth-Based ideology, and slightly more have now been raised to believe the Post-Truth ideology. In this sense, a historical ideological sea change is underway in our lifetime.[80]

Ideological Warring at the Spiritual and Supernatural Level. Warring ideologies are also fueled by the cosmic struggle between God and Satan, good and evil, truth and deception. Scripture describes Satan as active in deceiving the thoughts of populations.[81] Jesus, on the other hand, claims to be "the way and the truth and the life."[82] And Jesus said, "Everyone on the side of truth listens to me."[83]

So intertwined with human wisdom is the spiritual realm that the old Christian universities used to be known as "the light of learning." As Oxford's motto ("The LORD is my light") suggests, these Christian institutions brought a spiritual light of wisdom and understanding into regions of moral darkness.

Within the war of ideas, the human and supernatural levels overlap in ways that only the angelic hosts can see. Nero probably didn't know he was doing Satan's work when he burned Christians to light up his gardens at night. And Jesus' persecutors didn't realize the eternal significance of their actions when they crucified Him.

As Christians, we have in the Word of God everything we need to navigate this complex struggle. This is why one of our postures in a Post-Truth culture must be to **remain rooted to the Scriptures**.

In Revelation 12, God describes Christians who overcome the deceptions of Satan in this world—deceptions that we can expect to overpower nonbelievers.

> Then war broke out in heaven . . . The great dragon was hurled down—that ancient serpent called the devil, or Satan, *who leads the whole world astray.* He was hurled to the earth, and his angels with him.

Then I heard a loud voice in heaven say:

"Now have come the salvation and the power
    and the kingdom of our God,
    and the authority of his Messiah.
For the accuser of our brothers and sisters,
    who accuses them before our God day and night,
    has been hurled down.
They triumphed over him
    by the blood of the Lamb
    and by the word of their testimony;
they did not love their lives so much
    as to shrink from death."[84]

The believers who overcome the deceiver will do so because of three commitments. In our lives, we can overcome any cultural or intellectual deception from the enemy by the same three means:

1. **"By the blood of the Lamb."** We overcome the enemy by remaining anchored to the work of Christ on the cross as the ultimate solution to humanity's problems. In chapter 12, we will unpack how we do this today.

2. **"By the word of their testimony."** We overcome the enemy by staying true to our commitment to proclaim the Good News of Christ, no matter how unpopular it becomes. In chapter 16, we will unpack how we do this today. And we overcome the enemy by staying true to the Word of God itself.

3. **"They did not love their lives so much as to shrink from death."** We overcome the enemy by seeing that this world is a temporary precursor to eternity with Christ. The Holy Spirit will give us supernatural fearlessness in the face of persecution or death, as we will learn in chapter 20.

Christianity results in peace and love. But make no mistake, Christianity is a war in the realm of ideas and information. In this war, "we do not wrestle against flesh and blood, but against the rulers, against the authorities, against the cosmic powers over this present darkness, against the spiritual forces of evil in the heavenly places."[85]

If we hope to pass Christianity along to our children, we must understand that Christianity is a spiritual war waged in the battlefield of ideas. And we must understand that any argument to evict Christianity and absolute truth is ultimately satanic in origin, no matter how innocent it may appear.

CONCLUSION

In reality, it is not merely that some ideas have influence. It is not merely that ideas matter. It is that **nothing in all of human life matters as much as ideas.** Satan knows this, and that is why his tactic in destroying humans has been—from the Garden of Eden until now—to wage war against God in the realm of ideas, within the human intellect.

Note the highlighted words in this Scripture passage, identifying the battlefield on which we war with Satan: "For the weapons of our warfare are not of the flesh but have divine power to destroy strongholds. We destroy *arguments and every lofty opinion* raised against *the knowledge* of God, and take *every thought captive* to obey Christ."[86]

While we do not want to be argumentative people, we must "destroy arguments" against Christ in our own minds and lives. If deadly arguments are not destroyed, then it is people who end up being destroyed as a result of their believing satanic lies.

If we don't do this in our personal lives, then we are surrendering intellectual battles to the enemy. During the last century, these intellectual battles were surrendered in the halls of the great American universities. How tragic that so many of those universities were founded by Christians, with the Bible as their core required textbook.[87]

In a generation led to believe that ideas do not matter, we must be separate from the world on this issue. We must value ideas as powerful for good or for evil, as matters of life and death.[88] **And we must anchor our minds in the ideas of God, which lead to life, given to us objectively in the written Word of God.**

Every genocide, every policy-induced famine, every mass killing, every unnecessary war, every murder, rape, and pillaging the poor to profit the rich—these are all the fruit of ideas enacted.

Perhaps the simplest truth about ideologies—and the most important—is this: **The dominant ideologies in world history all claim to be exclusively true and superior**. Lenin's Marxism sounded benevolent in 1917 when Russians adopted it. But like any muscular ideology, its claims required the subjugation of other ideologies. From that sprang the murder of millions, the abolishing of Christianity and Judaism, and the demolishing of tens of thousands of churches and synagogues.

Communism has affected the regions where it has been adopted because it claims to be superior to other ideologies. Communism does not claim to be an equal among ideas. Hinduism also claims to be superior. So does Islam. And so does Christianity.

The real question is not if a strong ideology claims to be superior. The enduring strong ideologies all do. The real questions for a society are, "How does an ideology treat those who disagree with it?" and—especially once it becomes the dominant controlling power—**"How does an ideology treat the people who choose a different, 'inferior' ideology?"** Disagree with the dominant ideology in many cultures, and you will be sentenced to the Gulag, beheaded, or see your church burned to the ground. Such violent repression of other beliefs has been the norm rather than the exception throughout history's dominant civilizations.

Here is where the Christianity of the United States stood apart as the most inclusive of all the muscular ideologies in history. Its ability to disagree and yet "tolerate" became the cultural fabric of the true melting-pot nation. That was back when tolerance meant its literal definition—"to overtly disagree but allow and respect an opposing opinion."

Now, in the Post-Truth era, we see daily that tolerance is being redefined to mean "the celebration of all Post-Truth values, even those that contradict each other." Tolerance now requires the denial of any serious truth claim that threatens the "openness" of the Post-Truth view.

The Post-Truth idea that all ideologies are created equal and will coexist without conflict is not only an anomaly in world history; it is also an absurdity. Speak to a sincere Muslim, and you will find that he or she does not believe other ideologies are equal to Islam. Muslims believe their ideology is superior. And why shouldn't they? They have staked their soul on it being correct. The same is true of a sincere Christian, of a sincere communist, and of a sincere Hindu. This is not surprising beyond the insulation of a university campus and hypothetical scenarios. This is normal human behavior.[89] Most ideologies throughout history have claimed to be superior to their counterparts. They claim that they are right and that other ways of thinking are wrong.

Again, what makes an ideology noble is how it treats those who disagree with it—particularly when it is in a position to punish those dissenters. Post-Truth Americans are unable to understand what motivates 86 percent of people in the world today, because many people alive today believe the ideas of Hinduism, Islam, Christianity, or communism to be the exclusive, superior way of seeing the world.

In part 2 ("Where Will It Lead?"), we will consider some likely results of this struggle between ideologies. In chapters 8 and 9, we'll look at some likely consequences within the United States and globally.

In summary, then, what we sense in many of the surrounding social changes today is a war of ideologies. In the United States and Europe, a great civil war is taking place, of which many remain ignorant—the struggle between the old Truth-Based ideology and the new Post-Truth ideology.

Meanwhile, as these two ideologies war for the soul and resources of the West, other muscular and subjugating ideologies are also growing and battling around the world. These two ideological struggles— the internal struggle within the US and the global struggle beyond— will continue to mix and combust within our lifetime to bring about widespread and unpredictable changes for nations and individuals.

Chapter 6

FORCE 4: WESTERN CIVILIZATION IS UNRAVELING

> "I gave you a land on which you did not toil and cities you did not build; and you live in them and eat from vineyards and olive groves that you did not plant."
>
> JOSHUA 24:13

Here is a great irony. Many American thought leaders who enforce the anti-Christian and Post-Truth ideology pride themselves on their connections to Harvard, Yale, Princeton, and other Ivy League universities. The most prominent anti-Christian, Post-Truth thinkers are connected by degrees they have earned or by positions they hold within these great universities, which rank among the top ten in the world. The status derived from being associated with such universities is a point of pride and even identity for leading proponents of the post-Christian, Post-Truth ideology.

It is a tragic paradox—when you zoom out to consider it—that these men and women who vehemently swing their axes at the roots of Christian truth are, in fact, educated by institutions that were founded by Christians for the purpose of Christian education.[1]

The irony is this: the men and women who are most engaged in demolishing Christianity in the intellectual and ideological domains are depositing paychecks, maintaining offices in buildings, and enjoying social cachet—all of which exists because of Christian predecessors who created the institutions they so proudly enmesh with their personal identity.

These critics of Christianity have never founded a college of their own. They have never created an influential university. They did not get their hands dirty clearing a forest to build the buildings, as the Reverend John Harvard and other Puritans did. Rather, from a place of inheritance, they use their position of influence to criticize, minimize, or satirize the sacred beliefs of the very people who built the institutions that put bread on their tables, money in their retirement accounts, and social pride in their identities.

So this is the scenario: the acclaimed professor who is revered because he works at Harvard and who profits from the Harvard name and history is using his position and education to destroy the foundational ideas on which Harvard was created—a scenario repeated many times over, and one that personifies popular American culture today at the broadest level.

The professor swinging his axe at the foundations of his own university offers a small picture of what is happening on a national level in America. Incoming generations that have inherited great wealth now criticize and deride the predecessors who passed it down. **We eat from fields we did not cultivate. We enjoy courts and economies we have not founded, and we (my generation of Americans) are trained to have contempt for those who labored to create what we now freely inherit and enjoy.**

The people who are the most free, prosperous, and healthy in world history—as a result of Christian ideas—are now in a position of either ignoring these Christian ideas, mocking them, or labeling them as dangerous, ignorant, and backward.[2]

Our generation is not the first to inherit great wealth from godly ancestors—and then to despise both those ancestors and their God, even while getting fat on the inheritance. Scripture describes God's people in a similar posture, thousands of years ago, not long after this was written: "I gave you a land on which you did not toil and cities you did not build; and you live in them and eat from vineyards and olive groves that you did not plant."[3]

With its visceral, blood-spilling danger, violent strains of Islam may seem the most dramatic threat to life in Europe and the United States. Indeed, Islam is the fastest-growing ideology in the world, and it increasingly intertwines with state and government militaries in ways that Christianity no longer does.

But outside ideologies are not the gravest threat faced by the US or the West. In fact, the most dangerous threat to the West is its own self-induced unraveling as it embraces the Post-Truth ideology and completes the final turn away from Christian influence. Abraham Lincoln predicted this when he said, "If [danger] ever reach us, it must spring up amongst us. It cannot come from abroad. If destruction be our lot, we must ourselves be its author and finisher. As a nation of freemen, we must live through all time, or die by suicide."[4]

The reality is that the United States and Western Europe have inherited weaponry and infrastructure more than capable to defeat any external threat. However, if a nation is blinded, divided, or incapable of discerning reality, then the best weaponry in the world won't be able to protect that nation. Such a people will need protection from themselves just as much as they need protection from outside forces.

We are witnessing in our lifetime a self-inflicted deconstruction of Western civilization that would have been unthinkable to our predecessors. European and North American societies have achieved unrivaled prosperity, freedom, human rights, and scientific advancement.

Such advances include electric lights and appliances, vaccines, modern hospitals, airplanes, automobiles, the modern university, widespread literacy, dramatic advances in women's rights, the global abolition of slavery (which had been a global norm for thousands of years), and the computer and internet, just to name a few exclusively Western innovations.

It is a fact that these advances have grown in the last few hundred years from a geographically focused portion of the world—those civilizations built expressly on Christian beliefs.[5] And yet today, many inheritors of these blessings have not been taught a basic understanding of this. Nor have they been taught

- how the world works beyond the West
- what human life was like before Western advances
- how unique Western advances are
- what ideas produced these advances
- how to protect and perpetuate these advances

Like limestone cliffs relentlessly eaten away by powerful ocean waves, the Judeo-Christian foundations of American universities, laws, and society are now eroding. The Post-Truth currents of moral relativism, anti-Christian humanism, unrestrained hedonism, and social unrest daily weaken the underpinnings of a prosperous and free society in Europe and the United States.

We somehow find ourselves in a position where our most formally educated do not understand the ideas that produced this inheritance of wealth. Even worse, more and more thought leaders are being taught to proactively destroy the ideas on which this exceptional civilization was built. The most educated nations in world history, the very nations that boosted social literacy from 12 percent to 100 percent, have now failed to remember the elementary lessons from the fall of Rome, the fall of Troy, and dozens of other decadent, wealth-inheriting civilizations that also seemed too big to fail.

The West's foundation pillars are groaning. And the reality—barring some radical change—is that a gradual deterioration is now underway. Each day of continued deterioration, the unthinkable possibility of sudden, dramatic collapse becomes slightly more possible.[6]

I suggest that never before in history have inheritors of such wealth and prosperity so intentionally detonated the very foundations on which their society is built. Like the "invincible" ancient city of Troy, infiltrated by the Trojan horse and then burning at night amid the screams of women, children, and groggy-eyed Trojan warriors, the West's eventual demise may be more sudden and unforeseen than its sleeping inheritors can imagine. Or like Rome's fall, the disintegration of the West may drag on in a slow, gradual, centuries-long deterioration of living standards, international power, and norms.

A host of great thinkers within the last fifty years have predicted the West's ultimate decline as it abandons its Truth-Based ideology for the Post-Truth ideology. I refer to the predictions of Francis Schaeffer (1976), Malcolm Muggeridge (1980), and incisive non-Christian thinkers such as Allan Bloom (1987), whom I quote extensively in this book.

To assess this claim—that the Western society we inherit is now unraveling—let's consider three questions.

1. Is it accurate to claim that Western civilization is unraveling? Or might such a claim be dramatic, overstated, and possibly even impossible to verify?
2. By what means can we measure Western civilization's trajectory?
3. What are the key factors driving Western civilization's present trajectory?

IS WESTERN CIVILIZATION REALLY UNRAVELING?

"Son of man, I have made you a watchman for the people of
Israel; so hear the word I speak and give them warning from me."

EZEKIEL 3:17

When I was an editor for the *Scottsdale Times* in Arizona, I began
writing a new car auto review, which meant that auto manufacturers
supplied me with a different brand-new automobile every week. I was
in my early twenties, fresh out of college, and I must admit that
my favorite weeks were those when I drove around in a brand-new
$150,000 BMW, a $120,000 Jaguar, a $135,000 Audi, or a $115,000
Range Rover.

It was a blast to take my dates and friends out on the weekends.
We'd visit the luxury shops and hotels, valeting the cars at high-end
restaurants. We lived those weekends like the top few percenters of
the world, if only for a few hours. Travel the country today—from
Silicon Valley to New York City, from Atlanta to Dallas, from Naples
to Orange County—and you can witness overwhelming wealth and
opulence in the United States, from sea to shining sea.

Visit the gleaming new retail stores in the wealthy suburbs of
any major American city, and you will not get the impression that
this grand society could be deteriorating. Walk past the luxury cars.
Drive through neighborhoods of custom high-end homes rising from
the earth. Observe the healthy economic activity and shops, and you
might even laugh at the suggestion that Western society has peaked
and is now descending. Such peaceful prosperity is so overwhelming
in those neighborhoods and many middle-class neighborhoods that
we can get the sense—materially—that this way of life is just too big
to fail, too established to be shaken.

Americans continue enjoying—even during economic down-
turns and global hiccups—a standard of living that is exponentially
higher than what most humans in history ever experienced (or, for

that matter, ever imagined). In light of this, how can I possibly suggest that Western civilization is unraveling? Isn't that a bit dramatic? Possibly overstated? What sort of doomsdayer thinks such a powerful society could ever unravel?

The answer depends on our means of measurement. If we view the world materialistically, that is, if we consider material evidence the primary measure of reality (as a Marxist or a Darwinist does), then the most obvious material evidence does not suggest that this society is threatened or declining.

Note that some material economists do argue that if you dig deep into the material realm, you will find troubling signs in national currencies ripe for inflation, global debt expanded beyond reality, and other "material" factors, but those arguments are not part of my case that Western civilization is unraveling.[7] Those factors, to the degree they may exist, are in fact results of the ideology we aim to measure.

There's another way to measure societies. If we measure humanity from an ideological point of view, we will see things differently. **Viewing reality through the lens of ideology, we see that this overwhelming prosperity does not originate in the material world. Rather, the material reality is the result of values, norms, and ideas that previous generations planted into the soil of American society. The ideology of past Americans, while imperfect, has resulted in the largest accrual of wealth, personal freedom, and societal stability in human history. They sowed an ideology, and we reap its material benefits.**

Lest we forget, superior natural resources and weather existed materially in the world in sixteenth-century Arabia, eighth-century North America, tenth-century Africa, and eighteenth-century China. It is ideology that has broken humanity loose from its slavery and darkness. It is ideology that has allowed humanity to leverage and harvest resources that were nothing more than rocks in previous generations. The banking, commerce, education, retail norms, and social safety we enjoy in the West are all fruits of a society built by our predecessors. And while it is rarely taught or understood today, our predecessors wove unseen values into the fabric that produced this society.

To know whether this society—Western civilization as we know it today—is evolving or devolving, improving or declining, we must identify and measure those values that produced this societal fabric and this vast wealth.

I should hasten to say that to measure the health of a society only by its present material wealth is shortsighted. Measuring a society's trajectory by its present material comforts would be like measuring the well-being of the *Titanic* by the gleam of the crystal chandeliers in its ballroom or the opulence of its first-class cabins. That material measure would have been accurate for a time, but it also would have been foolish.

That is, all was well on the *Titanic* according to material measures—until all wasn't well. And once trouble was evident by internal material measures, it was far too late to avert disaster. The more accurate measure on the *Titanic* would have been to look beyond the ship and out into the cold, chilled air to see the ship's trajectory. And that's what we aim to do here in regard to Western society broadly and American society specifically—to trace the trajectory that delivered these grand successes and to measure whether those foundational values are still driving this society, or whether the society is turning onto a different course.

Allan Bloom foresaw the coming decline of the West in the realm of ideas when he wrote, "As an image of our current intellectual condition, I keep being reminded of the newsreel pictures of Frenchmen splashing happily in the water at the seashore, enjoying the paid annual vacations legislated by Léon Blum's Popular Front government. It was 1936, the same year Hitler was permitted to occupy the Rhineland."[8]

Intoxicated with their material view of reality, France's paid vacationers in 1936 had little awareness of how world ideologies were warring or how a post-Christian Germany could invade and destroy their entire way of life. Those splashing vacationers could not have imagined they would be crawling through muddy battlefields, burying their loved ones, stumbling into concentration camps, or witnessing Nazi armies march to the Eiffel Tower within years.

Invisible Threads, Unseen Forces

In 2017, physicists snapped a photo of "dark matter" for the first time.[9] Dark matter is an invisible force that holds the galaxies and planets together.[10] Using gravitational lensing, scientists were able to create the first image of a dark matter "bridge." It reveals that galaxies and solar systems are all interconnected by an invisible spiderweb-like network of unseen dark matter that literally holds the universe together.[11]

Dark matter is unseen, and previous generations denied its very existence. But even though it is unseen, dark matter is the force holding planets and solar systems in place. In fact, scientists now believe that "dark matter is about five times more abundant than the matter that we can see."[12] In a similar way, the unseen, nonmaterial values of a culture hold a society together. Far more than what is materially visible, it is the unseen values and ideology of a civilization that shape its future.

The Post-Truth American ideology includes a materialistic view of the world, as opposed to a spiritual or ideological view. If we're not careful, this materialistic way of defining reality can bleed into our own thinking as Christians. Like our Post-Truth neighbors, we can easily fall into measuring our society by its material wealth and comfort rather than by God's standards.

The dangers of this are many. But chief among them is that a materialist interpretation of reality limits our ability to properly see all of reality. It limits our ability to understand the trajectory of society. Going back to the *Titanic* analogy, a materialist interpretation of society is akin to measuring the *Titanic*'s trajectory by the shine of the crystal chandeliers in the ballroom. **The materialist view will not know that danger is upon it until it's too late. A materialist view will not know that anything is wrong until everything is wrong.**

Just as dark matter invisibly holds galaxies together in space, ideology invisibly holds cultures together in human history. Ideological threads weave together to form a web, a social fabric that makes a society what it is. Of course, these ideological threads will vary from culture to culture. A Muslim culture has very different threads of value shaping it than, say, a Hindu, communist, or Christian culture.

Different threads produce different results for women's rights, economic prosperity, social stability, the value of invention, education, personal property, free speech, and every facet of life. In each culture, we can measure whether that culture will hold together or unravel by examining the health of its unique essential threads (its values). If we wish to measure the future course of Western society, we must identify which ideological threads produced the social fabric on which today's freedom and wealth rest.

Cultures always change as they transfer from the older generations to the younger. And so we must ask, "Are the cultural changes we're witnessing in America simply the normal evolving of a culture as one generation passes it down to another? Or, like post-Christian France, post-Christian Germany, and post-Christian Russia, are these changes more foundational? Are these changes that rip and remove the essential threads that have held this society together?"

To measure whether Western civilization is simply evolving or is in fact unraveling, we must identify the unique, invisible threads that have made Western society what it is, and then we must measure the well-being of those threads.

HOW WILL WE MEASURE WESTERN CIVILIZATION'S TRAJECTORY?

Righteousness exalts a nation,
but sin condemns any people.

PROVERBS 14:34

Acclaimed economist and scholar Deirdre McCloskey, in the pinnacle work of a decorated career, identifies seven values or virtues that created the social fabric of Western society as we have inherited it.[13] She concludes from social and economic research that these values produced the great wealth and freedom we inherit. McCloskey is not a traditional Christian, but she argues that Christian virtues produced Western cultural gains as we've inherited them. McCloskey concludes that Christian virtues—adopted by a majority in Britain, the United States, and the West—resulted in the greatest wealth production in history.

McCloskey found that the average daily wage in the US was just $3 per day in 1800, and that it is now about $200 per day (adjusted for inflation). She estimates that the Western nations have built 99 percent of all humanity's wealth throughout history, and we have done so within the last 1 percent of time.

From where did all this wealth originate so quickly? McCloskey argues that it all began with an ideology—a set of ideas. As a scholarly economist, she argues that Christianized civilization created a unique incubator for ideas, which in turn profited society more than any other era or ideology in world history. Specifically, McCloskey credits the **seven Christian virtues—faith, hope, love, justice, courage, temperance, and prudence—as shaping the society that has most tangibly improved global humanity**.

McCloskey concludes that these values were lifted up as an ideal. And while no one person perfectly exemplified these virtues, the societal embrace of them as the ideal resulted in human rights, freedom, security, and well-being that produced unprecedented innovations such as the Industrial Revolution, the airplane, and so much more. In summary, "The upshot [of this ideology] since 1800 has been a gigantic improvement for the poor, such as many of your ancestors and mine, and a promise now being fulfilled of the same result worldwide—a Great Enrichment for even the poorest among us."[14]

McCloskey's assessment is that without these seven virtues, the West would not have produced its great wealth and innovation— fruits that have been exported to other parts of the world. She specifically argues against the now popular materialist idea that the wealth of Western nations is a mere consequence of having better weather or better raw materials. Instead, McCloskey gives all the credit to a society that embraced the seven Christian virtues and in so doing created a unique incubator for innovation, human dignity, and wealth creation.

If McCloskey is correct, then we can measure Western society's next future by measuring the well-being of these unseen values, the seven virtues that McCloskey expertly ties to our abundance.

- faith (or diligence)
- hope (or compassion)
- love (or generosity)
- justice (or patience)
- courage (or humility)
- temperance (or abstinence)
- prudence (or chastity)

If raising these seven virtues as the ideal created unrivaled prosperity, as McCloskey argues, then where does Western society stand today in regard to them? To answer that question, let's note that each of the seven Christian virtues has an opposite, a historical counterpart—known as the seven deadly sins.

- faith (or diligence)   sloth
- hope (or compassion)   envy
- love (or generosity)   greed
- justice (or patience)   wrath
- courage (or humility)   pride
- temperance (or abstinence)   gluttony
- prudence (or chastity)   lust

Because of Force 1 (the depravity or sinfulness of humanity), we know that every world culture will lean toward the seven deadly sins more than toward the seven virtues. So it's not surprising to see envy, pride, gluttony, and lust around us today. Those sins also existed during the era of exponential wealth production that the economist McCloskey documented. We make no false assumption that the past was a golden era free of problems or prejudices.

But what we are attempting to gauge is whether the invisible strings of these virtues as a societal ideal are being strengthened or are being snipped and shorn in our generations.

Here are the incisive questions: Which of these lists is most lifted up and encouraged in our mainstream society today? Which of these lists is most praised by a society's cultural leaders? Which of these lists is most openly the standard for the incoming young?

McCloskey argues—not as a theologian but as an economist— that the unique progress we have inherited is the result of a culture that had ingrained the seven virtues as the high standard to which every boy and girl should attempt to rise. From that ideology resulted great wealth, freedom, and innovation. Those threads—invisible but more powerful than the material world—wove a society that, while not perfect, created a foundation of trust and commerce, economy, freedom, and productivity unlike any other society in history. These unseen values produced innovation, liberty, human dignity, and personal property rights.

Most sincere Christians will agree with McCloskey's conclusion because we have experienced it in our own lives. We have seen that when we follow the paths of lust, gluttony, greed, sloth, wrath, envy, or pride, it reduces our own personal wealth and freedom. It negatively affects our careers, our productivity, and our relationships. And it affects our children, spouses, and neighbors.

Every drunk driver who kills a child demonstrates—painfully—that one life embracing vice rather than virtue will dramatically affect other lives too.

More positively, we have also experienced that we achieve increasing freedom, peace, and prosperity when we pursue faith, hope, love, justice, courage, temperance, and prudence (ideally, with God's help, as fruit of the Holy Spirit).

We have witnessed the difference between these two lists of ideals. We have witnessed the difference in our lives, families, and communities. It does not take a moral genius to multiply such a positive impact outward across ten thousand families and lives and then across a society with millions of people.

Philosopher Vishal Mangalwadi summarizes well how Christian beliefs resulted in the prosperity of capitalism, and also how capitalism is running off course now that American society has been severed from its founding Christian values:

> Submitting orientations of our sinful nature to supernatural laws was the secret of Capitalism's success. Secularization of Capitalism has destroyed the dikes that channeled America's creative energies. Gordon Gekko's dictum, "Greed is good," in Oliver Stone's movie *Wall Street* tells us that the secular mind has become incapable of differentiating ambition from greed.[15]

In the early years of American post-Christianity (circa 1950–1980), many Americans still lauded the seven virtues as an ideal. Sure, they may not have lived up to the virtues themselves, but the virtues were still held as a societal ideal. They could still be found in popular culture, from *Little House on the Prairie* to Elvis Presley singing gospel hymns to *The Brady Bunch*.

Good people lived the ideal, and society affirmed it. Society enforced an invisible peer pressure toward the Christian virtues. This was reflected in popular TV shows, novels, and even music as recently as the 1970s and 1980s. Unabashed greed, lust, wrath, and pride existed, but they were not openly flaunted. They existed as countercultural fringes.

Meanwhile, while mainstream culture still lauded the seven Christian virtues, post-World War II academia was supplanting the foundation of those virtues in America's universities and ideological publications. **The erosion of the truth foundations began when the Ivy league universities gave up the authority of Christian Scripture and then further abandoned the Bible, giving up the relevance of Christian Scripture.**[16]

Following World War II, ironically and almost unbelievably, the great American academics began espousing the same Post-Truth thinking and ideology that infected German academia before World War II, including Friedrich Nietzsche, Martin Heidegger, G. W. F. Hegel, Sigmund Freud, and Karl Marx, among others.[17] This sounds impossible when stated so blatantly, but it is a fact, as recorded in the academic journals of the last century. Allan Bloom, who began his academic career in the late 1940s, describes this shift in America's academic thought leaders.

> The popularization of German philosophy in the United States is of peculiar interest to me because I have watched it occur during my own intellectual lifetime, and I feel a little like someone who knew Napoleon when he was six. I have seen value relativism . . . grow greater in the land than anyone imagined . . . The new American life-style has become a Disneyland version of the Weimar Republic for the whole family.[18]

Bloom summarizes the dechristianization of the American university: "There is now an entirely new language of good and evil, originating in an attempt to get 'beyond good and evil' and preventing us from talking with any conviction about good and evil anymore."[19]

There was a time when the old American virtues of charity, chastity, and temperance were so embedded that they were given as names for children. In addition to the virtues, a majority of Americans had "Christian" names such as Abraham, John, David, Samuel, Ruth, and Deborah. These children were named after characters from the Bible because the Bible was the truth standard inextricably connected to the cultural ideal. After all, the Bible was the source of Christianized America's social ideal. Today, some Americans bear Christian names without knowing their source, and children are just as likely to be named after the infamous stars of sex tapes, celebrities, or others who openly aspire to the seven deadly sins.

Back in that era (and again, it was not a perfect era, but it was a constantly improving era inasmuch as it pursued the truth standard), the question of religion was more often a binary one—Catholic or Protestant. And immigrants who wished to succeed in such an overwhelmingly Christianized society would quickly adopt either the Catholic or the Protestant interpretation of Christianity, at least externally. Christianity provided access into assimilation.

Today many young Americans ignorantly deny that America was ever "Christian" in any sense. They have been indoctrinated to believe this error. They have not been taught the difference between a nation that is formally and legally a "Christian nation" (such as England, Denmark, or Vatican City) and a nation in which a majority of people are devoutly Christian (the United States being the latter of the two options).

The evidence is overwhelming, not only in the historical record but also in architecture, cultural documents, and polling from the last eighty years, that the United States has always been a nation in which the majority identifies as Christian. **As recently as 1948, some 91 percent of Americans identified as Christian, either Protestant or Catholic.**

This is not to say that everyone was sincerely Christian or that these self-identified "Christians" were perfect in a spiritual sense. And this isn't to say that national policies overtly intertwined with a state church. Neither was the case, but equally clear is that the vast majority of Americans operated from a somewhat Christianized worldview, including a Truth-Based ideology.

The vast majority identified as Christian, and for better or worse, they exalted their interpretation of Christian values. These were times when students at Yale, Harvard, and Princeton still knew the Bible to some degree. They knew as a matter of fact passed down from parents and grandparents that American society and law had been built on Christian virtues. Many still attended Bible studies, and many schools still featured the Christian Bible as a central component in the curriculum.

These were times when stores closed on Sundays and many societal aspirations tracked—for better and worse—with Protestant Christian interpretations. Of course it wasn't a perfect society, because it was still a society of sinful people. As such, various groups had inaccurate interpretations of Scripture at various times, and sadly, some falsely used the guise of Christianity to justify hatred or prejudice.

Take a look at the Gallup polling data during the last seventy years that shows the percentage of Americans who self-identify as Protestant, Christian, or Catholic.[20] Pay particular attention to the column in which all Christian groups are combined. From the bottom to the top of the chart, note the gradual but very consistent decline of Christianity in the United States during the last seventy years.

The poll asked this question: What is your religious preference—are you Protestant, Roman Catholic, Mormon, Jewish, another religion, or no religion?

What Is Your Religious Preference?

YEAR	PROTESTANT	CHRISTIAN (NONSPECIFIC)	CATHOLIC	ALL CHRISTIAN (COMBINED)
	%	%	%	%
2016	37	10	22	69
2006	49	6	22	77
1963	69	n/a	24	93
1954	71	n/a	22	93

Source: Gallup data

Figure 6.1

Following World War II, some 93 percent of Americans identified as Christian—either Protestant or Catholic. That was only seven decades ago. On today's trajectory, it is almost certain that fewer than half of Americans will identify as Christian by 2048 (that figure includes very nominal and casual Christians). In a time of unprecedented peace and prosperity compared to historical averages, one of the most Christianized nations in history has steadily turned away from its faith.

If we were to trace the trend of Americans who identify as Christian from 1948 back to 1776, we would see that the overwhelming majority (more than 90 percent) of the citizenry in the United States and its preceding colonies were always Christian until very recently.

For centuries, the Christian Bible and its values tied together an

What Is Your Religious Preference? *(cont.)*

	JEWISH	MORMON	OTHER	NONE	NO ANSWER
YEAR	%	%	%	%	%
2016	3	2	5	18	2
2006	2	2	5	12	2
1963	3	n/a	2	2	*
1954	3	n/a	2	n/a	2

Source: Gallup data

Figure 6.1 *(cont.)*

otherwise disconnected populace. Immigrants brought with them competing cultures from France, Ireland, England, Germany, Russia, and elsewhere, but those cultures melded together within the boundaries of Christian ideals.

Allan Bloom, a secular scholar who isn't a Christian, connects the fate of America as a cohesive society to the embrace of the Christian Bible. He argues that the Bible had previously been the unifying ideological tie in American culture.

> Real religion and knowledge of the Bible have diminished to the vanishing point . . . The delicate fabric of the civilization into which the successive generations are woven has unraveled, and children are raised, not educated . . . *In the United States, practically speaking, the Bible was the only common culture, one that united simple and sophisticated, rich and poor, young and old . . . Without the book even the idea of the order of the whole is lost.*[21]

As popular culture began to turn away from Christianity (1950s to recently), American society still held the notion of Christian virtues at large, even as American academics deconstructed the foundation on which those virtues were built. Francis Schaeffer described this well in his book *How Should We Then Live?* in which he argues that the Bible was America's source of authority and absolutes, as well as the sole alternative to authoritarianism.[22] Schaeffer also predicted our present unraveling—as a result of abandoning the belief of scriptural authority—in his book *The Great Evangelical Disaster.*[23]

Are the Seven Deadly Sins (Vices) Actually the Overt Values of Young Americans?

As we make the Post-Truth turn, with the truth foundation deteriorating, there is no real reason for a wealthy generation of inheritors to cling to the old Christian virtues. They are not worth the work and grit required. *And besides, they are antiquated. After all, weren't those people who valued those things backward, uncivilized, probably racist, and uneducated?* Sure, the old values are convenient for publicity and for public appearances. They have some sentimental and emotional value, but they are not true cultural aspirations for the most part.

As a result, incoming generations may hold some tattered value in regard to some of the virtues—for example, compassion or justice in public contexts as it relates to applauding the good work of others. But when it comes to personal lifestyles, they are more likely to openly and shamelessly strive toward greed, applaud wrath, aspire to pride, and feed lust.

And here is the most important societal shift. New Americans will not chide or judge a person who does openly seek sloth, greed, pride, or lust as their life values. There is no longer any shame in open ambition toward sloth, envy, greed, wrath, pride, gluttony, or lust. The social peer pressure is gone.

In fact, measured by popular music and pop culture, many of

these vices are the stated values and ideals for incoming generations. It's hard to find a chart-topping pop song that is not about sex, porn, strippers, drugs, sloth, greed, lust, or money.

To avoid profanity, I will not quote the lyrics here, but consider merely the titles of these hit songs by American mainstream pop sensation Nicki Minaj—a favorite with American teens.

- "Cuchi Shop" (a profanity-laced "madam's" explanation of the features on the prostitutes for sale at her brothel)
- "F*** You Silly"
- "Sex in Crazy Places"
- "I Endorse These Strippers"
- "Get On Your Knees," with Ariana Grande, another chart-topping cultural phenomenon who has elementary to middle-school aged girls among her fans
- "Grinding Getting Money"
- "Feeling Myself," with Beyoncé, another mainstream hit among school-aged Americans
- "Get Your Money Up"
- "Stupid Hoe"
- "Pills N Potions"
- "Did It On'em"
- "Come on a Cone"

These songs are not fringe. This is mainstream American entertainment, featured on TV shows like *Good Morning America* and dominating the playlists, Spotify accounts, and YouTube views of young Americans, including prepubescent elementary students. This is material they think of not as dirty or edgy, but as normal. In addition to the Post-Truth worldview that American middle schoolers are learning in so many classrooms, these are the themes cycling through their earbuds, headphones, and iPhones.

It sounds old-fashioned to even document these cultural shifts, but they are real and almost so obvious that we can miss the dramatic shift in the cultural fabric. We who understand the power of ideology and ideas must not forget that such ideas will have consequences for individuals, families, and the network of individuals we call a society or civilization.

Consider the values in the most popular TV shows of past decades, shows like *The Brady Bunch*, *Little House on the Prairie*, and even 1990s sitcoms like *Full House*, which are embarrassingly wholesome, moralistic, and didactic by today's standards.

The mainstream ultra-popularity of *Game of Thrones*, even among many self-professed Christians, represents the same cultural shift. *Game of Thrones* and a host of similar shows are known for their violence and their ultra-graphic, extended, fully nude sex scenes. Non-Christian media reviewers have referred to these shows as the mainstreaming of pornography. Of course, pornography is nothing new, but we are living in the era of American history where it is stepping into the middle of the cultural stream rather than lurking on the banks.

Pop music and the mainstreaming of pornography are mere symptoms of a deeper cultural change to overtly embrace sloth, envy, greed, wrath, pride, gluttony, or lust. Where previous generations imposed social peer pressure away from outright exaltation of these vices, the incoming generations now praise them openly and aspire to them. More than that, the person in today's society who will be shamed is the one who asks, "Have we gone too far?" in any of these matters. Like the Post-Truth shift, this cultural shift can seem hypothetical, but it becomes all too practical on the streets, in living rooms, in college dorms, at high school parties, in workplace cultures, and among the millions of people who together shape a society.

Researchers have documented this shift objectively. Dr. Jean M. Twenge, professor of psychology at San Diego State University, has spent more than ten years researching the values of America's university students today. She compares their values to the values their parents and grandparents held when they were university students.

Twenge says the common stereotype of millennials as being more altruistic than older generations is actually not correct.

> Popular views of the millennial generation, born in the 1980s and 1990s, as more caring, community-oriented, and politically engaged than previous generations are largely incorrect, particularly when compared to baby boomers and Generation X at the same age . . . These data show that recent generations are less likely to embrace community mindedness and are focusing more on money, image and fame.[24]

When she compared freshman college student surveys from 1966 until now, Twenge found a dramatic swing toward overt greed. Where previous generations attended college primarily to "develop a meaningful philosophy of life," millennials identified "being very well off financially" as their number one motivator.[25]

Twenge's generational data is particularly interesting because she uses survey records that began in 1966. Today's millennials (and now Generation Z) are offered the same menu of multiple choice answers that their parents or grandparents were offered.

Data on Overt Greed. As for greed, only 45 percent of baby boomers surveyed between 1966 and 1978 identified "being very well off financially" as important to them when they were college students. That number jumped to 75 percent for millennials, who overwhelmingly identified "being very well off financially" as their most important reason for attending college. The millennials were surveyed between 2000 and 2009.

The *Los Angeles Times* summarized the research with this headline: "Money Top Goal for College Freshmen."[26] While the finding is not unexpected, the dramatic shift between generations is. It demonstrates quite strikingly the change in cultural values.

Data on Overt Pride. In a separate study, Dr. Twenge also found that narcissism is dramatically on the rise among incoming college students.[27] In the most recent generation of American college freshmen, Twenge and a fellow researcher identified "a 30% tilt towards narcissistic attitudes in US students since 1979" to the degree that now "one in four recent students responded . . . in a way which leaned towards narcissistic views of the self."[28]

In an interview about the significance of her findings on narcissism, pride, and greed, Twenge cited the changing values of American culture: "Our culture used to encourage modesty and humility and not bragging about yourself. It was considered a bad thing to be seen as conceited or full of yourself."[29]

Of course, some sociologists will argue that millennials are able to be honest about what boomers felt was inappropriate to say. And that is exactly the point. The moderating pressure of the societal values has changed. The broad, invisible fabric of cultural peer pressure has shifted from virtue to something else. Call it vice, or, more modestly, call it nonjudgmentalism. These findings are documentation of the shift in the fabric of society.[30]

Twenge's findings are not the conclusions of a moralizing preacher; they are the findings of a professor of psychology at San Diego State University.

So what's the big deal? The big deal is that a societal embrace of different ideals will produce an entirely different society. Large ships require time to change course. In a society as vast as the United States, the consequences of these new values (all seven of the old values abandoned, to various degrees) will not overtake us in a day. But the consequences will show in time. And much like it was with the *Titanic*, once these consequences do show in courtrooms, homes, businesses, and schools, it will be too late to reverse course. Like sowing and reaping, the consequences are not immediate, but they are eventual and irrevocable.

Quite simply, then, the openly espoused values of incoming American generations appear to be increasingly changing:

- from faith (or diligence) to sloth
- from hope (or compassion) to envy
- from love (or generosity) to greed
- from justice (or patience) to wrath
- from courage (or humility) to pride
- from temperance (or abstinence) to gluttony
- from prudence (or chastity) to lust

I'm not arguing that the world will end because of the millennials. After all, I'm a millennial myself, and I know many of my peers who break from these trends, as exceptions. But the trends above are the conclusions of a trained sociologist's dedicated work. They are not mere opinion. The point is that societal values are shifting dramatically, not according to anecdotal or individual impressions, but according to formal research.

Also, my point here is not to write a puritanical diatribe against an immoral society. These young people are not destroying society. They are simply expressing fallen human nature that is now unrestrained by any Christian self-denial, and they are simply living what they've been taught in Post-Truth classrooms—to "follow your heart" and "find your truth."

Most societies in history have been immoral (and also poor, uneducated, and brutal). My point is that counterintuitive Christian values—saturated into the moral consciousness of a society—raised Western society to excel far above the historical averages in wealth, prosperity, freedom, human dignity, and life expectancy.

And my point is that, with those Christian values now largely removed and increasingly exterminated, the opposite results will return in time. Sure, vestiges of the old values will linger like an aftertaste, likely for many generations. But with their foundation dismantled, those old values will not have staying power to direct the whole culture, as they once did.

As a result of this and other Post-Truth consequences, American and other Western cultures will slowly sink back down toward the historical averages of wealth and freedom. Where the Western way of life was exceptional—on global average—it will sink closer to normal and average. The gains in life expectancy and standard of living will not be erased overnight, for they have been affixed and are materially self-perpetuating for a season, but the invisible threads that produced those gains are unraveling.

Whether it's the safety of a woman jogging alone in the evening, the justice we expect from law enforcement (how many young Americans know that you must bribe an official to get a "fair" hearing in many other cultures?), the confidence to walk into a bank without attack, the basic human dignity of an elderly person, or the human respect we expect from someone who disagrees with us, America's forsaking of these Christian values will affect every dimension of American society in time.

We will notice this moral and cultural sea change in the various layers of American life: in local government corruption, in national politics, in neighborhood break-ins. We will notice it in opponents who cannot treat each other with dignity or respect. We will notice it in increased rape and child sexual assaults as a result of unbridled lust.

Traveling a different path of logic, Os Guinness reached a similar conclusion when he wrote these words:

In short, contrary to the founders—and in ways they do not realize themselves—Americans today are heedlessly pursuing a vision of freedom that is short-lived and suicidal. Once again, freedom without virtue, leadership without character, business without trust, law without customs, education without meaning and medicine, science and technology without human considerations can end only in disaster.[31]

Confession: As a millennial, I feel old, stodgy, and embarrassingly out of fashion to write these truths. And I suppose the social pressure on me to refrain from writing the things I am writing in this book is in itself a demonstration of the point I am making. The social peer pressure has changed, and the anti-Christian, antitraditional mood is more significant, more pervasive, and more saturated into the emerging fabric than we may be able to grasp.

WHAT ARE THE KEY FACTORS DRIVING WESTERN CIVILIZATION'S PRESENT TRAJECTORY?

Let's take some time now to consider both the human factors and the spiritual factors involved in the decline of Western society.

Human Factors for the Decline of Western Society

Human free will, infected as it is by the fall into sin (Force 1), is largely leading the Western turn away from Christianity, particularly now in America. I will be accused of oversimplifying here, but I stand by it. This turn away from the Christian truth standard correlates with America's change in societal values. That change in societal values will eventually lead to tangible losses in actual prosperity, freedom, and peace.

Above we saw the changing values of America's youngest generation. Now let's look at some separate studies to see how the dechristianization of societal values does in fact correlate with the dechristianization of individuals. With every younger generation, more Americans are forsaking the Christianity of their parents and grandparents.

The reason young Americans are not behaving like Christians is that they are not Christians. In 2014, a team of five academic researchers surveyed more than 11 million American teens and millennials and drew this conclusion:

American adolescents and emerging adults in the 2010s (Millennials) were significantly less religious than previous generations (Boomers, Generation X) at the same age . . . Twice as many 12th graders and college students . . . never attend religious services. Twice as many 12th graders and entering college students in the 2010s (vs. the 1960s–70s) give their religious affiliation as "none," as do 40%–50% more 8th and 10th graders.[32]

The researchers continue:

Recent birth cohorts report less approval of religious organizations, are less likely to say that religion is important in their lives, report being less spiritual, and spend less time praying or meditating. Thus, declines in religious orientation reach beyond affiliation to religious participation and religiosity, suggesting a movement toward secularism . . . Overall, these results suggest that the lower religious orientation of Millennials is due to time period.[33]

In other words, it is a national shift away from the Christian religion of their upbringing.[34]

Very simply, then, both at a national/cultural level and at an individual level, America is turning away from Christianity. The turn is not final and perhaps is not irreversible, but it has been well underway for more than fifty years. It is underway intellectually, where it seems most irreversible. It is underway culturally in ways that will feel more irreversible as baby boomers and older Americans age out of influence. And it is underway on the individual level, as has been undeniably documented by multiple researchers.[35]

When Nations Turn Away from Christianity, Disasters Follow

As we look back on the post-Christian catastrophes in both Germany and Russia, it's interesting that so few have noticed the correlation between casting off Christianity and the resulting societal implosion.

Not only is the correlation obvious, but brilliant minds, such as

Aleksandr Solzhenitsyn, have openly warned citizens of the West, including Americans. In an interview with the BBC on March 1, 1976, Solzhenitsyn said, "A people which no longer remembers has lost its history and its soul . . . One must think of what might happen unexpectedly in the West. The West is on the verge of a collapse created by its own hands."[36]

And then in his BBC address on March 26, 1976, he said, "One of the greatest dangers of all is that you have lost all sense of danger, you cannot even see where it's coming from as it moves swiftly towards you. You imagine you see danger in other parts of the globe and hurl the arrows from your depleted quiver there. But the greatest danger of all is that you have lost the will to defend yourselves." Later in the address, he added:

> We, the oppressed peoples of Russia, the oppressed peoples of Eastern Europe, watch with anguish the tragic enfeeblement of Europe. We offer you the experience of our suffering; we would like you to accept it without having to pay the monstrous price of death and slavery that we have paid.
>
> But your society refuses to heed our warning voices . . . And all of us are standing on the brink of a great historical cataclysm, a flood that swallows up civilisation and changes whole epochs.
>
> The present world situation is complicated still more by the fact that several hours have struck simultaneously on the clock of history. We have all got to face up to a crisis—not just a social crisis, not just a political crisis, not just a military crisis. And we must not only face up to this crisis but we must stand firm in this great upheaval—an upheaval similar to that which marked the transition from the Middle Ages to the Renaissance.[37]

The fact that many intelligent minds fail to correlate the West's present trajectory with the falls of Germany and Russia can be attributed to Forces 1 and 2: that humans are fallen and also that human intellect is blinded by "the god of this world"—Satan.

British journalist and thinker Malcolm Muggeridge, describing the post-Christianized culture of the West, wrote this toward the end of his life:

> So the final conclusion would surely be that, whereas other civilisations have been brought down by attacks of barbarians from without, ours had the unique distinction of training its own destroyers at its own educational institutions and for providing them with facilities for propagating their destructive ideology far and wide, all at the public expense. Thus did western Man decide to abolish himself, creating his own boredom out of his own affluence, his own vulnerability out of his own strength, his own impotence out of his own erotomania, himself blowing the trumpet that brought the walls of his own city tumbling down, and having convinced himself that he was too numerous, laboured with pill and scalpel and the syringe to make himself fewer, until at last, having educated himself into imbecility and polluted and drugged himself into stupefaction, he heeled over: a weary, battered old Brontosaurus and became extinct.[38]

No statement better summarizes all the research I've compiled on Western society's trajectory today than Muggeridge's final sentence above: **"Thus did western Man decide to abolish himself, creating his own boredom out of his own affluence, his own vulnerability out of his own strength, his own impotence out of his own erotomania, himself blowing the trumpet that brought the walls of his own city tumbling down, and having convinced himself that he was too numerous, laboured with pill and scalpel and the syringe to make himself fewer, until at last, having educated himself into imbecility and polluted and drugged himself into**

stupefaction, he heeled over: a weary, battered old Brontosaurus and became extinct."

Just a few decades later, Muggeridge's prediction is proving true in certain European nations that don't have sufficient young people to fuel their economies. Why have their populations shrunk? Because of the abortions to which Muggeridge alludes. And so, lacking enough laborers to row their own ship forward, they have in their old age become dependent on immigrants to come in and power the economy.

Immigration can be a wonderful thing for Western societies, of course, but when Westerners are "educated . . . into imbecility," those societies no longer understand the competing of ideologies or the difference between an immigrant who desires to assimilate into the culture versus one who despises Western culture and wants instead to import a usurping ideology.

———————————

Increasingly, within my generation (the millennials), my American peers have been taught to believe not only that America is not exceptional, but also that America is imperialistic, colonialist, slave promoting, predatory, and a long list of other derogatory accusations that make it sound like one of the worst nations in world history. Conversely, older and Truth-Based Americans see the US as the greatest nation ever.

This foundational disagreement about America's status is why arguments from history fall flat with younger Americans. They have been indoctrinated to believe that American history is evil or irrelevant; therefore, Abraham Lincoln's Christian faith—or anyone else's—doesn't matter to them. If anything, it only proves that "Christians had slaves" (even if the Christian in question did not have slaves, such as Abraham Lincoln or John Adams or hundreds of others), as well as other sweeping, inaccurate claims. Not only is history "so boring," but also there isn't much worth learning from those old racist, backward, closed-minded, bigoted white Christians of the past (or so the thinking goes).

A Parable: Four Generations of a Family Business

In my first years as a news reporter, I profiled the founders of prominent businesses in the Phoenix area, from national companies like Discount Tire, GoDaddy, and Cold Stone Creamery to regional family-owned restaurants.

I noticed a trend in family-owned businesses. The first generation often works tirelessly to build the business. By the end of their lives, they have lifted themselves and their children from poverty to middle-class prosperity.

Then the second generation, having seen the remarkable difference made in lifestyle, continues to lead the business with a good work ethic and perspective, building on the first generation's foundation. The second generation knows where they came from. They can remember the smaller home, the old neighborhood, the first humble business office, among other things.

By the time the second generation passes away, the family business is generating sufficient income to move the family from middle-upper-class to outright-upper-class, or in some cases to the top 1 percent of wealth holders.

The third generation of a profitable family business is born into significant wealth and inheritance—into a world where their father and grandfather already owned multiple stores and homes. They sometimes adopt the good values of the second generation, depending on how they are raised.

Rarely does a family business like this survive into the fourth generation if it remains under family management. In fact, researchers have found that fewer than 3 percent of family businesses survive into the fourth generation, regardless of how profitable those businesses were in earlier generations.[39]

As a reporter, when I interviewed various generations in family businesses, I'd often see these generational trends in posture, knowledge, and attitude about the work and value of the business, as well as the value of the employees and customers.

Why do most family businesses fail to endure into the fourth generation? I believe it is largely because this generation is born into absolute prosperity, and as a result, perspective and original values are lost. The fourth generation does not understand the "so what?" or the "why?" of the hard work and innovation required to keep a business competitive.

Whether a family business unravels in the third generation or in the fourth, the reason is often that the inheriting generation does not understand the work ethic that was required to build the business, nor does it comprehend how difficult life was for their ancestors. In other words, a values difference has very practical implications.

Very often, the inheriting generation enjoys such overwhelming material comfort that they don't feel that they need to work hard to maintain the pleasures and standard of living to which they are accustomed or addicted. The wealth was there when they were born, so they assume it will always be there.

This metaphor is imperfect, but it captures some of our contemporary national mood. For starters, we can think of the World War II generation ("the Greatest Generation") as the first generation of the American "family business" as we have inherited it. We can think of their kids as the second generation (baby boomers). Now the third generation (known as Generation X) and the fourth generation (the millennials) are taking the cultural reins in the US.

In 2016, two esteemed researchers announced a global warning in the *Journal of Democracy*. The percentage of young Americans and Europeans who consider democracy to be important has been falling since World War II and is now dangerously low, they warn.[40]

This graph shows the downward trend of Westerners who believe that living in a democracy is "essential." The decades noted at the bottom are the year-of-birth decades. So "1980s" represents those who were born in the 1980s—in other words, millennials like me (I was born in 1982).

"Essential" to Live in a Country That Is Governed Democratically

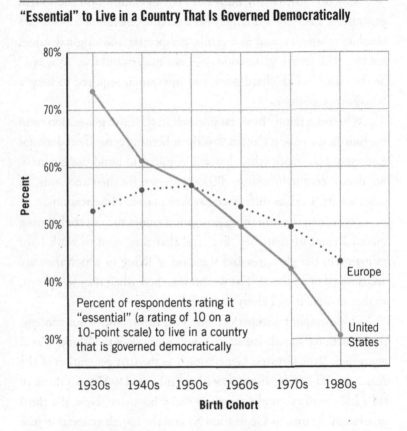

Percent of respondents rating it "essential" (a rating of 10 on a 10-point scale) to live in a country that is governed democratically

Source: World Values Surveys, Waves 5 and 6 (2005–14)

Figure 6.2

As you can see, only one in three Americans born during the 1980s believes it is important to live in a democracy—meaning that nearly 70 percent of younger Americans believe it is not important to live in a democracy. Astonished by these findings, the researchers commented:

What we find is deeply concerning. Citizens in a number of supposedly consolidated democracies in North America and Western Europe have not only grown more critical of their political leaders. Rather, they have also become more cynical about the value of democracy as a political system, less hopeful that anything they do might influence public policy, and more willing to express support for authoritarian alternatives. The crisis of democratic legitimacy extends across a much wider set of indicators than previously appreciated.[41]

The researchers continue, as they mark the difference between the first generation and the fourth generation as I've called them:

How much importance do citizens of developed countries ascribe to living in a democracy? Among older generations, the devotion to democracy is about as fervent and widespread as one might expect: In the United States, for example, people born during the interwar period consider democratic governance an almost sacred value. When asked to rate on a scale of 1 to 10 how "essential" it is for them "to live in a democracy," 72 percent of those born before World War II check "10," the highest value. So do 55 percent of the same cohort in the Netherlands. But, as Figure 1 shows, the millennial generation (those born since 1980) has grown much more indifferent. Only one in three Dutch millennials accords maximal importance to living in a democracy; in the United States, that number is slightly lower, around 30 percent.[42]

Similar trends exist regarding the importance of the Bible and the Christian faith. These have been well documented by David Kinnaman of The Barna Group and also by the Pew Research Center. I will not recite those statistics here, as they have become nearly obvious, but I will footnote some sources if you want to dig deeper.[43]

Baby boomers may not be as "Christian" as their parents and grandparents, but they grew up well aware of the power of evil and the power of ideologies. Boomers are the final American generation to have grown up with Christian prayer allowed or encouraged in their schools. It is their children and grandchildren who inherit both an anti-Christian education and an abundance of wealth and prosperity so as to eclipse the old Truth-Based understanding of reality and the ideology that produced America as we know it.

Within the next eight years, the fourth generation (millennials) will make up 75 percent of the US workforce. In the next presidential elections, millennials, who are far more liberal, progressive, and openly socialist than previous generations, will outnumber the baby boomers and older generations in the vote.[44]

As the Brookings Institute has found, "By 2020, Millennials will comprise more than one of three adult Americans. It is estimated that by 2025 they will make up as much as 75 percent of the workforce. Given their numbers, they will dominate the nation's workplaces and permeate its corporate culture. Thus, understanding the generation's values offers a window into the future of corporate America."[45]

And I would add that understanding the values of millennials offers a picture into the future of the United States—in part, because it is a numerically large generation, but also because the social trajectories move even further away from traditional American values with each younger generation below the millennials.

This metaphor of the four generations has its flaws. It is overly simplistic, to be sure. But it also captures the challenge of inheritors to understand where that wealth came from, what it took to generate the wealth, and why it even matters.

Another Parable: Fruit Trees in the Orchard

In 2015, I moved to California with my wife and young children. The house we rented had three healthy fruit-bearing trees in the backyard: an orange tree, a lemon tree, and a fig tree. Throughout the year, these trees produced an abundance of delicious fruit. The crop could be overwhelming for our little family.

My children enjoyed picking the oranges and lemons. The kids delighted in making hand-squeezed orange juice and lemonade. The quality of the oranges exceeded anything we've bought at the store since.

Now, we did not plant these trees. We did not water them. We did not do any of the hard work that created these trees. But we enjoyed their fruit. Somebody else dug the dirt. Somebody else planted the seedlings. Somebody else watered them and cared for them. All that hard work began very likely before anyone in our family was born. We moved into the house, and we enjoyed the delicious fruit of these trees. My children had no understanding of the hard work required to cultivate such trees—not until I taught it to them.

In a similar way, we are born into an American society where we did not plant the orchards. We did not clear the fields where our universities were built. We did not establish the courts or implement the healthy societal norms, but we eat the fruit from these trees every day—trees that others labored to plant.

Some of these fruits include

- hospitals
- schools
- courts and justice
- freedoms and laws that encourage fair living
- prosperity and opportunity
- scientific advances
- human rights and cultural values that dignify human life
- personal property and other basic rights
- women's, children's, and worker's rights
- a society where slavery no longer exists openly

What fewer Americans seem to understand is that all of these fruits are exceptions in world history. Fewer Americans seem to understand that not all people live in societies with fruit trees like these planted by their predecessors. For some decades now, the "parents" in our society have failed to teach these matters to the "children."

Not only that, but the incoming generations have been conditioned to rebuff any attempt to explain how unique and special American life is. Within my generation, any claim of exceptionalism is considered politically incorrect.

Regardless of the cultural mood, it is a fact that the human advances in the US and the West are exceptional. Increasingly, I find that immigrants understand this more than natural-born Americans, because immigrants have experienced life outside of the US. In this sense, immigrants can be great allies in exploring and then elevating the Truth-Based values that produced America's exceptional wealth and freedom.

Approximately 108.2 billion humans have lived on planet Earth.[46] The vast majority were born into societies that didn't have the fruits we enjoy and assume to be normal. Most people in history lived under unpredictable tyrannical rulers, with barely enough food and with no rights, no hospitals, no modern medicine, no electricity, no cars, no airplanes, and no appliances. They had no ability to break out of slavery or break out of slave-like peasant classes. It was a world of physical abuse, widespread disease, and malnourishment where a majority of people died by age ten. And those strong enough to live past age ten were fortunate if they lived to fifty-five.[47]

Aware that we are enjoying the fruits of a historical anomaly, we do well to ask these questions:

- Who planted these trees that make our lives so different?
- Who planted the seeds that became modern colleges and universities?
- Who planted the seeds that abolished slavery?
- Who planted the seeds that became modern hospitals?[48]

As we consider the trajectory of the Western society we now inherit, we find that the ideological roots from which American society grew have been neglected for the past few decades. Even with its roots neglected (1950s to recent times), the trees have continued to bear fruit—much like the neglected trees did in my backyard in California.

But now, a new generation is emerging, and increasingly this generation has been trained to wield sharpened axes. They have been indoctrinated by leading American universities to swing their axes at the very roots of the civilization they inherit.

Enjoying the Fruits While Neglecting the Roots

Now, let's intentionally mix two metaphors. I described the fruit trees in my backyard. I did nothing to care for these trees, but they continued to produce fruit, even as I neglected the roots.

If we multiply these trees outward, we can picture a sprawling orchard. Let's imagine this sprawling, fruitful, and profitable orchard as the family business in our earlier analogy of the four generations of family business. Since this orchard represents the wealthiest economy in all of world history, let's imagine it as a miles-large orchard that generates immense wealth for the generations that inherit its land, its crops, its efficient production, and its business assets.

The inheritors live in a comfortable home on the expansive grounds—a home built by their grandparents. These inheritors are the Post-Truth thinkers now taking over the helm of society in the US.

Increasingly, Post-Truth and post-Christian Americans do not accept the Christian values that produced the society they inherit, the very values that enable their economy to function. As Allan Bloom, Thomas Sowell, and Jean Twenge document, lost on these inheritors is the basic understanding that America grew out of a society in which Christian values were the connective tissue. Lost is the understanding that a vast majority of past Americans were profoundly influenced by Christianity and the Bible.[49]

Additionally, these inheritors do not realize just how unusually fruitful their land and culture are. When I describe my travels to nations like Haiti or Belarus, I find that some Post-Truth thinkers can't comprehend what life is like outside of the United States. There are so many classes on multiculturalism, yet somehow there is no basic understanding of actual daily life in other cultures. Instead, the multiculturalism classes have indoctrinated America's young to recoil at any Christian truth claim and to never speak negatively about any other culture, regardless of a culture's record on human rights abuses or women's rights.

So unaware of basic history are so many in the incoming generations that few realize how Western Europe was once Christianized, how it was largely dechristianized during the 1800s, and how significant this dechristianization was in what came next—World Wars I and II. These are basic facts of our inheritance and history.

Post-Truth Americans today do not realize they are still eating the fruits from the very trees on which they are condemning the roots. There is so much fruit and profit from the orchard that many generations could neglect the care of the trees for quite some time. But the turning point may be upon us, for the emerging generations are not content just to neglect the roots. Increasingly, they are set on chopping the roots, on uprooting the trees. They've been taught that the orchard will look better without those unsightly, scraggly roots on the ground.

- Why so many steeples on the horizon?
- Why so many old rich white men?
- Why so many bigots allowed in places of influence?
- Why so many tax breaks for those bigoted conservative Christians?

To take just one example, consider a Northwestern University scholar's recent conclusion that Christianity poses a greater threat to

America than Islamic terrorism.[50] For additional examples, visit your closest state university and audit a few first-year courses.

Using the orchard analogy, it may not be until new generations sell off the land, burn the trees, or chop out all the roots that they finally realize the wealth and provision they had taken for granted. We are standing at the beginning of this deconstruction of the American orchard at the popular level.

Intellectually, the deconstruction has been underway in American universities for at least eighty years. But now the ideas have moved into the fields. Now the axes have moved from diagrams on whiteboards and chalkboards to become steel and Kevlar in the hands of an eager generation that is ready to clear the orchard and make its mark.

We find ourselves today in the midst of generations that have been taught to deconstruct and destroy the roots of Christian society. Little do they understand what the consequences of that destruction will be. The chopping of the roots may take fifteen years, or it may take fifty or more.

Post-Christian France took mere decades to move from Voltaire's and Rousseau's ideas to the guillotine. Historian Mark A. Noll elaborates:

> On November 10, 1793, France's greatest church, the Cathedral of Notre Dame, witnessed an unprecedented spectacle. For over six hundred years . . . it had served as a symbol for the Christian identity of the nation. But now in the enthusiasm of revolution the cathedral had been renamed the Temple of Reason. A papier-mâché mountain with Greco-Roman motifs stood in the nave. Historian Simon Schama describes what happened next: "Liberty (played by a singer from the Opéra), dressed in white, wearing the Phrygian bonnet and holding a pike, bowed to the flame of Reason and seated herself on a bank of flowers and plants." This inverted "worship service"

was a high point in the French Revolution's program of dechristianization, whereby leaders of the revolution attempted to throw off what they felt to be the heavy, dead hand of the church. In Paris, the revolutionaries renamed 1,400 streets in order to eliminate reference to saints . . . Priests, bishops, and other religious were forced to leave their posts.[51]

Referring to that time, Alexis de Tocqueville wrote, "Though Christianity was attacked with almost frenzied violence, there was no question of replacing it with another religion. Passionate and persistent efforts were made to wean men away from the faith of their fathers, but once they had lost it, nothing was supplied to fill the void within."[52]

Post-Christian Germany took about sixty to ninety years to move from the philosophies of Marx and Nietzsche to the Weimar Republic, depending on how you measure it. Post-Christian Russia's revolution was even quicker and even more destructive in body count and aggressive dechristianization. Of course, each of these examples had a different culture and a different expression of Christianity than what we inherit in the US.

The United States is a massive orchard—the largest, wealthiest, and most fruitful economy ever planted in all of human history. Its history of religious freedom, free speech, and civil rights is unprecedented. Many of those values will continue on, to some tattered extent, in Post-Truth America, despite the uprooting of the foundation. What will be lost is the ability for the society to sustain and protect those values, because they can only sprout—as we've known and enjoyed them—from a Christianized and Truth-Based society.

We cannot predict how many years will ensue between the chopping of the roots and the potential cultural revolution or devolution that may follow. What we can say with certainty is that eventually if the roots are continually destroyed, then the fruits of prosperity, freedom, and a functioning society as we have inherited them will be lost to some degree. The orchard is large enough that there will still be fruit for some time, because it is vast. But eventually, the consequences will begin to be felt in stomachs and store shelves and monthly income. Eventually.

Rodney Stark contrasts today's college focus—to make money—with the old intents that (ironically) produced Western prosperity, leisure, and liberty: "The most fundamental key to the rise of Western civilization has been the dedication of so many of its most brilliant minds to the pursuit of knowledge. Not to illumination. Not to enlightenment. Not to wisdom. But to knowledge. And the basis for this commitment to knowledge was the Christian commitment to theology."[53]

Documenting the newly educated ignorance, with its refusal of knowledge, Allan Bloom writes from within the Ivy educational system, concluding (again, as a non-Christian):

> We are like ignorant shepherds living on a site where great civilizations once flourished. The shepherds play with the fragments that pop to the surface, having no notion of the beautiful structures of which they were once a part. All that is necessary is a careful excavation to provide them with life-enhancing models. We need history . . . to make the past alive . . . and make a future possible. This is our educational crisis and opportunity. Western rationalism has culminated in a rejection of reason.[54]

My generation consumes food it did not plant or harvest, and it uses the energy from that food to mock and scorn the ancestors who sacrificed for our prosperity. Nowhere is this more apparent than in the post-Christian and Post-Truth beliefs of the incoming generations. Here is where we stand. **My generation has been taught to despise and deconstruct the foundations on which American society was established.**

Barring some radical change of course, if this deconstruction continues, the entire system may in time collapse inward upon itself. Or the system will become so weakened that, much like a family business, a more muscular group will overtake it.

Spiritual Factors for the Decline of Western Society

Looking back down the hallway of history, we can see with clarity the turning point for America's cultural demise. It was the moments when the great American universities abandoned a supernatural view of the Christian Scriptures.

So essential were the Christian Scriptures—embedded into the crests of Harvard, Yale, Princeton, Johns Hopkins, and most other early American colleges—that even those who turned their backs on the authority of the Bible may never have imagined there would come a day when graduates of their institutions never once read the Bible or even had basic familiarity with it.

Even more unthinkable to those founders would be the day when Christianity is mocked and ridiculed in their institutions, while rampant debauchery, lust, and hypersexuality are openly encouraged. That day is today. And it has been for some time.

Yale was the first to fall.[55] Then Harvard. And most recently, Princeton. If we could go back in time and throw ourselves into the debate regarding the authority of Scripture in these institutions, we would, I believe, alter the course of American history. The removal of this foundational truth standard has led inevitably to the Post-Truth and post-Christian absurdities we are witnessing today. The trickle-down has been slow but consistent and now, after a full century of it, irreversible in academia.

As in Germany and Russia, the defeat of Christianity within the university did not immediately affect the mainstream culture. But it was the watershed turning point. In *The Great Evangelical Disaster*, Francis Schaeffer describes well the delayed watershed effect of surrendering scriptural authority.

Not far from where we live in Switzerland is a high ridge of rock with a valley on both sides. One time I was there when there was snow on the ground along that ridge. The snow was lying there unbroken, a seeming unity. However, that unity was an illusion, for it lay along a great divide; it lay along a watershed. One portion of the snow when it melted would flow into one valley. The snow which lay close beside would flow into another valley when it melted.

Now it just so happens on that particular ridge that the melting snow which flows down one side of that ridge goes down into a valley, into a small river, and then down into the Rhine River. The Rhine then flows on through Germany and the water ends up in the cold waters of the North Sea. The water from the snow that started out so close along that watershed on the other side of the ridge, when this snow melts, drops off sharply down the ridge into the Rhone Valley. This water flows into Lac Leman—or as it is known in the English-speaking world, Lake Geneva—and then goes down below that into the Rhone River which flows through France and into the warm waters of the Mediterranean.

The snow lies along that watershed, unbroken, as a seeming unity. But when it melts, where it ends in its destinations is literally a thousand miles apart. That is a watershed. That is what a watershed is. A watershed divides. A clear line can be drawn between what seems at first to be the same or at least very close, but in reality ends in very different situations. In a watershed there is a line.[56]

The surrender of scriptural authority was a watershed moment in American history that led inevitably to cultural disaster. Downstream from the surrender of scriptural authority has been the eventual surrender of Christian ideals and values. Following the surrender of the truth standard (Scripture), we see a post-Christian culture embracing a Frankenstein-mutant mixture of some Christian ideals (still valuing justice and caring for the poor, while simultaneously rejecting the foundations). Once the complete rejection of foundational Christian ideals reaches the mainstream culture (as is now happening in the US), it is nearly irreversible by human means alone.

During the last century, most of America held to the Christian ideals, valued the Bible, valued the seven Christian virtues, and even valued the role of the church. Meanwhile, the great American seminaries, which had become the great American universities, deconstructed the foundations of those societal foundations.

For about a century, we have lived in dissonance. An aftertaste of the virtues continues as a hazy hangover in the mainstream culture, even as leading academic thinkers in America's best universities mock, scorn, or deny those foundational ingredients.

This dechristianization of the leading American universities hit full steam soon after World War II and has been progressing at a feverish pace ever since. And now, while sincere Christians remain a lively portion of the American population, sincere Christians hold few positions of influence at the leading edges of culture.

Because the most prestigious universities disproportionately produce the cultural thought leaders, the last forty years have seen a gradual saturation of Post-Truth thinkers into every leading edge of the culture. As a result, those who now lead the culture in film, journalism, academia, Silicon Valley, entertainment, many government posts, and pace-setting metropolitan cities are almost wholly indoctrinated into the post-Christian and Post-Truth ideology. If only we could turn back the hands of time on this matter. These are well-intentioned, highly intelligent, kind, and highly skilled people who occupy these positions of cultural influence, but they increasingly view the world through a flawed Post-Truth ideology taught to them in their most vulnerable, formative years of education.

While the spiritual causes for America's cultural turn away from God are many (including idolatry and dozens of other factors), it is my belief that one primary spiritual factor—the surrender of the authority of Scripture—is most directly correlated to the unraveling of Western civilization as documented in this book.

CONCLUSION

In summary, then, we have seen that the societal fabric of Western civilization is indeed unraveling when measured by ideology and cultural values. We have considered some of the human and spiritual factors that drive this decline.

In part 2, we will look at where all of this may lead. But first let's anchor ourselves in some hope, for there is an even more powerful force at work in the universe, which we will focus on in the next chapter: "Christ and His People are Prevailing."

Chapter 7

FORCE 5: CHRIST AND HIS PEOPLE ARE PREVAILING

"On this rock I will build my church, and the gates of hell shall not prevail against it."

JESUS, IN MATTHEW 16:18 ESV

Aware of the Five Forces shaping humanity and their potential to wreak destruction, we need not whimper beneath a defeatist mentality. We do not crumple or collapse into a pessimistic outlook. Why not? Because we know with confidence that our Father and our Savior will prevail. We know with confidence that all of this is working precisely as Christ predicted—toward a climactic moment when every nation and tribe and people and tongue will see the glory of Christ, the Prince of Peace, and the goodness of God, the provider of "every good and perfect gift."[1]

One can wonder if God were to replay the history of humanity on judgment day, how humanity might gasp when it sees with clarity how overtly the Christianized societies have turned away from the God whose truth produced their prosperity. One wonders if seeing this with stark clarity, humans will realize that, indeed, humanity has rejected God, His ways, and even His blessing. Perhaps humanity will also see God's compassion and patience in how He waits to allow those who hate Him even more time to repent yet today.

In light of such blatant rebellion, how much more glorious will the sacrifice of the cross be when humans realize how God sacrificed Himself so painfully—not to help people who are inherently good, but to redeem people who are so inherently selfish and blind as to turn away from the light of God!

Not only do we know that all of this will end well for the Christian, but we also know that every apparent obstacle in this world is an opportunity spiritually. God has ordained for you and me to be alive at this time, at this historic cultural moment. This is our opportunity in the story of human history. Out of all the continents and cultures and centuries of history, God placed you and me here, now.

And it is not by accident. God has an important role for us to play during this cultural sea change. Some Christians will miss the great opportunity—perhaps our greatest opportunity—because of fear or apathy.

As we saw in the Pew projections, in about thirty years, two out of five Christians will live in sub-Saharan Africa. The global church will be significantly poorer, even as Islam and communism thrive in the rising economies and regions of the world.

From a scriptural view of the "seven churches" that Christ addresses in Revelation, we could summarize it this way: in the next thirty years, the center of the global church will move from a Laodicean church (wealthy, self-indulgent, and lukewarm) to become more like the church in Smyrna (persecuted and poor, but faithful and resolute).[2]

Those of us in America are inheriting the wealthiest church in world history. In the coming decades, if America's light dims globally and if American Christians face social challenges, we will be presented with the opportunity and responsibility to invest our disproportionate wealth and gifts into Christ's kingdom rather than into our own kingdoms.

No matter what continent we find ourselves on, we aim to seize the opportunity to live for Christ now and to live for Christ in the next decades. Doing so requires us to see world events with a God-aligned perspective. With the global rise of Islam and Chinese communism, as well as the Post-Truth turn that may socially discriminate against Christians in the US and West, it may seem like the great truths of the cross are not prevailing after all. Yet, among all world ideologies, we happen to know which one ideology will prevail in the very end when the books are closed on human history. Back when Christianity only represented a few dozen people, Christ predicted that the journey to His ultimate victory and kingdom would pass through uncertain times—through wars, famines, persecutions, and difficult territory.[3] To his fearful disciples and also to us, Jesus said, "In this world you will have trouble. But take heart! I have overcome the world."[4]

Jesus, who is almighty God, came into this world as a gentle lamb, a vulnerable baby. He came as a suffering servant. He will soon return in great contrast, as a Mighty Warrior leading an army of supernatural beings. He will return as the Judge with fire in his eyes. He will return as King of kings and Lord of lords, before whom every knee will bow in submission and every tongue will confess His lordship.[5]

Note Christ's pattern: chosen humility precedes universal glory. Christ intentionally humbled himself, and this preceded His future universal glory as the central Star of the universe. We have only ever seen Christ at His physically weakest, much like Lucy and Susan watching Aslan, the Christ-figure, sacrifice himself on the stone table in C. S. Lewis's *The Chronicles of Narnia*. This, of course, was a chosen weakness. Christ exhibited the strength to humble Himself in self-sacrifice for the rescue of others.[6]

Christ's return, His second coming, will be in contrast to the humility of His first. That moment will explode in a demonstration of physical and supernatural might far greater than the world has ever seen or imagined, a power of higher order and magnitude than any nuclear blast or cultural revolution.

Christ's chosen humility precedes His universal glory. And now, Christianity follows the same pattern. The Christian ideology may appear at points in history to be a victim or to be impotent or weak. But **Christianity is only weak inasmuch as Jesus Himself chose to appear weak in His first coming. For nearly two thousand years, the ideology of Christianity, though appearing weak at moments, has been unstoppable even in the face of atrocities.**

- Nero impaled Christians in his gardens and lit them as torches for evening parties.
- Romans gathered to place bets as they fed Christians to lions.
- Adolf Hitler sent true Christian activists like Dietrich Bonhoeffer and Corrie ten Boom to the concentration camps.
- Joseph Stalin sentenced Christians to freeze in the Siberian Gulags.
- Mao Tse-tung had Christians murdered in the fields.
- Dictators have vowed to eradicate Christians from the planet.
- Muhammad's most devoted followers have beheaded thousands of Christians for 1,400 years.

Together, these forces have stripped millions of Christians of their earthly lives.[7] They have inflicted unthinkable suffering and pain in this temporary earthly life. But together, these forces have not killed a single Christian's eternal soul. Nor has the combined force of these fearful powers slowed the Christian ideology.

Consider the massive size, the rumbling tanks, and the intimidating power of the USSR in the 1970s or of China today. None of these have been able to shout louder than the gentle whisper of "Come to me, all you who are weary and burdened, and I will give you rest."[8] No army of millions, no Roman legion, no band of sword-wielding terrorists, no military power with nuclear warheads, has been able to stop the gentle Shepherd who welcomed children onto His knee.

No empire, dictator, philosopher, or cultural leader has been able to stop Christ's ideology. Back when Christians numbered fewer than a graduating high school class, Jesus predicted that His followers would spread to the ends of the earth. And now, Christianity boasts more followers than any other ideology in world history. It has spread to every continent, precisely as Jesus predicted—far outpacing the growth rate or the reach of any other ideology in all of history.

"You will be my witnesses," Jesus predicted—those who will spread His message "to the ends of the earth."[9] This is a remarkable ancient prediction, documented by ancient texts, and now this very prediction is undeniably proven to have come true among the 2.4 billion self-declared Christians in our time.

And so as we assess various threats to our way of life, as we uncover the latest tactics of the enemy who prowls about, we do so in the knowledge that every seeming victory for the enemy is temporary. And every seeming defeat of the cross is limited, both in time and dimension. *The gates of hell shall not prevail.*

Christ's final victory is sure. His final victory will be unlimited in all dimensions, stretching into heaven, hell, and the new heaven and new earth. Christ's victory will be unlimited in time also, extending infinitely into future and past time. In this sense, Christ has already won. In this sense, truly, "It is finished."[10] And yet, we get to join in his sufferings now in this present and temporary era,[11] if we will move our wills to join His eternal kingdom by faith.

With 2.4 billion followers in our lifetime, the ideology of Christianity is already the most viral, generous, unstoppable movement in world history. It owns more real estate than many nations, and it has done more to better human life and rights than any other movement.

But here is the point: Christianity is presently in its humblest and weakest form. Christianity is presently following the mocked and scorned Nazarene who stumbled under the weight of His cross on the path to Golgotha. Christianity is presently in the form of Aslan the lion of Narnia—shaved, shorn, mocked, and scorned. The present humility of Christianity will, when Christ

returns, be traded for outright glory. And so, despite the opposing forces we may face in our earthly life, the message of Christ will continue marching uninhibited, proving in every epoch of history the truth of Jesus' prediction: "I *will* build my church, and *the gates of hell shall not prevail against it*."[12]

By faith, heroes of the Christian faith have believed this larger reality in every epoch. Hebrews 11 describes Christian heroes who have remained faithful to believe this, even as they shivered under the sword's blade, under the lion's breath, under starvation's sting, under persecution's injustice. We know of Roman military officers who, when commanded to slaughter a Christian village, surrendered their own Roman insignia and walked alongside their Christian brothers and sisters.[13] We know of faithful Christ followers in Hitler's Germany, in Stalin's Russia, in Mao's China. And we can choose to stand with that faithful remnant now.

Whether we face gradual moral decay under the power of Post-Truth materialism or we face abrupt social chaos, we can be faithful Christ followers now. Whether faced with the challenge of hypersexual immorality, of legal persecution, or of outright war, we can find our security in "a kingdom that cannot be shaken."[14]

Now is our turn to play our role in the church's outlasting of Rome, of Russia, of Muhammad, and a thousand other opponents. It is our turn to march forward in Christ's peaceful way of "grace and truth," the most powerful, the most muscular, the most peaceful, the most undefeatable ideology, in all of human history. Present and future tragedies only reinforce what God assures us about our temporary assignment in this sin-infected world: "Our citizenship is in heaven. And we eagerly await a Savior from there, the Lord Jesus Christ."[15]

In part 3 of this book, we will examine practical postures to help us live out such a faith today. We will determine together to be God's righteous remnant in our day. For now, let us resolve to have a heart of faith and a spirit of confidence in Christ's guaranteed return.

Together let us continue anchoring into this firm belief. Let us become unshakable in our resolve that our Savior will have the victory. We will learn to live fearlessly in Christ's invincible way of life. We will not be intimidated.

Nations may tremble. Kingdoms may wage war. Mountains may fall into the seas. But ours is a kingdom that cannot be shaken.

PART 2

WHERE WILL IT LEAD?

Chapter 8

WHAT CAN AND CANNOT HAPPEN

We began chapter 2 with a description of the Kristallnacht ("Night of Broken Glass") in Germany in 1938. A full decade before that eruption, before the bursting glass of shopwindows, before the fires and beatings in the streets, many sincere Christians and Jews in Europe sensed that calamitous times were coming. They sensed this because they had an intuition about the cultural climate and its ideology. They understood the principle of sowing and reaping. They connected the dots between what children were being taught and how those beliefs would affect society once those children led society.

Some foresaw the calamity of the Holocaust simply by playing out the Nazi ideology to its logical end. They realized that isolated attacks on Jews were not sporadic problems that would resolve themselves. No, the isolated attacks were pre-tremors or foreshocks preceding a much larger tectonic shift, the eruption of a social army that genuinely believed it was its duty and destiny to kill Jews and dominate Europe.

Many Christians and Jews sense similar evils taking root in various cultures around the world today through violent interpretations of Islam, government persecution of churches, and social prejudice against Christians. In countries surrounding Israel, it is a fact that there are classrooms where kindergarteners are trained to kill Jews, Christians, and homosexuals.[1]

In other parts of the world, sincere Christians warn of anti-Christian motivations in the unpublicized policies of the Communist Party now leading China—the world's fastest-growing economy. Many Americans are blissfully unaware of the thick government censorship in China that blocks internet access to sites with words like *Jesus, Christianity,* or even *God* in many instances. And while many underground churches thrive, other churches have seen their buildings demolished and steeples physically toppled by government order.[2]

Christians in some regions of India—on a path to become the #2 economy in the world during the next thirty years—also experience violent persecution in many regions from strains of Hinduism that burn church buildings and punish converts to Christianity, as well as from some strains of Islam. Christians are no safer in Indonesia or in most of the Middle East and North Africa.

As of today, the safest place for Christians to flee to is the territory held by the once-Christian Western nations and their allies. But if Western society's rejection of Christian truth develops into policies that limit Christian expression, there may be few places on the planet where persecuted Christians can find safe haven or worship with the freedom we've known as normal in the West in our lifetime. In addition to potential social persecution, Western society's cascade of Post-Truth choices in morality, sexuality, ethics, and government may in time produce an upset of the broader stable society we have known.

SEVEN PLAUSIBLE SCENARIOS FOR THE NEXT THIRTY YEARS

Compressing everything we've learned, we can venture ahead with some potential scenarios that range from cataclysmic to benign. I present these with the caution that the future is fundamentally unpredictable.

Potential Scenario 1: At the dramatic end of the spectrum, we could build a case that global calamity is possible, perhaps as extreme as a world war or a global economic depression. Consider Graham Allison's 2017 book *Destined for War*, in which the Harvard scholar argues that historically, during the last five hundred years, whenever a #2 economy has overtaken a #1 economy, it has led to war twelve out of sixteen times.[3] Thus he concludes that China and the US are statistically likely to engage in a war during the next fifteen years as their economies swap roles as number one and two in the world.

Beyond Allison's academic prediction, potential scenarios include international conflicts ignited by competing ideologies or by rising nations as they compete for limited resources. Financially, we inherit a global economy founded on Western principles but now severed from the Truth-Based values that made the economy stable and mutually beneficial. As a result, we could build a logical case that the global economy is increasingly vulnerable to dramatic collapse.

Potential Scenario 2: Also at the dramatic end of possibility are "wild card" factors such as North Korea, Turkey, Pakistan, and Iran, which each hold enough military power, superpower allies, and militant ideologies to upset the delicate global equilibrium.

Potential Scenario 3: In contrast, one could argue that the Truth-Based foundation is so robust in the United States and that the peak of Western civilization is so vast that life may tick along in a somewhat normal manner for Americans and Westerners during the next thirty years. Perhaps, then, the only changes will be internal. These would include Post-Truth cultural consequences, which will degrade the standard of living, but maybe they will be limited to a gradual decline of prosperity and public safety and a gradual deterioration of religious liberty, Christian rights, and free speech in Western nations.

Potential Scenario 4: Within the United States, we could build a case from generational demographic findings that the Post-Truth preference for socialism will land a socialist government in

Washington at some point in the next thirty years, and that, as has happened in many other nations, socialism may eclipse individual rights as we've known them. In the event of a crisis such as a war or an economic downturn, socialism has proven to be the repeated on-ramp to authoritarianism (note that Benito Mussolini, Joseph Stalin, Adolf Hitler, and Fidel Castro were all socialists in their early years).

Potential Scenario 5: We can and should pray for Christian revival. With our focus on movements beyond Christianity, we can lose sight of the reality that Christianity remains the largest ideology in the world, and Christianity will still be, by small measure, the largest ideology in 2050, even if revival does not occur. Let us pray for a supernatural revival of Christianity that upsets these other trajectories and sees the church of Christ prevailing spiritually in the US and across the globe.

While the church in the United States and the West may be smaller than in previous generations and may wield less cultural influence, the reality remains that there is a vibrant remnant here in the US—that the millions who are still committed to Christ are often committed at the deepest levels. Additionally, the US church still holds more wealth than any other church in world history.

Jesus seemed to prefer a dozen or so committed disciples to many hundreds of casual followers.[4] In this sense, we are well positioned to lead a genuine revival as the world shakes around us. The young American Christians who remain in the faith are, in my experience, some of the most committed and genuine Christ followers I've met. I have great hope for the church in the West and in the world, based on the sincere commitment of such "remnant" Christians.

Potential Scenario 6: As believers in Christ, the "wild card" scenario we most pray and hope for is Christ's return to deliver His people and establish the fullness of His kingdom of earth. This is our "blessed hope,"[5] and Christ repeatedly taught us to prepare for this imminent return. Indeed, as Islam grows to dominate militarized nations, and as these nations join forces against Israel, the prophecies of Revelation, Daniel, Ezekiel, and of Jesus in Matthew's gospel will be wound like a tight spring, ready to catapult the apocalyptic end of days.

Potential Scenario 7: Of course, history demonstrates that world events may unfold in ways we could never anticipate today—either disastrously or wonderfully. We should hold our research and global projections with humility, knowing that only God knows the future. He has shared the end of the story with us, but He has been intentionally silent about details and timelines. The human scenarios above, while entirely logical, are mere conjecture. **The spiritual scenarios above cannot be timed or predicted by humans, but the certainty that Christ will prevail is sure**.

Thankfully, we can do something more practical than attempt to predict future global events.

WHAT WE CAN KNOW WITH SOME CERTAINTY

While we cannot know the future, what we can know with near certainty are the social currents of today. And we can trace these currents forward as we follow their paths into a likely future.

In any of the potential global scenarios, our neighbors in America will increasingly think as they think today—from a Post-Truth ideology. And so if we prepare ourselves to live for Christ in a Post-Truth America and to live in an uncertain global world, then we will be prepared to maintain a Christlike posture, no matter what scenario the future delivers. We will be prepared to minister to our neighbors in feast or in famine. We will be prepared to hold a Christlike posture in peace or in war, in persecution or in apathy.

The global events of the next thirty years are beyond our control. What we can control is our intent to live for Christ in the emerging Post-Truth American culture and in the emerging reshuffling of the world order. If we see reality as Jesus describes it, then we are not placed on this earth to merely survive or to protect ourselves.

We are placed here to serve an eternal purpose in the specific events of our lives.

Based on the Five Forces we examined in part 1, we can venture some predictions about the social currents ahead for America and the West in the next thirty years.

In America and the West

Here are *some currents we may witness in America and the West*:[6]

- the deconstruction of many foundational Christian and Truth-Based morals, values, laws, and aspirations
- increasing societal unrest and division as the absurdities of Post-Truth thinking soak deeper into actual lives, institutions, governments, and societal norms—an unrest that may demonstrate itself in riots and protests in urban areas
- increasing corruption among people in power who will make regulatory and legal decisions based on Post-Truth opinions and whims rather than objective written rule or the Constitution
- continued ideological division among Americans as evidenced in political and social conflict. The conflict between Truth-Based thinkers and Post-Truth thinkers overlaps with this, though it is not the only social conflict we will see. The present split is about 57 percent Post-Truth thinkers and 43 percent Truth-Based thinkers, but with Post-Truth thinking increasing in every younger generation, the Post-Truth ideology is on track to become a stronger majority by the mid-2020s and an overwhelming majority by the 2030s.
- social and political division within individual Western nations (see Spain, the United Kingdom, and the United States as examples of these ideologically divided populations)
- the dissolving of some formerly allied Western nations collectively (see Brexit and the European Union)
- a hypersexual society untethered from moral absolutes

- a society in which former moral guides, such as a traditional family, church association, aspirational Christian values, and law enforcement, are continually abandoned and scorned
- ignorance in the new West regarding what made the West strong
- self-hatred in the West toward traditional Western values and institutions, including Christianity, Christian organizations, institutions, and churches
- ignorance in the new West regarding hostile and conquering ideologies at home and abroad
- inheritor generations increasingly unable to generate actual wealth or produce innovation to the degree of previous American generations
- a West that may become less competitive in technology and finance than emerging nations like China and India
- a West ill-equipped to discern, define, or defend against existential threats
- an America that continues squabbling internally, even as its global position deteriorates
- an American populace ignorant of the extraordinary benefits that Americans presently enjoy as inheritors of the world's #1 economy and go-to reserve financial currency
- an American populace surprised by the consequences as the United States declines and becomes less insulated from massive shifts in other nations

Around the World

Here are *some currents we may witness globally*:

- the reshuffling of the world's largest economies—away from the West and into the East—with potential 2050 rankings:
    a. China (communist)
    b. India (Hindu)

    c. United States

    d. Indonesia (Muslim)[7]

- a geographic reorientation of world power from West to East
- an ideological reorientation of world power from West to East
- a reshuffling of the world's most powerful militaries as it relates to practical power to grab and hold land areas
- a China as anti-Christian as the recent USSR, yet a nation that Western nations continue to make wealthy and on which Western nations are increasingly dependent for financial stability and for the basic commodities of war (steel foundries, semiconductor fabrication, rare earth element production, etc.)
- the global spread of Islam as the fastest-growing ideology on the planet
- the global growth of ideologies that dominate, subjugate, and conquer other religions or cultures, with this growth set to occur among massive populations and on a scale we may struggle to comprehend
- As conquering ideologies prevail, some may demonstrate that, while they were happy to take Western weapons and technology for their purposes, they are not open to Western tolerance, the West's globalism ideal, or Christianity; in some cases, the conquering ideologies will not tolerate the West, Israel, or Christianity once they are in a position of physical superiority. Indeed, this is already the case in many parts of China, India, Indonesia, and Turkey.
- the increasing cohesion of fundamentalist Islam among advanced military nations such as Turkey, Pakistan, Iran, and Indonesia
- eventually, the likelihood of one or more unified transnational Islamic military forces, the size and power of which may surpass that of World War II armies and surprise many Westerners who remain ignorant of the military buildup in nations like Turkey and Pakistan and of the ideological education toward

conquest among hundreds of millions of young people stretching from Morocco to Indonesia

- a vulnerable world economy that is interconnected in increasingly complex ways

WHAT WE CAN BE QUITE SURE WILL NOT HAPPEN

History is fundamentally unpredictable. Only God knows the future. But barring radical supernatural intervention, here are three things I believe with a high level of certainty *will not happen* in our lifetime—based on the trajectories we've considered.

Impossible Scenario 1: The status quo will casually continue without hiccup. What I'm describing in this book—an understanding of past and emerging global ideologies—is a large-scale, complex system. It's not linear. Factor in the intense pressures that are building, and some inevitable shift is likely coming.

Impossible Scenario 2: A socialist-Marxist utopia will arise in the United States. While many young Americans are excited about socialism and Marxism, the reality is that the dream of a Marxist utopia simply will not happen in the United States in any sustainable manner. It can't happen because the ideology doesn't work. It has been tried, and it has failed every time. The sad conclusion reached by many Post-Truth thinkers is that a Marxist utopia will right the wrongs and injustices of America, the West, Christianity, and humanity as they have been taught them. We can't say for certain if a Marxist experiment will actually emerge in the US, but we can say with certainty that if such an experiment does take place, it will end in tragedy and death, as it has on every other continent.

Impossible Scenario 3: An easy return to the "good ole days" of Christianized America will take place. I meet many well-intentioned Christians who share a common sentiment: that somehow we're going to return to the good ole days when most Americans respected the

Bible and shared Christian values and morals. Humanly speaking, this is impossible for at least three reasons:

1. The rate of cultural change.
2. The overwhelming percentage of Post-Truth Americans.
3. Post-Truth's domination in every leading edge of the culture, now including K-12 education, universities, film, TV, journalism, influential coastal metropolises, and Silicon Valley.

These combined factors make such a rewind to the cultural values of the past impossible, humanly speaking. Only God can bring about a miracle of revival or societal change.

CONCLUSION

In the coming years and decades, the combined effect of the above factors (both abroad and within the West) will affect each of us, our children, and our neighbors. We cannot predict how these trends will affect us, but we can say with some certainty that many of these trends will be in play, in varying degrees, during the next thirty years. And in one way or another, some of them will affect us.

In the next chapter, we will condense all of our research into nine specific trends we will face in our lifetime. Then in part 3, we will look to God's Word so that we can shine for Christ in the coming darkness.

Chapter 9

THE NINE POST-CHRISTIAN TRENDS WE WILL FACE

We began our journey at the top of a giant global funnel—an expanse spreading across centuries, continents, and cultures. We started at that broad cosmic level. We considered global realities through the biggest lenses possible—ideology, Scripture, and historical trajectory.

We learned about the Five Forces that will shape world events in our lifetime. Then we journeyed down the funnel in our analysis. Here, at the bottom of the funnel, we find nine simple, concrete trends that are presently developing. Barring a radical change, we can expect to witness these trends during the next years and decades.

1. A WORLD THAT IS POST-CHRISTIAN

In America and the West, we can expect a society that moves from ignoring its Christian foundations to demeaning or dismantling those Christian beliefs and institutions that contradict the Post-Truth mood of tolerance and moral relativity. Beyond 2020, the shift may begin evidencing itself more dramatically, with the potential for social backlash against individual Christians who hold to moral absolutes on sexuality. Such Christians may be labeled as prejudiced in some universities, cities, or corporations.

189

Globally, the center of economic and military power is set to drift away from the formerly Christian/Western nations.

2. A WORLD THAT IS POST-TRUTH

In America and the West, we can expect a society where truth and morality are feelings-based and crowd-sourced. This so-called "truth" can be contradictory, dangerous, and even absurd, as long as it is not judgmental toward protected classes. Historical Western social morals will be challenged and disregarded in many instances, as a majority of people in the culture genuinely believe "you must decide for yourself what is right and wrong." The culture's definition of right and wrong will be increasingly mob-driven. In some circles, the greatest threat to society may be defined as Christians, conservatives, or other Truth-Based thinkers who take unpopular stands on moral issues.

3. A WORLD THAT IS POST-KNOWLEDGE

In America and the West, we can expect a society of educated ignorance and blindness, already having taken root at the influential universities and now trickling down into the whole of the culture. Increasingly, many of the most educated will be ignorant of basic factual history in the West and of global ideologies, including Islam, Hinduism, and the emerging world powers.

4. A WORLD THAT IS POST-CHURCH

Based on generational trends, Pew Research projects a continued massive exodus from Christianity and a migration into agnosticism and nonbelief in America and the West. We can expect a society that may uproot the old tax exemptions and other social privileges once granted to Christians and clergy—a society where churches are largely ignored, as long as they do not challenge the status quo or "discriminate" against protected classes. Eventually, there may be retaliation against those churches or Christian organizations that do not compromise their ancient beliefs about morality.

Globally, as a result of warring ideologies and declining Western influence, we are already seeing a world where Christians in the fastest-growing economies (China, India, Indonesia) are increasingly persecuted, often having their buildings burned or physically demolished. The church is on track to spiritually thrive in poor and developing regions, including sub-Saharan Africa and portions of South America.

5. A WORLD THAT IS POST-DECENCY

We can expect a society in which Truth-Based versus Post-Truth Americans are deeply divided by ideological disagreements, prejudiced stereotypes, reactive impulses, and mob mentalities. The old Western idea that you can disagree with an opponent and respect them with graciousness may continue to fade away, because it is a Truth-Based value.

6. A WORLD THAT IS POST-HUMAN

In America and the West, we are already seeing a society where Truth-Based thinkers are vilified and where the Christian values of human dignity and respect slowly deteriorate. People will be valued or not valued based on their class within the Post-Truth scaffolding or on their conformity to the Post-Truth ideology, not on their inherent humanity.

Globally, we can expect a world where human dignity as we hold it today slowly dissolves, largely because human dignity and value are Truth-Based values, but also because human consumption may exceed supply in some regions and because machines will become more valuable than humans for most practical work, satisfaction, companionship, assistance, and economic production. As a result, in some circles, human life will be seen as a liability and a cost (mouths to feed) rather than as an asset and an opportunity.

7. A WORLD THAT IS POST-PROSPERITY

In America and the West, there is the potential for a plateaued and then declining economy and a standard of living that is also increasingly vulnerable to rapid decline.

Globally, we can expect a world competing for limited resources and driven by fear, competition, unrest, scarcity, and an ever-opening power vacuum created by the decline of the West.

8. A WORLD THAT IS POST-LIBERTY

As the world becomes less predictable and secure, incoming Americans and Westerners may trade traditional American rights such as personal liberty, freedom of speech, and freedom of assembly in exchange for promises to keep society safe, achieve peace, or better the masses.

9. A WORLD THAT IS POST-PEACE

In America and the West, we may see a society that is internally less stable and more susceptible to internal riots and violent demonstrations than recent generations.

Globally, we can expect an increasingly armed world that is divided by ideology, terrorism, and competition, resulting in an increased likelihood of terror attacks, as well as an increased chance of war or armed conflict.

PART 3

HOW WILL WE LIVE?

Chapter 10

WHAT WE CAN AND CANNOT CONTROL

All we have learned has the potential to cause despair. We can feel hopeless. But God has a better plan for us.

And so now, as we unpack nine positive manifestos for Christ's people (chapter 11 and the chapters that follow), we are going to make an intentional pivot in our hearts and minds. We are going to build a supernatural, biblical, and practical hope. It will not be a hope of blanket denial or of blind delusion that "things will just be problem-free." Instead, we will build a genuine, sincere, and God-given hope that leads to fearless courage and to bold action.

In his book *Necessary Endings*, Dr. Henry Cloud writes about the importance of hopelessness.[1] When we finally become hopeless in regard to a situation, we are ready to change, to risk, and to try something new.

Drug addicts have to hit the hopelessness of "rock bottom" before they can experience a true recovery. In the same way, hopelessness can force us to make positive changes.

Hopelessness often precedes true hope.

Hopelessness often precedes true change.

Hopelessness often precedes fearless resolve.

As you read through the following nine manifestos, let the hopelessness of the world apart from Christ motivate you to trust in Christ

195

alone. And let the hopelessness of the human condition drive you to act on these clear scriptural teachings.

Dr. Cloud writes that hopelessness becomes a gift when we use it to properly define reality and then to step toward something better. But it is a personal choice to turn hopelessness into a stepping-stone rather than let it be a stumbling block. Nobody else can make this pivot in your heart for you.

Dr. Cloud tells a personal story from 2007 and 2008, after the economic collapse known as the Great Recession. When the stock market crashed, many formerly successful businesspeople felt that the financial conditions were so out of their control that they could not possibly succeed in such a broken economy.

But Dr. Cloud describes others who managed to find sales and success, even in the financial downturn. Here's what set those people apart: "Their focus was different. They did not spend their time and energy focused on all the things that were falling apart that they could do nothing about. Instead, they thought hard and fast about what they *could do*."[2]

The people who excelled and thrived within the crisis were able to acknowledge what they could not control, and then they focused their energies on *what they could control*.

However, those who were overtaken by the crisis had the opposite outlook. They got stuck as they focused on *what they could not control*.

Dr. Cloud describes the mental state of those who became paralyzed by fear: "In a learned-helplessness model, the brain begins to interpret events in a negative way, thus reinforcing its belief that 'all is bad' . . . When someone with this vulnerability is put in a position where things that they cannot control, such as the economy, are affecting them, they shut down and do not execute *in the activities that they can control*. This is where it all begins to go downhill."[3]

In our journey through this book, as we acknowledge massive forces beyond our control, it is important that we do not fall into a "learned helplessness" mentality. We do not assume that all is bad or

that things will only get worse. In fact, we know the very opposite—
**that our God is the most powerful force in the universe, that He
is good, and that even if things get worse temporarily, all things
will ultimately lead to His return. The end for us is very good.
And as God's people we can walk this earth knowing that the
best is truly ahead of us.**

We also know that our God will sustain and strengthen us—not
merely to survive, but also to thrive in serving Him and others during
this unique moment in history. He is a God who brings good from
evil and life from death. He has filled us with His very Spirit, who
brings joyfulness, peace, love, and kindness.

Dr. Cloud offers a specific strategy to move from feeling out of
control to taking control. He suggests making two lists. On one list,
you have permission to write every terrible thing that you cannot
control. In some ways, parts 1 and 2 of this book have been a long
list in that column of things we cannot control.

Our list of things we cannot control includes nations, ideologies,
economies, other people, and forces that are out of our hands. It is
important to understand these. God never calls us to be ignorant of
our surroundings. **But it is equally important to move to the next
list:** *the things we can control.* **This is where we will choose to
spend our mental and moral energy. This is where we will spend
our days, months, and years.**

For example, I cannot control what the world will look like when
my eight-year-old son, Jack, is an adult, but I can control how I raise
Jack. I can prepare Jack to live for Christ in that future world. If I
spend my days envisioning Jack in some bleak apocalyptic future,
then I become fearful, edgy, and defensive, but if I focus on preparing
Jack to be a man of character who can thrive for Christ and serve
others well, then I become purposeful, energized, and engaged. The
difference is the focus on what I *can* control.

Here's an example of two lists I made the other day as I was
processing the material in this book.

Things I Cannot Control

- I cannot control if North Korea launches nuclear missiles.
- I cannot control China's military, economy, or treatment of Christians.
- I cannot control the US stock market.
- I cannot control ISIS or radical terrorists who seek to kill Americans.
- I cannot control what children are being taught by American society at large.
- I cannot control the fact that great Christian institutions beyond my influence continue to be lost intellectually and morally.
- I cannot control the direction of cultural change in the US.
- I cannot control the future.
- I cannot control the global order.
- I cannot control the world my kids will inherit.

In contrast, here is *my list of things that I can affect, influence, or control.*

Things I Can Control

- I can control my response to all these things—whether it is a response of faith or not.
- I can control if I am modeling faith and confidence to my neighbors.
- I can control what my kids learn and value.
- I can control what I teach my kids and model for them in our home.
- I can control, or at least influence, many great Christian institutions that have not abandoned scriptural authority, and I can encourage these institutions to remain intellectually and morally faithful.
- I can control the moral direction of my own life.

- I can control what I will do with my day, my thoughts, and my future.
- I can influence who my kids will become as people.
- I can control whether I will pray for my neighbors and for Christ's kingdom to come.
- I can control whether I will live by faith or by fear.
- I can control how I will lead my family.
- I can control how I will use my finances.
- I can control how I will use my gifts of communication, research, and teaching.
- I can choose to believe that every obstacle is an opportunity when I am rightly related to Christ in faith.
- I can prepare to minister to my neighbors when future events frighten or unsettle them.
- I can work to fortify the Christian communities I belong to.
- I can choose to believe that God has placed me here, now, for a reason.

Using my lists as an example, you can personalize this exercise whenever you need to move from a spirit of fear to a spirit of faith regarding any issue in your life. The two lists (what you can control versus what you cannot control) provide you with a tool that shifts your focus toward the productive and actionable in every domain of life.

If you find yourself falling into despair about world events or morality, I encourage you to get out a pen and paper and start writing a list of the things you *can* control. The remainder of this book—the real spiritual heart of it—is such a list.

The nine manifestos discussed in the following chapters are a positive, actionable list of things you can control as you choose to trust in Christ and follow Him in these times. As God's Spirit prompts, allow these manifestos to move your feet into specific faith-filled actions. Allow the map of Scripture to move you from

dwelling on what you cannot control to *living out what you can control*.

That, in my experience, is when you will begin to taste the supernatural fearlessness and heaven-sent courage that biblical heroes like Moses, Deborah, Daniel, Peter, and Paul knew so well. Those godly heroes were people of understanding, people of faith, and people of action. Having gained understanding in parts 1 and 2 of this book, let us now commit to be people of faith and action. As we absorb the following nine manifestos, let's choose to build our lives around the Christ who is the Hope of Nations.

Chapter 11

THE NINE MANIFESTOS
WE CAN EMBRACE

H ow, then, do we be Christian now?

In response to the nine post-Christian trends, we determine that we will intentionally posture ourselves in these nine biblical and Christlike ways. We cannot control the course of nations or civilizations, but we can choose to adopt each of these nine postures and embody them in faith today and in the future.

TREND WE WILL FACE	OUR POSTURE
POST-TRUTH	**I: We will remain rooted to the Christian Scriptures.** In a world where truth is feelings-based, **we will remain rooted to the Christian Scriptures** and their life-giving direction.
POST-KNOWLEDGE	**II: We will train our young.** In a society of educated ignorance and blindness, **we will train our young** in the freedom, knowledge, and power of Christian truth.
POST-CHURCH	**III: We will be known for doing good.** In a world where Christians are labeled as bigots or backward, **we will be known for doing good**, serving the least of these and loving our neighbors.

TREND WE WILL FACE	OUR POSTURE
POST-HUMAN	**IV: We will dignify all people as image bearers of God.**
	In a world where people are treated as commodities or as opponents, **we will dignify all people as image bearers of God**.
POST-CHRISTIAN	**V: We will be ambassadors.**
	In a post-Christian world, **we will be ambassadors** to foreign tribes, behaving diplomatically toward neighbors who have been told the worst about Christianity.
POST-DECENCY	**VI: We will love our persecutors.**
	In a world where opponents are vilified and crucified, **we will love our persecutors**.
POST-PROSPERITY	**VII: We will remain calm.**
	In a world competing for limited resources, driven by fear, unrest, and scarcity, **we will remain calm**, confident that our Father provides our daily bread.
POST-LIBERTY	**VIII: We will be invincible.**
	In a world where we are discriminated against, prejudged, and even persecuted, **we will be invincible** as we serve God's purposes for which we are placed here, now.
POST-PEACE	**IX: We will be fearless.**
	In a world divided by violence, terrorism, and war, **we will be fearless**.

In the following chapters, we will unpack each of these nine manifestos. Each chapter concludes with a weblink to a free video message I have delivered on that specific manifesto. The links include study notes and resources. These are gifts to help you and your family, ministry, or community begin the conversation about how to be Christian now. I encourage you to make full use of these free resources and to share them freely with others, using the hashtag #HopeOfNations.

And do this, *understanding the present time*: The hour has already come for you to wake up from your slumber, *because our salvation is nearer now than when we first believed. The night is nearly over; the day is almost here.* So let us put aside the deeds of darkness and *put on the armor of light.* Let us behave decently, as in the daytime . . . *clothe yourselves with the Lord Jesus Christ.*

ROMANS 13:11–14, EMPHASIS ADDED

Chapter 12

ROOTED TO SCRIPTURE IN A POST-TRUTH ERA

> All your words are true;
> all your righteous laws are eternal.
>
> PSALM 119:160

> Let the word of Christ dwell in you richly, teaching and admonishing one another in all wisdom.
>
> COLOSSIANS 3:16 ESV

In a world where truth is feelings-based, **we will remain rooted to the Christian Scriptures** and their life-giving direction.

The foundational rupture in the tectonic plates of Western civilization is the breakage along the fault line of truth. The very concept of truth as we have known and inherited it is a Judeo-Christian concept.

Germany became a post-Christian nation after its seminaries and universities rejected the Scriptures as God's perfect, revealed

204

truth. The United States has become a post-Christian nation after its best seminaries and universities—founded as teaching centers for the Word of God—rejected Scripture as God's perfect, revealed truth.

As American culture drifts further and further from anything Christian, the pressure to abandon the authority of the Bible will increase proportionately, even within churches and Christian institutions that once elevated God's Word. Where the old view of Scripture as the Word of God was once tolerated, it will become increasingly offensive, out of style, scoffed at, and scorned.

We must remember that this pressure to abandon Scripture is not only social; it is also supernatural and satanic. Already within mainstream media and large metropolitan cities, it is tolerable to be a "Christian" in a relaxed sense. The dividing line is those Christians who take the Bible seriously. The "fundamentalists" are the dangerous ones—so the thinking goes.

As culture passes the Post-Truth tipping point, we will see some churches and ministries cave under pressure to make less of the Scriptures. Some recently popular teachers have already caved under this pressure. Every few months, we see another prominent Christian thinker, writer, blogger, artist, or leader become so zealous to be "relevant" that their cultural sensitivity first eclipses scriptural authority and then expels scriptural authority entirely.

In our ministries and on our boards, we must bear in mind that many incoming younger Christians who sincerely love Jesus will not have been taught the importance of the infallibility of Scripture or related doctrines that elevate the Word of God as the authority for all we do and believe. Many young Christians have placed their faith in Christ, but they are still thinking from a Post-Truth paradigm that has been deeply indoctrinated into them by the culture.

And so, aware that this will be the cultural drift, not only in the broader culture, but also within Christian institutions, **we must**

resolve to remain rooted in the Christian Scriptures as the authority for all we will do and believe. Scripture must be our authority on every issue in the culture, as well as our life-giving guide for every facet of our lifestyles.

We must resolve this on a personal basis. We must teach this in our discipleship and training. We must make this the anchor for our Christian families if we wish to stand strong amid the currents of a post-Christian and Post-Truth culture.

We must resolve to keep the authority of Scripture a top priority, written and elevated in our selection of board members, pastors, and faculty. No amount of charisma, gifting, or proven effectiveness can justify a Christian leader who degrades the Word of God by making it anything less than the sole standard for all we will do and believe.

As a millennial, I know that some of my peers will call me closed-minded or outdated for writing these things. I invite them to do so, and I will take it as a compliment. The historical record is clear. Beyond nations like Germany, we can look to the mainline American denominations that abandoned the doctrine of inerrancy during the early 1900s. Today those denominations are empty, dead shells of their former selves. In addition to their empty parking lots and vacant real estate, most openly praise the moral opposites of God's best designs.

Whether we feel it in our bones or not, we must always operate with this awareness: **any ministry or family that abandons the authority of Scripture (no matter how noble the argument for it) is one generation away from abandoning Christianity entirely.**

And so for these reasons, we do here declare with purpose and resolve that in a world where truth is feelings-based, we will remain rooted to the Christian Scriptures and their life-giving direction. No matter the cost, we will elevate the Christian Scriptures as the standard for all we do and believe. We do this because:

- We love our children, and we want them to experience the life, light, and truth found only in the pages of the Bible.
- We love our Savior, and we would not know His words or His heart apart from the Scriptures.
- We have seen that the words of God lead to life.
- Our enemy the devil functions primarily in the realm of ideas and deception, scheming from Eden until Revelation 20:10 to undermine the words of God, the promises of God, and the very Living Word of God.[1]

Lest we forget, it was Jesus who said, "The reason I was born and came into the world is to testify to the truth. Everyone on the side of truth listens to me."[2] If we lose the doctrine of Scripture, we not only abandon being on Jesus' side in the great struggle, but we also lose the ability to even know what His side looks like—since His words are recorded in Scripture.

God reminds us repeatedly that the violent conflicts of human history are waged in the battlefield of ideas: "For the weapons of our warfare are not of the flesh but have divine power to destroy strongholds. We destroy arguments and every lofty opinion raised against the knowledge of God, and take every thought captive to obey Christ."[3]

And again God warns us, "But mark this: There will be terrible times in the last days. People will be lovers of themselves, lovers of money, boastful, proud, abusive . . . not lovers of the good . . . conceited, lovers of pleasure rather than lovers of God—having a form of godliness but *denying its power*. Have nothing to do with such people."[4]

In the 1800s, the German universities were the pinnacle of science and intellect. As they rejected God and His Word, they retained a form of godliness, empty of spiritual power. History has proven—time and again—the deadly end for every people who reject the authority of God's Word.

And so we resolve:

In a world where truth is feelings-based, **we will remain rooted to the Christian Scriptures** and their life-giving direction.

I recently made a presentation about this for a millennial-aged audience. A free video of that message is available at the link below. I encourage you to watch and share the video.

Find the video message and more tools to inspire this posture at:

www.HopeOfNations.net/Scripture

Chapter 13

TRAINING OUR YOUNG IN A POST-KNOWLEDGE ERA

Be careful, or you will be enticed to turn away and worship
other gods and bow down to them . . . Fix these words of mine
in your hearts and minds; tie them as symbols on your hands
and bind them on your foreheads. Teach them to your children,
talking about them when you sit at home and when you walk
along the road, when you lie down and when you get up. Write
them on the doorframes of your houses and on your gates, so
that your days and the days of your children may be many in
the land the LORD swore to give your ancestors, as many as the
days that the heavens are above the earth.

DEUTERONOMY 11:16, 18–21

In a society of educated ignorance and blindness, **we will
train our young** in the freedom, knowledge, and power of
Christian truth.

The education of our Christian young people has never been
more important in the American church than it is today. Aware of

the aggressive currents of ignorance and anti-Christian sentiment sweeping across the nation, we must acknowledge that if we are not expressly intentional in how we educate our children, we will lose their minds. And if we lose their minds, we lose their souls, their lives, and their eternal life.

Those Christian families and churches that do not adopt an explicit plan to counter the ideology of the day may find that their children join the ranks of the two out of three American Christian young people presently abandoning the Christian faith between ages eighteen and twenty-nine.[1]

Exactly how we apply this will differ among various families and churches, but what is not optional is our need to overtly declare an objective like the following: "In a society of educated ignorance and blindness, we will train our young in the freedom, knowledge, and power of Christian truth."

Such training includes demonstrating how Christian truth produces freedom in our lives and how Christian communities produce good works that benefit society.[2] Most importantly, such training must be rooted in the Christian Scriptures. However flawed we may be at educating our children, "every word of God is flawless."[3] The Word of God as we plant it in the hearts and minds of our children and grandchildren will be for them a shelter, a guide, a protector, and a refuge long after we leave this earth and can no longer shelter, guide, or protect them.

We must resolve to financially bolster those churches, ministries, and institutions that commit to stand firm in training our young in a Christian worldview. We must prepare these institutions through endowments, through wise planning, and through the appointment of next-generation board members who remain committed to both grace and scriptural authority.

The day is likely coming when many of these Christian schools, churches, camps, colleges, and universities will lose any state or federal funding they presently receive through federal student loans or state grants. The day may even come when some are denied basic operating licenses, accreditation, or other necessities—on the grounds that the organization is "discriminatory" in its views on morality. The day will almost certainly come when some are stripped of tax-exempt status. We who have the means of talent or fortune must bolster and endow these institutions now—before the storm.

We have a closing window of world peace and of religious liberty. We possess more earthly wealth than any other church in world history. And the question is, "How will we who have so much earthly wealth choose to use that wealth?"

As Jesus taught in Scripture, "From everyone who has been given much, much will be demanded; and from the one who has been entrusted with much, much more will be asked."[4] How will we use what we have been given during our time on earth?

Through bequeathal and legacy gifts, will we invest this earthly wealth when we graduate to the next life? We need patrons to identify and provide for the prophetic clarion voices and institutions that will declare the truth of God during the coming decades, no matter how unpopular, difficult, or deadly that might become.

The Post-Truth worldview is so pervasive, so slippery, so all-encompassing in media, entertainment, and cultural assumptions, that we cannot assume our Christian children will emerge into adulthood with a Truth-Based, Christian view of reality. Quite the opposite. We must assume that, short of overwhelming intentional effort and concerted prayer, our children will absorb the spirit of this age and the Post-Truth ideology that accompanies it.

Christianity is at its best when it is an overtly countercultural movement. And this is now the position in which we find ourselves—if we're honest about the realities around us. We must begin thinking, behaving, and planning accordingly.

If we want our children and grandchildren to be among the one-third who retain the faith beyond age twenty-nine, we must equip them with an intellectual and spiritual foundation of such reinforced fortitude as to stand unweathered through a lifelong storm of oppression.

It is imperative that we bolster, endow, and invest in those Christian churches, ministries, and educational institutions that are committed to hold fast to the ancient Christian beliefs regarding morality and our unchanging religion. These institutions will likely face cultural pressures greater than we can imagine. It is imperative to bolster them in their appointments of board members who are orthodox, in their formation of faith-filled leadership, and in their financial coffers so they can be prepared to weather the coming storms. The same is true for our K-8 and K-12 Christian schools, universities, and discipleship-oriented churches and ministries.

It is imperative that national legal ministries be well funded, well organized, and well led so that Christian ministries and ministers can defend their constitutional rights in courts. It is imperative that we encourage our able-minded young people to pursue serving Christ as attorneys, civil servants, and lawmakers. When I think of my eight-year-old son and his sharp mind and conquering spirit, I pray that God will perhaps use him as one in his generation to lovingly argue for the truth and for the actual good of his neighbors.

The apostle Paul summarizes our mission well: "The things you have heard me say in the presence of many witnesses entrust to reliable people who will also be qualified to teach others."[5]

FINDING INSPIRATION IN OUR HERITAGE

Harvard, Princeton, Yale, and many others have fallen spiritually. We can lament that these once-great Christian universities have lost their way. But we have in our possession the same Scriptures on which they were founded. And we have the opportunity to found, fund, and further a new generation of Harvards in our day by founding, funding, and furthering high-quality Christian education within our families, churches, and institutions.

If the Reverend John Harvard and his Puritan Christian brothers could physically clear the forest to begin their Christian college, then we can surely roll up our sleeves and get our hands dirty to fortify, fund, and when necessary found a new generation of institutions that will be great because of their focus of study—the Word of God.

If local, state, and federal policies begin to penalize Christian institutions, many Christian schools and universities will struggle to stay afloat financially, particularly if federal student loans become unavailable for students at Christian colleges that hold the biblical position on morality. Within the collective assets of America's Christians today, we have more than enough funds to keep these institutions open and flourishing, but most of these funds sit in retirement accounts and in other assets held by individual American Christians—the wealthiest generation of Christians in world history.

The question for all of us who will "depart and be with Christ"[6] is this: "Do we want to leave behind our worldly wealth in a way that will enable Christian education and ministry at this key moment in American history, or do we not?"

I suggest that endowments, bequeathals, and legacy gifts are the make-or-break issue for Christian institutions as they face public backlash and legal entanglements in coming decades. Those institutions with leaders of personal integrity, high character, and biblical ideology will be more than sufficient to lead through these upcoming decades, as long as the lights are on and the bills are paid. Let us equip them with sufficient funds to keep the lights on and the attorneys paid.

Harvard University was the first college founded in the United States. It was founded by a group of Puritan pastors for the express purpose of training clergy and state leaders whose ideology would be Christian. Given the anti-Christian sentiment among Harvard graduates today, these facts of history can seem ironic. But much of Harvard's original purpose and roots remain etched into stone.

Engraved above one of the most heavily trafficked stone gates into Harvard Yard are these words from the King James Version of Isaiah 26:2: "Open ye the gates, that the righteous nation which keepeth the truth may enter in."

What prophetic words for these times! We are witnessing in our lifetime a nation founded by a majority of Christians—a nation with unprecedented wealth because of Christian values—now turning overtly away from that faith.

As we resolve in our churches and families to educate our children and grandchildren to be citizens of a higher kingdom, let us consider these verses from Isaiah 26:

> We have a strong city;
> > God makes salvation
> > its walls and ramparts.
> Open the gates
> > that the righteous nation may enter,
> > the nation that keeps faith.
> You will keep in perfect peace
> > those whose minds are steadfast,
> > because they trust in you.
> Trust in the LORD forever,
> > for the LORD, the LORD himself, is the Rock eternal.
> He humbles those who dwell on high,
> > he lays the lofty city low;
> he levels it to the ground
> > and casts it down to the dust . . .
>
> The path of the righteous is level;
> > you, the Upright One, make the way of the
> > righteous smooth.

Yes, LORD, walking in the ways of your laws,
    we wait for you;
your name and renown
    are the desire of our hearts.
My soul yearns for you in the night;
    in the morning my spirit longs for you.
When your judgments come upon the earth,
    the people of the world learn righteousness.
But when grace is shown to the wicked,
    they do not learn righteousness;
even in a land of uprightness they go on doing evil
    and do not regard the majesty of the LORD.
LORD, your hand is lifted high,
    but they do not see it . . .

LORD, you establish peace for us;
    all that we have accomplished you have done for us.
LORD our God, other lords besides you have ruled
  over us,
    but your name alone do we honor . . .
You have enlarged the nation, LORD;
    you have enlarged the nation.
You have gained glory for yourself;
    you have extended all the borders of the land . . .

Go, my people, enter your rooms
    and shut the doors behind you;
hide yourselves for a little while
    until his wrath has passed by.
See, the LORD is coming out of his dwelling
    to punish the people of the earth for their sins.
The earth will disclose the blood shed on it;
    the earth will conceal its slain no longer.

Because we love our children, our grandchildren, and the work of Christ among them, we do hereby resolve:

> In a society of educated ignorance and blindness, **we will train our young** in the freedom, knowledge, and power of Christian truth.

I recently delivered a twenty-minute TED-style message to inspire us toward this opportunity. You can find it and other free tools at:

www.HopeOfNations.net/OUR-YOUNG

For a list of trustworthy Christian ministries and institutions to consider leaving a bequeathal, legacy, or trust gift to, visit:

www.HopeOfNations.net/FOUNDATION

Chapter 14

KNOWN FOR DOING GOOD IN A POST-CHURCH ERA

Live such good lives among the pagans that, though they accuse
you of doing wrong, they may see your good deeds and glorify God.

1 PETER 2:12

> In a world where Christians are labeled as bigots or back-
> ward, **we will be known for doing good**, serving the least
> of these and loving our neighbors.

We must have the humility to acknowledge that in American
culture today, Christians are often prejudged as closed-minded,
opposed to progress, and careless toward the rights and feelings of
others. Whether we like it or not, we are often known for what we
oppose rather than for what we support. Sometimes this is the result
of spiritual deceit, but other times we have earned this reputation.

God clearly describes how we are to behave in a culture that
becomes hostile, antagonistic, and even violent toward us. As we
browse the record from Scripture, note the common theme (emphasized in italics) throughout these words from God to us:

"In the same way, let your light shine before others, *that they may see your good deeds and glorify your Father* in heaven."

MATTHEW 5:16

Do not be overcome by evil, but *overcome evil with good*.

ROMANS 12:21

And God is able to bless you abundantly, so that in all things at all times, having all that you need, *you will abound in every good work*.

2 CORINTHIANS 9:8

Let us not become weary *in doing good*, for at the proper time we will reap a harvest if we do not give up. Therefore, as we have opportunity, *let us do good to all people*.

GALATIANS 6:9–10

For it is by grace you have been saved . . . For we are God's handiwork, *created in Christ Jesus to do good works*, which God prepared in advance for us to do.

EPHESIANS 2:8, 10

Command them to *do good*, to *be rich in good deeds*, and to be generous and willing to share.

1 TIMOTHY 6:18

Remind the people to be subject to rulers and authorities, to be obedient, to be ready to *do whatever is good* . . . And I want you to stress these things, so that those who have trusted in God may be careful to *devote themselves to doing what is good* . . . Our people must learn to *devote themselves to doing what is good*.

TITUS 3:1, 8, 14

And let us consider how we may *spur one another on toward love and good deeds.*

HEBREWS 10:24

Live such good lives among the pagans that, though they accuse you of doing wrong, they may *see your good deeds and glorify God* . . . For it is God's will that *by doing good you should silence* the ignorant talk of foolish people.

1 PETER 2:12, 15

Do not repay evil with evil or insult with insult. On the contrary, *repay evil with blessing* . . . Who is going to harm you if you are *eager to do good?* . . . *Do this with gentleness and respect*, keeping a clear conscience, so that those who speak maliciously against *your good behavior in Christ* may be ashamed of their slander. For it is better, if it is God's will, to suffer *for doing good* than for doing evil.

1 PETER 3:9, 13, 15–17

Our good deeds should never be severed from the Good News, as happened in the American denominations that abandoned the authority of Scripture during the 1900s. Those denominations emphasized good deeds at the cost of the Good News. In retaliation, some sincere and biblical Christians have now moved the pendulum to an opposite extreme. They have sacrificed good deeds in order to re-elevate the Good News.

The reality is that these two work in tandem: good deeds demonstrate the power of the Good News. They are oxygen and carbon dioxide. They are water and sunlight. They are symbiotic in producing supernatural life. The two interrelate to prove the effectiveness of the gospel to change people and to emphasize the clarity of the gospel.

In a culture where Christians are thought of as villains, we resolve to be known for our good deeds. And we resolve to tie our good deeds to the Good News: that Christ came into this world to reconnect humanity back to its Creator.

Writing about this in my book *The Great Evangelical Recession*, I summarized the "good deeds" as follows:

> Such unfair accusations can roil our human defensiveness. It's instinctive to protect ourselves, stand up for our rights, and demand fair or reasonable treatment. But we didn't typically see Jesus do this when he was misunderstood.
>
> So how do we silence unfair accusations hurled against us? Let's start with Scripture. Living in a pagan and hypersexual culture may be new and frightening to us, but it was the norm for New Testament churches. Homosexuality and hypersexuality were nothing new to New Testament cultures or Christians. Time and again, God repeats His strategy: Live "good" lives *among* pagans . . .
>
> How do we silence unfair accusations hurled against us? Answer: by our good deeds (1 Peter 2:15). Unfortunately, we have hidden most of our good deeds under the bushel. I speak of the old children's song, "Hide it under a bushel? No!"
>
> Jesus said that our "good deeds" will praise our Father in heaven (Matthew 5:16), but not if we hide our good deeds under a bowl, or bushel. It has not been our intent, but so many of our good deeds take place within the bushels of our churches, or they take place on other continents. Many of the "pagans" living on our same streets in the United States don't ever see our good deeds. Instead, they see our absence, or worse, our defensive reactions to the changing United States culture. They see our antagonism against their tribe, against *them*. We give the impression of insecurity, self-protectiveness, and hate on the outside, even as we secretly conduct good deeds in the safety and shade of the bushel.

On accident, we have huddled under the bushel. We have hidden the light of the world from some of the tribes that most need that light—tribes in the United States of America. And within the United States, we have told some of these people groups that they are evil and should work harder to be more righteous in their own strength. We have claimed to love them from a distance, but we have failed to show them directly and personally that we are selfless, loving, and good. We vocally oppose them in mass media. We are absent in their personal lives, and then we claim with our words that we love them unconditionally.

Resurrecting God's mandate for good living among the pagans does not require a particular political position. But it requires that regardless of political conviction or doctrinal system, we re-elevate the goodness of our lives lived out *"among"* the pagans in our local communities—no matter what tribe those pagans belong to. That's what God repeatedly commands Christ's followers to do. That's His public relations plan.[1]

In summary then, we resolve to be known for our good deeds, even as we share the Good News. We resolve to carry out God's public relations plan. And so,

> In a world where Christians are labeled as bigots or backward, **we will be known for doing good**, serving the least of these and loving our neighbors.

Find a free video message and more articles explaining this posture at:

www.HopeOfNations.net/GOOD

Chapter 15

DIGNIFYING ALL PEOPLE IN A POST-HUMAN ERA

> Therefore, as God's chosen people, holy and dearly loved, clothe yourselves with compassion, kindness, humility, gentleness and patience. Bear with each other and forgive one another if any of you has a grievance against someone. Forgive as the Lord forgave you. And over all these virtues put on love, which binds them all together in perfect unity.
>
> Let the peace of Christ rule in your hearts, since as members of one body you were called to peace. And be thankful.
>
> COLOSSIANS 3:12–15

In a world where people are treated as commodities or as opponents, **we will dignify all people as image bearers of God**.

Christ was known for loving and accepting sinful individuals to the point of what seemed to some to be absurd. But in many instances, we Christians are now being outloved by our non-Christian neighbors. Many of our Post-Truth neighbors are more accepting, kind, dignifying, and valuing of all people than we Christians are.

Rather than merely separating the sin from the sinner, we must also inject back into our view of humanity a biblical dignity and respect for all people as made in the image of God—no matter how broken or enslaved those people are by the corruption in this world.

In a world where humans are measured by their output or practical value, where automated machines are preferred to human workers, where opponents are vilified, we resolve to dignify all people—no matter their race, self-identification, hostility toward us, or religious creed.

We will treat all people as inherently valuable—made in the image of God and eternally valuable to Him. All people are eternally valuable to us. We will treat people with dignity and respect. We will be kind. We will be thoughtful. Empowered by the Holy Spirit, we will be patient, gentle, forgiving, slow to anger, and abounding in love and faithfulness.

Because of what God tells us about humanity—that all people are image bearers of God—we will dignify and value all people, regardless of their race, creed, religion, abilities, disabilities, gender, self-identifying label, overt sin, covert sin, or any other factor. **In short, we will love in the manner Jesus described as fulfilling "all the Law and the Prophets."**[1]

Unintentionally, the Post-Truth world will drift toward valuing people by materialistic measures. The value of a human will be their output, their contribution, their existence in a protected class, or their conformity to the Post-Truth system. Conversely, those who do not provide material value and particularly those who will not take their stand on the Post-Truth moral platform will be discarded or disregarded.

In a world where people are treated as problems, we will refuse to see any human being from a merely materialist ideology. We will see people as they are—eternal souls whom God loved so extravagantly as to inject Himself into humanity and willingly be tortured and killed in His offer to reach and redeem them.

GRACE AND TRUTH

It is possible to understand the truth, to know the truth, and yet to not be loving. The apostle Paul warns that such a position—possessing the truth while lacking love—is never a truly Christian position. Indeed, if we gain great knowledge in understanding the times and in understanding ideologies, but if we then fail to hold that knowledge in love, we will "gain nothing," according to 1 Corinthians 13:3.

If we aim to see the world as Christ sees it, then we will not see any human as our true enemy. We will see Satan, the great adversary, as our enemy. And we will see the humans who do Satan's work as they actually are—slaves of demonic forces, conscripted to perform the adversary's works of destruction. Christ came to set captives free, and as we follow Him, we will set captives free too.

If our goal is truly to live like Christ in these changing times—and that *is* our goal—then we do well to consider that Christ came into the madness of this world as the One "full of grace and truth."[2]

In the divine order, grace is the prerequisite to truth. The prerequisite to understanding our broken age (and I mean *spiritual understanding*) is compassion for those who are enslaved in the chains of sin, those who are blinded by the ignorance of the spirit of this age, those who will be caught beneath the collapsing structures, those who will be trapped in the grinding gears of war and injustice. We must invite the Spirit of God to fill us with His fruit of love so that we will have God's heart of compassion toward those who may call us their enemies.

In the long march of Christian history, the narrow path of Christlikeness is littered on both sides with Christians and churches who have embraced truth while ignoring grace, or, on the other side, by Christians who have veered off the path to embrace grace while ignoring truth. Christ came into this world "full of grace and truth." And our journey to be Christian now will be no different. When we supernaturally love all people in a balance of grace and truth that only God can provide, we prove that we do indeed have the Hope of Nations.

As our minds grasp these intellectual truths about our times, we must also pray for the Holy Spirit's fruit of love, joy, peace, patience, kindness, goodness, faithfulness, gentleness, and self-control to occupy our hearts.[3]

These supernatural characteristics become all the more important in times of controversy and conflict. We all know some Christian Truth-Based thinkers who defend the truth, but who do so without any of the fruit (love, joy, peace, etc.) evident in a Spirit-filled Christian. When we face fearful realities, we need the Spirit of God living inside us to anchor us simultaneously in both God's truth and His grace. Even in the face of unthinkable evil. *Especially* in the face of unthinkable evil.

May God divinely fill us with His love for those who unwittingly and ignorantly invite their own demise. In our human nature, we could be blunt, frustrated, and even angry toward our neighbors' willful ignorance and opposition of the truth. We will, of course, be courageous and unflinching in defending Christ's kingdom and the Christian truth. But if we aim to follow Christ, we must also invite His Spirit to fill us with compassion for the very people who malign us, falsely accuse us, and even persecute us.

As we work for the freedom and protection of our neighbors, we will at times be attacked by the very people whose well-being we are striving to protect. It's an odd position to be in. And it is precisely the position from which Jesus lived out His days on earth. Jesus came to set people free. And yet those very people turned on Jesus and attacked Him. They were blinded by ignorance. They were blinded by self-righteousness. They were blinded by hatred and sin. In response, Jesus prayed, "Father, forgive them, for they do not know what they are doing."[4]

And so the mature Christian posture in this Post-Truth, anti-Christian era will be not only a position full of the truth, but also a posture full of grace. Grace is unmerited, undeserved forgiveness. Grace is favor directed toward our accusers and adversaries when they do not deserve it.

How this applies will vary from situation to situation, but let us determine as a way of life that we will strive toward this divine ideal to be "full of grace and truth." Let us determine that we will never hold truth at the expense of grace, for in so doing, we are contradicting the central truths of Christ.

Let us seek the heart of Christ in grace just as eagerly as we seek the mind of God in truth regarding these times.

We resolve:

In a world where people are treated as commodities or as opponents, **we will dignify all people as image bearers of God**.

Want more insight on this posture? Find a free video message, audio recordings, and more about this posture at:

www.HopeOfNations.net/DIGNIFY

Chapter 16

AMBASSADORS IN A POST-CHRISTIAN ERA

All this is from God, who reconciled us to himself through Christ and gave us the ministry of reconciliation . . . *And he has committed to us the message of reconciliation. We are therefore Christ's ambassadors, as though God were making his appeal through us.*

2 CORINTHIANS 5:18–20, EMPHASIS ADDED

In a post-Christian world, **we will be ambassadors** to foreign tribes, behaving diplomatically toward neighbors who have been told the worst about Christianity.

We can either constantly bemoan the reality that our pagan, non-Christian neighbors are behaving like pagan non-Christians, or we can acknowledge that we are now ambassadors in an ideologically foreign land, in a post-Christian society.

In some ways, our task in America and Europe today is more difficult than the task of a missionary to a people who has never heard of Christianity. We are now missionaries to a culture that has been told

227

lies and half-truths about Christianity—to a land where a growing number of people believe that Christians are historically oppressors, slave masters, and inhumane conquerors. It is simultaneously a land that inherits such wealth and comfort that there seems to be little need for help from any "God."

The once-Christianized United States of America is no longer prevailingly Christian in its ideology, values, culture, or aspirations. As Scripture states, those who do not know Christ are indeed blind in their thinking and trapped in a bondage of spiritual oppression. Paul puts it bluntly: "Their foolish hearts were darkened."[1]

As such, we are interacting daily with pagans who are spiritually as blind and lost as the unreached people groups in the jungles of Papua New Guinea or in remote sub-Saharan Africa. The differences spiritually are that our mission field enjoys the highest standard of living in history and is also prejudiced against Christianity before we ever meet them or open our mouths.

There was once an "American" way of thinking. There was a center for the majority of Americans—a somewhat monolithic set of Christian values that most Americans shared. Back in that era, we Christians could expect that our neighbors would know basic truths about Jesus, the Bible, and Christian morality. Our neighbors respected the concepts of church, pastors, and the Bible. Connected to these were aspirational morals such as faithfulness in marriage, honesty, and charity.

Many of us—and many of our churches—still operate from the assumption that our neighbors share these and related "American" values. But this is no longer the case. We are now surrounded by foreign thought tribes in the United States. Each tribe has a competing ideology—atheism, Islam, Post-Truth pluralism, and so forth. Even in the Midwest and the South, where some of the old Christian values remain intact, these shared values are consistently melting away as a result of the Post-Truth shift.

If we assume that our American neighbors share our values,

assumptions, and language, we will become frustrated with their thinking, their conclusions, and their behavior. Very simply, our neighbors are viewing reality through the lenses of their post-Christian and Post-Truth ideologies.

AMBASSADORS

When the world around us changes, it is only natural to respond with fear and anxiety. When our Christian rights are challenged, it is natural to respond with fear. And when we see society embracing policies that will harm our children and grandchildren, it is natural to respond with emotions of concern and self-protection.

But we must become more intentional, more spiritual, and more biblical in our posture toward our neighbors. Do we believe that almighty God placed us here and now for a purpose? If we believe the Word of God, we will choose to believe that we are "foreigners and exiles" here on earth.[2] The United States is an important and noble citizenship. However, the United States is not our highest citizenship. As Scripture states, "But our citizenship is in heaven. And we eagerly await a Savior from there, the Lord Jesus Christ."[3]

Why has God left us on planet Earth after we've trusted in Christ? Why were we not immediately teleported to heaven at the moment of salvation? The answer is that God has work on earth for us to do.[4] We continue the work that God the Father gave to Jesus and that Jesus has now given to His "body," the church. In the remaining fifty years, fifteen years, or five years that each of us has on earth, God has called us to be diplomats and ambassadors from heaven.

Where we cannot do this directly, we can invest into ministries that are. Our aim on earth is not to store up as much disposable wealth as possible and be as comfortable and secure as possible; our aim is to be successful diplomats from heaven to earth.

No passage better summarizes this than 2 Corinthians 5:18–20 (emphasis added).

God . . . reconciled us to himself through Christ and gave us the
ministry of reconciliation . . . *And he has committed to us the
message of reconciliation. We are therefore Christ's ambassadors,
as though God were making his appeal through us.*

The most significant posture change we Christians can make in
the Post-Truth era is this: **We are not here to attack or fight our
neighbors when they disagree with us; we are here to be diplomats
and ambassadors to them.** Diplomats are not surprised when cultural
differences cause confusion or even suspicion from the people they
hope to reach. Diplomats take the time to understand the values,
assumptions, and culture of the people group to which they are called.

Where our human response would be anger or defensiveness, God
has a better way. He does not call us to be aggressive in our posture toward
those lost in spiritual darkness. Instead, He calls us to be ambassadors
to them. This does not mean we lack courage or conviction (we will
see plenty of courage in the other manifestos), but it does mean we
exhibit tact, patience, kindness, and a winsome, diplomatic manner in
dealing with non-Christians. It means we have compassion for their
brokenness. We have patience for their spiritual blindness. It means we
become intentionally diplomatic rather than reactionary and defensive.

In other words, we will adjust our expectations. We will
acknowledge that we are now cross-cultural ministers within the
United States. Whether we have a relative who identifies as LGBTQ,
a neighbor who identifies as Muslim, or a coworker who identifies
as "open to everything" (that is, a Post-Truth thinker), in all of these
cases we are doing ministry that must cross over the boundaries and
barriers of conflicting cultures, of contradicting ideologies.

GOOD DEEDS AND GOOD NEWS

In some settings, the American church is very effective at cross-
cultural ministry. We've been sending missionaries to foreign tribes

and cultures since before the American Revolution. Countless hospitals, orphanages, schools, and universities exist in Africa, India, and around the world today because of American Christian missionaries who understood cross-cultural ministry to foreign tribes. Indeed, many American missionaries have become experts at crossing the boundaries of culture in order to share the Good News of Christ.

The challenge is to apply the steps of successful cross-cultural ministry right here at home in the United States. Here, in summary, is how the best missionaries bridge cultural barriers to be ambassadors for Christ. We can see ourselves as ambassadors in the United States, sent from heaven to the people God loves here.

Step 1: Go to the Foreign Tribe

In the same way that Jesus left the comfort of heaven and came down into the mess of humanity, the best missionaries go into uncomfortable regions to meet the lost where they are. When our neighbors, relatives, or coworkers do not share our Christian values or ideals, we can make it a point to reach out to them by entering their world with the following steps in mind. Whether our neighbor is a Muslim, an atheist, or a former Christian, God loves that neighbor.

In these divided times, we may fear the potential conflicts that can result when we engage a person from a foreign tribe. But the Word of God reminds us that "perfect love drives out fear."[5] Where our human nature might paralyze us in fear of conflict, our call to be God's diplomats compels us to reach out to these neighbors and begin a relationship. In our present context, with so many preconceived evils associated with Christianity, the adage about wildlife applies to us: "They are probably more afraid of you than you are of them."

Step 2: Demonstrate God's Love through Actions

The best missionaries prove God's love through actions long before they begin talking about sin, the cross, Jesus, or even creation. It's normal for foreign tribes to be suspicious of others, and our non-Christian neighbors will often be suspicious when we begin reaching out to build relationships. In the Post-Truth context, suspicions about Christianity run especially deep.

In undeveloped areas, successful cross-cultural ministers begin by demonstrating God's love through actions—for example, by building a medical clinic, digging a well, or giving the gift of modern tools to the tribe. The point is that long before we begin talking about Jesus and God, we show undeniable love through actions. We should not move to step 3 until we suspect we've gone overboard on step 2 ("Demonstrate God's Love through Actions"). As a good rule of thumb, when we think we have done step 2 too much, we may be one-third of the way toward completing it.

What does this look like with our neighbors, relatives, or coworkers? It could begin by having them over for dinner and listening to their story, their past, their passions. It could look like mowing their lawn, raking their leaves, or snowblowing their driveway. It could look like caring, helping, bringing them coffee or their favorite dessert—all without saying anything about God or Jesus at that point.

In our settings, we must first show God's love through good deeds to soften the soil so that it may receive the seed of the Good News of Christ. This is best done when we listen to the needs and values of the people we are called to reach. For a tribe that needs medicine, medicine becomes the greatest opportunity. As you listen to the actual hurts, wounds, and needs of the people God has placed in your life, you can pray for wisdom and resources to meet those needs so that you can demonstrate God's unconditional love for them.

Step 3: Build Relationship

This step results from step 2, but it's more. It's intentionally taking an interest in others. It's appreciating their culture, their values, their food, their language, their children. It's asking questions like:

- What do you love?
- What do you fear?
- What motivates you?
- What are your favorite things about your favorite holidays?
- What keeps you awake at night?
- What delights you?
- What values, hobbies, or interests do you have in common with me or with someone you love?

In each of these, we can seek common good and look for the ways in which this person's culture overlaps with God's values.

Step 4: Learn the Language

While a successful cross-cultural minister builds relationship, she or he is also learning the language. In some contexts today, this is a literal "other language." Often in America today, this step applies to cultural assumptions about what "homosexuality" is, what a "Christian" is, who "Jesus" is, and so forth. You cannot learn a language without listening, and at this step, you are listening to discover what the person believes about morality and Christianity. Your aim is to learn what their words mean to them.

If we really listen, we may be surprised to hear that the person thinks "Christian equals Republican," or that they've been told that God hates homosexuals, or that they were personally abused by someone who claimed to be a Christian. They may have been taught one of the common lies of the incoming generations—for example, that all Confederate slave owners were Christians or that all Union activists and soldiers were not Christians. You won't know what they've been taught and what they believe until you ask and then commit to listen.

In this step, we must control the urge to correct or instruct. Our goal is not to speak, but to hear. As James wrote, "Everyone should be quick to listen, slow to speak and slow to become angry."[6] We want to fully understand how this person sees the world and what certain key words such as *God*, *Jesus*, and *the Bible* mean to them, so that we can eventually speak their language when we share the Good News.

Step 5: Present the Gospel, or Good News

As the relationship develops, having been proven through undeniable good deeds and further demonstrated through genuine relationship, we pray for the moment when we can turn a conversation toward Christ.

Because we have been listening to the person's actual needs, hurts, values, and assumptions, we will have a better inroad than this generic example. And because we have learned what key words mean to them, we will be prepared to connect God's truth to their way of thinking. As the Spirit leads, it may begin along the lines of saying something like this:

> Can I tell you something crazy? I believe there's a Designer who created all of us. I believe He designed me and you, and I believe He sent me into your life to tell you that He loves you and wants to be in relationship with you. If there were a way for you to be brought into a fulfilling personal relationship with the One who made you, would you want to know it?

If curiosity is not expressed, then a sensitive cross-cultural ambassador doesn't push it. We wait and pray for God to soften the soil and prepare the heart. When curiosity is expressed, we then share the Good News. Exactly how this is done and with exactly which Scriptures will again depend on the unique relationship and the person's real needs. Often there is a parallel in the physical needs that we were able to meet during steps 1–4. Ultimately, we want to share the basics of the Good News, including the following:

- that humanity was designed to be in perfect relationship with God

- that an enemy invaded and separated humanity from God, resulting in evil, pain, and death
- that God, looking on humanity's plight, chose to enter our world and take the penalty for all of our mistakes in the person of Jesus Christ
- that Jesus died on the cross, rose from the grave, and now offers forgiveness and eternal life to all who trust in Him
- that I have tasted this personally and have found it to be true, life-giving, and stabilizing

All of this is building to an eventual invitation from heaven, delivered by us as ambassadors: that God invites all people everywhere to turn from the emptiness of evil and to receive the fullness of Christ by professing their need for Christ's forgiveness and salvation.

Step 6: Disciple Those Who Believe

We begin to spiritually nurture those who trust in Christ as newborns. We teach them the basics of baptism, the value of Scripture reading, and the importance of living in a Christian family that will help them grow. As they grow, they can experience freedom from sin and fullness of life in Christ.

Step 7: Expect Those Who Don't Believe to Continue Behaving as Slaves to Sin

When our neighbors or loved ones choose to reject the Good News, we do not expect them to practice Christian morality. We must remind ourselves that God did not send us into this world to carry out "behavior modification." He does not command us to be the morality police for our non-Christian neighbors.

Instead, He calls us to show and share the Good News. The only way any person ever says no to sin is by trusting in Jesus Christ and being set free from the bondage of sin. Our call is not to morally reform people who do not trust in Christ; our call is to get them to the foot of the cross. Those who trust in Christ will be capable of supernatural moral reform because their spiritual dynamics have changed.

However, those who reject Christ will only be frustrated if we constantly command or expect them to behave as if they are not slaves to sin.

Step 8: Define Success Biblically

Diplomats are not ultimately responsible for how the foreign nation responds to their message. They cannot control the will of other people. A diplomat's job is to deliver the message as smoothly as possible. In the same way, we are not responsible for how our neighbors respond to the Good News of Christ. Just as a diplomat is responsible to clearly communicate the wishes of the ruler he or she represents, so we are responsible to clearly communicate heaven's message of reconciliation to earth.

God does not hold you responsible to save anyone's soul; He simply holds you responsible to share the Good News with the souls He places near you. In this way, we define if we are spiritually successful, not based on how people respond, but based on how clearly and lovingly we shared the Good News of salvation in Christ.

Let us not forget that when Jesus perfectly communicated God's kingdom, He was betrayed, falsely accused, publicly stripped, beaten, and then murdered. All this was a response to His message that the kingdom of God was at hand. Did that response from the people make Jesus a failure? Not at all. Jesus' definition of success was to complete the work the Father had assigned Him to do.

Our work today is to be ambassadors from heaven to the various ideological tribes around us in the United States today. If we show and tell the Good News of Christ consistently and clearly, then we are spiritually successful, no matter how anyone responds.

As I've traveled around the country, interacting with Christians of various traditions and with nonbelievers in Silicon Valley and in the news media, I have found that this single paradigm shift—seeing ourselves as ambassadors—alleviates most of the tension surrounding questions like, "How do I love my neighbors without condoning their behavior?"

Missionaries who visit foreign tribes rarely worry about whether the tribe will perceive the missionary as "condoning" their cannibalism or polygamy. The missionary digs a well for the cannibals, not worrying if that will be perceived as approving of cannibalism.

The old Christian question ("Will people perceive my love as condoning their sin?") is a question from a Christianized culture in which people had a concept of sin and condoning it and in which people sought Christian approval. The world around us has moved beyond all of that. It doesn't even use these words or this paradigm, nor does it seek our approval as Christians.

For scriptural context, see 1 Corinthians 5:9–11, where Paul writes about separating from a self-professed Christian who is living in open, immoral, ongoing sin. But of *non-Christians* we are taught:

> I wrote to you in my letter not to associate with sexually immoral people—not at all meaning the people of this world who are immoral, or the greedy and swindlers, or idolaters. In that case you would have to leave this world. But now I am writing to you that you must not associate with anyone who claims to be a brother or sister but is sexually immoral or greedy, an idolater or slanderer, a drunkard or swindler.

In other words, God never sees it as a bad thing for Christians to mingle with sinners who have not professed Christ. How else can we get to know them, love them, and share the Good News of Christ with them?

Perhaps this is why Jesus did not seem preoccupied with the thought that his presence might be condoning sin as he ate and associated with tax collectors and prostitutes. Jesus did, however, seem preoccupied with demonstrating God's unconditional love. He was preoccupied with forcing a decision to either accept or reject the Good News of the kingdom.

To fulfill God's purpose for us on earth, we must become less preoccupied with whether people think we are "condoning" their sin and become more preoccupied with whether people sense a warm, unconditional love—a spiritual love proven through our actions and our truthful words. If we can achieve this, we will be able to effectively share the Good News in a Post-Truth culture.

Let us choose to take up our calling as God's divine ambassadors, placed here on earth as diplomats. We have been sent from heaven for eternal purposes and equipped with infinite resources to accomplish our calling.

For this, we resolve:

In a post-Christian world, **we will be ambassadors** to foreign tribes, behaving diplomatically toward neighbors who have been told the worst about Christianity.

Note: I believe that this manifesto is the single most important paradigm shift we can adopt to become more biblical in these changing times. I have taught on this topic at length, and I invite you to watch the free video message with much more content at the link below.

Find the video message and more tools to inspire this posture at:

www.HopeOfNations.net/Ambassadors

Chapter 17

LOVING OUR PERSECUTORS IN A POST-DECENCY ERA

The Word became flesh and made his dwelling among us. We have seen his glory, the glory of the one and only Son, who came from the Father, full of grace and truth.

JOHN 1:14

> In a world where opponents are vilified and crucified, **we will love our persecutors**.

We Truth-Based thinkers must acknowledge a blind spot within our own behavior. I include myself when I write that *our actions* often contradict *our own "truth"* as it relates to loving our neighbors. Among the chief truths of Scripture, Jesus commanded, "I tell you, love your enemies and pray for those who persecute you."[1]

We Truth-Based thinkers sometimes value being right (being correct) over being loving. Being right is important. It is a matter of life or death in spiritual issues. Nonetheless, Jesus and the New Testament apostles clarify that it is never Jesus' plan for us to be right at the cost of being loving.

I'll expand on this in a moment. But before I do, I must point out one of the oddities of the Post-Truth conflict with Truth-Based Christians: we Christians are often outloved by our pagan neighbors.

Christianity is, of course, the message that "God so loved the world that he gave his one and only Son, that whoever believes in him shall not perish but have eternal life."[2] When we are at our best, we Christians are the most genuinely loving people group in all of humanity. However, we must acknowledge that many Christians today are not at their best. Fearful of the rapidly changing times, many sincere Christians operate from motives of fear, anxiety, and self-protection rather than from faith in Jesus' radical truth claims.

In my experience, Christians can be the best of people, and some self-described "Christians" can also be the worst of people when it comes to treating others with basic human dignity and kindness.

Here is where our faith gets revealed as either genuine or superficial. Do we actually love our enemies and pray for those who spitefully use us? Heaven's command on this matter is just as clear as the commands to "not get drunk on wine" and to "not covet."[3] And yet many of us who claim to be committed to Christ's truth seem to think His command to "love your enemies" is optional.

Now, loving our enemies does not mean we never stand up for our rights, nor does it mean we never protect ourselves from physical or legal harm. Paul clearly claimed his legal rights as a Roman citizen when he was being persecuted.[4] And so we have a precedent to claim our legal and constitutional rights as citizens of the United States. And in the face of physical violence, many Christians in good conscience will love the potential victims of violence enough to neutralize an attacker.

And yet, protecting ourselves—physically and legally—should never come at the expense of loving our enemies in daily peacetime interactions. We love them in the sense that we truly long for their best. We long for them to be reconciled to God. And as we pray for them, we request God's heart toward them. God answers such prayers. He can develop within us a genuine compassion and concern for the emptiness of our attackers' lives and eternities.

Here, I believe, is one factor in the exodus of young Christians from Christianity. The rate of two out of three young people quitting Christianity between the ages of eighteen and twenty-nine is documented by multiple researchers and further explored in my book *The Great Evangelical Recession.*

Here it is: Many Post-Truth pagans are more loving in real life than many sincere Christians. Many atheistic and agnostic pagans are kinder, more decent people than some of the most grounded Christian Truth-Based thinkers.

Here's an example. When I worked as a journalist for a liberal-progressive newspaper, the two editors I reported to (as well as the rest of the staff) were not Christians. They cussed others out for making mistakes, not hesitating to drop tirades of f-bombs and other profanities. This was a work environment where writers kept vodka bottles on their desks. And yet those editors treated me with a sense of human dignity, respect, and honesty that is sometimes absent when I deal with conservative Christians who disagree about various interpretations of "the truth."

Some Christians become so obsessed with being correct that they fail to treat their opponents (or even their allies) as dignified bearers of God's image.

I'm not suggesting that all of us conservative Christians are completely failing at loving our neighbors, but I am saying that, in my experience, many conservative Christians I've interacted with do not love their neighbor in basic ways—and again, I include myself in this condemnation.

For all the errors and dangers of Post-Truth thinking, it is an ideology that strives to accept everybody. As a result, many young Christians have found more unconditional love and acceptance in the gay community than in the Christian church. I speak here even of "straight" individuals. My brothers and sisters, this ought not to be. We should not be outloved. As we abide in Christ, we should exhibit supernatural fruit in our lives—the fruit of "love, joy, peace, patience, kindness, goodness, faithfulness, gentleness, self-control."[5]

I think many of our young American Christians are experiencing what I experienced with my loving and accepting newspaper editors. As they move through high school, college, and into employment, some young Christians are experiencing more dignity and acceptance from non-Christians than from committed Christians.

Because Post-Truth thinkers do not judge anyone, they can be incredibly accepting and kind. The virtue of their love for other humans should be applauded. After all, Post-Truth thinkers are not villains or enemies. They themselves are people whom God loves dearly, and the kindness of their acceptance may actually be a cultural Christian vestige, as well as the tattered remains of the likeness of God's nature within them.

Because Post-Truth thinkers do not connect consequences of ideology with choices, they can be absurdly loving, even toward people whose ideology is against them. For example, it wouldn't surprise me to find in the San Francisco Bay area, where I recently lived, a homosexual protesting for the rights of a fundamentalist Muslim from Pakistan to live in his neighborhood. The protestor does not realize this fundamentalist Muslim holds a literalist interpretation of the Quran—that homosexuals should be stoned to death for their immorality—nor does the Post-Truth protestor care. The Post-Truth thinker has simply been indoctrinated to accept all people, no matter what.

And there is a bit of irony here, because when Christianity is at its best and most radical raw expression, it is Christians who are the most accepting of the people who would persecute and punish us.

My point is that Christians should be the best people in the world at loving others, including our enemies. We are not uncommitted to the truth if we love our enemies. Nor are we condoning sin if we love our enemies.

Even more, being committed to the truth *demands* that we love our enemies. For Jesus gave the command, "Love your enemies and pray for those who persecute you."[6] And so we must answer this question: "Am I actually committed to the whole truth of God's Word, or only to those portions that affirm my outlook on life?"

Just as Post-Truth thinkers function with self-contradictions, we Truth-Based thinkers can unintentionally function with self-contradictions as well. If we believe Jesus' words to be the great truth that leads humanity to life and freedom, then we must obey the truth that Christ taught as the greatest commandment: "'Love the Lord your God with all your heart . . .' and, 'Love your neighbor as yourself.'"[7]

Christian love does not ignore the consequences of people's ideologies or choices. Christian love does not require sitting in silence if humans are being harmed or are harming others—quite the opposite, in fact. But in our knowledge of the deadly consequences that will follow Post-Truth choices, we should never respond without a motive of love.

How would Jesus respond? He would respond with compassion toward those who are choosing ways of blindness and sin that will lead to their death and destruction. Do you remember when Jesus wept physically for Jerusalem as He foresaw where that group's rebellion toward God would take them?

> As he approached Jerusalem and saw the city, he wept over it and said, "If you, even you, had only known on this day what would bring you peace—but now it is hidden from your eyes. The days will come upon you when your enemies will build an embankment against you and encircle you and hem you in on every side."
>
> LUKE 19:41–43

How, then, do we be Christian now?

We respond with compassion toward those who are choosing ways of blindness and sin that will lead to death and destruction. Knowing the truth—and the true end of all who die apart from Christ—should propel us to love in extravagant and self-sacrificing ways. The apostle Paul spoke of sacrificing his earthly rights and comforts if it would gain eternal life and salvation for his persecutors who were separated from God.[8] When was the last time we felt this way toward our oppressors or neighbors?

In short, we who follow Christ should be the very best at loving our neighbors and our enemies. And if we're honest, as it stands today, many of our nonbelieving Post-Truth neighbors are better at loving their neighbors than we are. I don't think—when viewed through the lens of Jesus' teachings and emphasis—that this is acceptable. We Christians should be outdoing everyone with our love for others (by God's definition of love, of course).

We should be the ones who are absurd in our pattern of respecting, dignifying, and honoring the people who disagree with us. We do so, not because we agree with them or because their views or actions are innocent, but because they are made in the image of God. And if God loved them enough to die on the cross for them, then certainly we can love them more than our pagan Post-Truth neighbors do.

On this point and many others like it, we Truth-Based Christians must do an honest self-examination to ensure that our own Truth-Based ideology is in fact the ideology of Jesus and not simply a conservative political ideology that embraces some of Jesus' teachings while ignoring others.

Keep in mind that there are conservative Truth-Based thinkers in America who are Americans first and Christians second. They are more committed to a scaffold of conservative American values than to the teachings of Christ. As with any ideology that is placed before Christ, that position is idolatry.

We must be sure to cast down any idol that would come before

Christ in our own lives, even if that idol is good conservative policies held in a non-Christlike manner. Where our Christian Truth-Based thinking overlaps with some conservative principles, we must commit to be followers of Christ first and citizens of the United States secondly and subordinately. Never the other way around. Scripture is clear that we have our highest citizenship in Christ's kingdom.

If we are truly Christian in our Truth-Based thinking, then we will embrace and embody clear scriptural mandates, such as these from Paul's letter to the Romans:

> Bless those who persecute you; bless and do not curse. Rejoice with those who rejoice; mourn with those who mourn. Live in harmony with one another. Do not be proud, but be willing to associate with people of low position. Do not be conceited.
>
> *Do not repay anyone evil for evil. Be careful to do what is right in the eyes of everyone. If it is possible, as far as it depends on you, live at peace with everyone.* Do not take revenge, my dear friends, but leave room for God's wrath, for it is written: "It is mine to avenge; I will repay," says the Lord. On the contrary:
>
> > "If your enemy is hungry, feed him;
> > if he is thirsty, give him something to drink.
> > In doing this, you will heap burning coals on his head."
>
> *Do not be overcome by evil, but overcome evil with good.*
> ROMANS 12:14–21, EMPHASIS ADDED

Good Christians will disagree about how exactly to demonstrate the love of Christ to immigrants, refugees, Muslims, and the LGBTQ community and in many different situations. And that is okay. From the beginning Christians have disagreed about the application of good intentions in pagan cultures. When we disagree with other Christians about how to show Christ's love, we can look to Romans 14. This passage clearly predicts that in every era, good Christians will disagree about the finer applications of Christian principle to local culture. The great point of Romans 14—for those who ate meat offered to idols and for all of us today—is that we commit to never divide the body of Christ over our personal opinions on a cultural or subordinate issue.

Different Christians will be called to reveal Christ in different ways to our LGBTQ neighbors, to our Muslim neighbors, and to other thought tribes. What we must have in common, if we are truly a Truth-Based people, is that we love all people as God the Father does—not because of their merits or agreement around various issues and not because of their likeability, but because they are made in the image of God. This doesn't mean we are ignorant of the consequences of ideology or actions, but it does mean we live out the truth standard God has clearly mandated in Scriptures.

How do we actually do this? What does it look like in real life?

To answer these questions, I recommend reading or listening to an audio edition of Corrie ten Boom's *The Hiding Place*.[9] When confronted with the evils of Nazi fascism during World War II, ten Boom first experienced the normal human emotions of hatred for her Nazi persecutors. But as she bathed her emotions in prayer and Scripture, God placed in her heart a compassion for her Nazi persecutors that was truly supernatural.

And it can happen today, just as it did some seventy years ago for Corrie ten Boom. Corrie's compassion for Nazi persecutors did not arise from her human disposition or from her political beliefs. It arose as she read Scripture and prayed for God's perspective toward the Nazi guards who had brutalized her and killed her family.

Corrie never approved of the Nazi ideology and never ignored the reality that it led to death and destruction. She spoke openly against that ideology. She was as shrewd as a snake[10] in working against the satanic persecution of the Jews. She defied authority.

She broke laws. She told outright lies to those who would have killed the Jews she was hiding in her home.

And yet Corrie ten Boom was able to see even the vilest of Nazi persecutors as broken image bearers of God. She saw them as they were—enslaved souls in desperate need of salvation and restoration. She was able to hold this supernatural, superhuman view because the Word of God dwelled in her richly and the Spirit of God was aflame within her.

Believing that the same Spirit of God can be aflame within us, and longing for the Word of God to dwell in us richly, and believing in the God who has carried Christians through countless persecutions on every continent and century, we do declare:

> In a world where opponents are vilified and crucified, **we will love our persecutors**.

Find a free video message and other free tools inspiring us toward this posture at:

www.HopeOfNations.net/PERSECUTORS

Chapter 18

CALM IN A POST-PROSPERITY ERA

"Give us today our daily bread."

MATTHEW 6:11

> In a world competing for limited resources, driven by fear, unrest, and scarcity, **we will remain calm**, confident that our Father provides our daily bread.

There may come times when everything in our human nature fears what is happening. Yet we will remain calm during times of fear, unrest, and scarcity because our future as followers of Jesus Christ is secure.

There is no power in hell and there is no power on earth that can change our final destination. No marching of army or turning of economy, no empty grocery store shelves or ruptures of society, can change where we are going to spend eternity. We anchor ourselves in this reality. We find hope in this.

We live in this world, knowing that we are in a season of waiting for Christ's final victory. We have great hope that no

matter how uncertain things ever get here, we have a certain future. We don't have to fear tomorrow because our Father is already there, providing enough.

We cannot live in tomorrow and today at the same time. But our God can. Our God is not limited by time. He is above it. He is already in tomorrow, and He is already providing enough for us there.

We will do our best to prepare provisions wisely, but we choose to ultimately depend on our Provider more than on our provisions. Our best plans can be knocked over. The rug can be pulled out from under them. But our God cannot be knocked over. The rug cannot be pulled out from under Him. So even as we plan wisely for our needs on earth, we place our faith in Him. We place our faith in the reality that He is already in tomorrow and He already knows what we are going to need, tomorrow.

We may need more patience. We may need more peace. We may need more love. We may need daily bread, protection, or wisdom. We may need financial provision. Whatever it is that we will ever need, He knows, and He is already there, providing enough.

DAILY BREAD

As the Israelites traveled from the sand and slavery of Egypt toward their promised land, they lacked sufficient food. When they called out to God, He promised to provide them with daily bread.

But the promise came with a condition. Each day they could take only as much as they needed for that day. God wanted them to travel light. God intentionally kept them from stockpiling so that they would look to Him *daily* as their provider.

God does not command us to never stockpile or prepare today, but He does command us to place our ultimate faith and hope in the reality that He is our Provider. And so we trust in the same God who provided daily bread to the Israelites as they journeyed for forty years through the desert on their way to the promised land.

We believe He will provide our daily bread, every day, for every year of our journey to the promised land of heaven. We believe our Father is in tomorrow, providing enough. And if our resources ever dwindle, if we ever find ourselves worrying about tomorrow's bread, tomorrow's freedom, tomorrow's peace, or any other thing in tomorrow, we will remind ourselves that our Father is already in tomorrow. And our Father can be counted on to provide enough for us.

He delivered Israel to their promised land, and He will deliver us to ours.

As we pray, "Give us today our daily bread," we will begin to understand and say, "Things are going to change. Things may even get difficult, but every day, God is going to provide enough for what I need *today*. Enough money for *today*, enough peace for *today*, enough strength for *today*, enough love for others, enough perseverance when my calling is difficult. He will always give me enough."

Jesus taught us to pray for daily bread because He wanted us to grow in confidence that God will provide again tomorrow.

As we learn to really cry out to God for today, we will see, day after day, that He is faithful for today, and then our confidence will grow that God is also in tomorrow. We will stop trying to control tomorrow because we know our Father is already there, and He is already providing enough.

So today, in this shaking world, let us voice our emotion to God:

Father, give us today our daily bread. As we make our way through this desert, we have real needs. We have hungry stomachs. We have lonely nights. We have difficult circumstances. We live in a dangerous and unpredictable world. Lord, You know all this, and You desire every day to meet our needs.

So, Lord, where we are afraid of tomorrow, will You help us to see that You are bigger than tomorrow, that You are already in tomorrow? And, Lord, where our human nature is to put our faith in our provisions or plans, will You help us to put our faith in You—as our Provider? Help us to live as sons and daughters who know that our kingdom is certain and our Father is certain and our future is certain.

Father, we will not fear tomorrow because You are already in tomorrow, providing more than enough. Help us live this way, Lord, tomorrow and today. Help us live this way this next week and in this present moment as we ask for our daily bread.

Aware of this principle in Jesus' teachings, and claiming the certainty that we have a Father and a kingdom awaiting us, we do hereby resolve:

In a world competing for limited resources, driven by fear, unrest, and scarcity, **we will remain calm**, confident that our Father provides our daily bread.

Watch a free video message at the link below:

www.HopeOfNations.net/BREAD

Chapter 19

INVINCIBLE IN A POST-LIBERTY ERA

"You would have no power over me if it were not given to you from above."

JESUS, IN JOHN 19:11

In a world where we are discriminated against, prejudged, and even persecuted, **we will be invincible** as we serve God's purposes for which we are placed here, now.

We may face social pressure to conform and to abandon our Christian principles. Whether this pressure is merely social—or legal or physical in the future—we resolve that we will continue to choose Christ, no matter the cost. We will be loving, and we will have a servant's heart toward our neighbors, but we will be as fearless as lions, bold and courageous, when it comes to following Christ, no matter the cost.

A MODERN-DAY EXAMPLE

In the San Francisco Bay area known as Silicon Valley, some leading technology companies have cultures in which Christians thrive;

others have cultures in which Christians are challenged or demeaned for their sincere faith. A friend of mine serves as an executive at one of these companies. She's a strong Christian who is open about her Christian faith. She does not use her position to impose her faith on subordinates, but she openly posts on social media about her Christian activities. My friend is very involved in her church and in Christian ministries.

Recently, the director of human resources at her workplace came into her office and said, "It's come to our attention that you are really open about your Christianity. As an executive here, you represent the company, and you can't be doing that."

Now here's the question—with a mortgage on the line, with raising children and facing other practical life expenses—How would you respond? What would you feel? What would you say?

This sister in Christ gave a model response. She didn't get angry or defensive, but she was bold and courageous. She looked the HR director square in the eyes and said, "You know I care about you, and I care about this company. I would never do anything to harm this company. But I can also tell you that what I do on my own time as an expression of my private religious belief is none of this company's business. In fact, I'm pretty sure that if I were a follower of any other religion, you wouldn't be having this conversation with me. So unless you can show me a specific way I've violated the law by practicing my religion on my own time, I think this conversation is done."

My friend's story is a fantastic example of fearless living in the face of discrimination or prejudice. She continues to be known for her love and kindness, including to her HR director. But she was fearless. And when an attack came against her, she behaved as if she is invincible until God has finished His purpose for her in that environment.

As the Post-Truth turn continues to redefine American culture, more and more of us may have confrontations like this—subtle discrimination in workplaces, universities, and other settings, a discrimination that says, "Your beliefs are out of style. What you do is out of style. Either abandon those old ways or get out of here."

Now, in my friend's case, she kept her job. But she gave her reply, knowing it could have cost her that job. She was willing to stand by who she is as a Christian and what she believes, regardless of the consequences. Her proven track record as an excellent employee who genuinely cares about her coworkers surely played a factor.

We resolve to live in this same manner. We resolve to prepare ourselves courageously—mentally and spiritually—to view ourselves as invincible while we strive toward fulfilling God's purposes for us on earth.

What can we do when we are hated because of our Christian faith? What can we do when we are treated unjustly, held to a different standard, or falsely accused? What can we do if proclaiming Jesus makes us a target for violence?

Jesus answered this question overtly: "Do not be afraid of those who kill the body but cannot kill the soul. Rather, be afraid of the One who can destroy both soul and body in hell."[1]

In other words, we will not fear people, because we know they will soon give account to our Father. The only force we fear in the universe is God, and we know He is on our side. And so we walk in this world, knowing we are invincible until God has accomplished His purposes through us on earth. Once we complete the good works He has prepared in advance for us to do, then no matter how we leave this world, we are off to a much better home, a better body, and a better kingdom in the presence of our Father.

Every day we wake up on earth, we can know this: We are still invincible. We are invincible to fulfill God's purpose for our lives. And so if there's a fire in your neighborhood and if God is not done with you, then your house will still be standing when all the other ones are burned down. If a terrorist walks into a restaurant where you're eating dinner and if God is not done with you on earth, then you will be alive at the end of it.

You will be completely protected. You are invincible until God has served His purpose for you on earth. And what is His purpose? It is to be faithful to Him, to love Him, and to declare His Good News of salvation to those who don't yet know Him.

EXAMPLES FROM BIBLE TIMES: ESTHER, JESUS, AND PAUL

God provides an example in the life of Esther. Esther found herself as part of a prejudged religious minority living in a wealthy and pagan society. Esther was discriminated against on multiple fronts. Her gender, her race, and her religion each brought about discrimination in the culture and country where she was placed.

In the video mentioned at the end of this chapter, I unpack at length Esther's story and her courage in the face of opposition. She became queen to the most powerful man in the world—a king named Xerxes. And it turns out that God had placed Esther in that place, at that time, so that she could serve God's purposes and ultimately deliver God's people from a genocide.

In summary here, let us consider the life-or-death moment when Esther could have kept silent. Her life would have been comfortable and safe if she hadn't chosen to follow God. Instead, with great courage she opened her mouth, identified herself as one of God's people, and risked her own likely death.

When Esther surrendered her life to fulfill God's purposes, God injected into her a supernatural fearlessness. And as a result, she prevented a genocide against God's people. Esther shows us how to have the courage to open our mouths and follow God, no matter what discrimination, prejudice, or even violent persecution we may face.

I have a friend who escaped from Iran when she was being hunted for being a Christian. She tells me she is not particularly brave or courageous in her human disposition. She never thought she would have the courage to be publicly identified as a Christian. She never expected she would have the bravery to leave her possessions and family to follow Christ. But when the moment came, she chose God. And in that moment, God injected into her a fearlessness, a sense of invincibility, that was strong enough to carry her across national borders and through a life-or-death crisis. And we, too, when we face persecution, prejudice, or injustice, can claim the promise that God will inject a supernatural sense of invincibility into us that is sufficient to weather any crisis.

At the climax of Esther's story, she drew a line in the sand. She declared, in essence, "I am not defined by these riches. I am not defined by my position in this world as queen of Xerxes. I am not defined by my wealth or comfort. Rather, I am a daughter of the King of kings, and I will stand up for God's people. I will risk my life, and I'm willing to follow God, knowing it may cost me my earthly life."

With Esther, we can make that same declaration: "If I perish, I perish."[2] We can be bold, knowing that God desires to inject the same fearlessness into our lives. We can learn from Esther's life if we wish to have God's courage injected into our souls.

When we live through persecution, God has a plan for us to be there. Esther's life reminds us that our lives are not incidental. Rather, they are ordained. When we find ourselves in a workplace, in a family, or in a nation where God's people are being persecuted, it's not coincidental. It's not accidental. It is strategic.

We have been placed by God to represent Him and to represent His people. And so each of us can note today that our race is not an accident. Our profession is not an accident. Where we were born, the time in history we've been born into—none of it is by accident. God has a plan for us.

Chaotic times are not comfortable times, but chaotic times are times of great spiritual opportunity. In Esther's story, when Xerxes's first queen was banished, there was great unrest. That unrest and even injustice created an opening for God to work. Today, when we see unrest in the world, when we see difficulties and turmoil, we can see the human turmoil with the spiritual eyes of faith. We can believe that, while God is not the author of evil, He is a God who can work good and redemption from any human evil.

We will choose by faith to be God's agents of redemption within the chaos. We believe that every turmoil opens an opportunity for the kingdom of God. We believe that our God is capable and wise enough to bring good from any evil. As Joseph declared in Genesis (and I'm paraphrasing), "What others meant for evil, God is able to repurpose for good."[3]

God can work through anything He chooses, even the drunk impulses of a pagan king, to accomplish His purposes. Every foolish and deadly move by pagans in our era—whether by Kim Jong-un in North Korea or by any other earthly leader—can become an opportunity for the kingdom. World events that are tragic and beyond our control are already known by God. He has already prepared faithful believers to play a crucial role in each specific turmoil.

We are here not just to survive; we are here to serve God's purposes. Esther's life also inspires us to believe that we are not here to merely survive. As the wealthiest Christians in world history, we can have difficulty making this shift in our view of reality. Most Christians in history have lived through experiences of famine, sickness, and physical suffering that we struggle to comprehend. For them, the prospect of heaven was always a welcome hope.

Having lived through an era of unprecedented wealth, health, luxury, and freedom on earth, we must choose by faith to prefer the coming kingdom. And we must resolve that our highest aim in this life is not our mere survival on earth, but rather the serving of our eternal purpose—the playing of our part in this grand story of God and humanity.

And so we resolve to stop merely surviving and to instead start serving our God-ordained purposes in this era. Like the Christ we follow, we resolve to complete the work the Father has given us to do. We are here to serve God's purposes.

When we truly believe this, it resets the priorities in our lives. Our top priority in life is no longer to endure everything that is happening in the world. Rather, as our faith grows, we grow to believe that this world is not our home. And as our faith grows, we believe the kingdom of God will be so much better than this life. We start to realize that our daily goal is to discover, "God, what good works did You place me here to do today?" This is how Jesus lived.[4]

Perhaps you remember the scene where Jesus says to His disciples, "My food . . . is to do the will of him who sent me."[5] At the end of His life, Jesus declared to the Father, "I have brought you glory on earth by finishing the work you gave me to do."[6] Jesus said, in essence, "I'm ready to go back to heaven."

Similarly, at the end of his life, the apostle Paul declared, "I have fought the good fight, I have finished the race, I have kept the faith. Now there is in store for me the crown of righteousness."[7]

We resolve to live this way. We resolve to strive toward it. We are imperfect, but we will point our compass in that direction. We raise this, rather than the American Dream, as our ideal.

And so we pray, "God, we want to be faithful to everything You've given us to do in this world. We want to be Your agents of redemption within the chaos, and once we've accomplished our work on earth, we're ready to get out of this world, because it is a broken world, a painful world."

In this world, our bodies feel pain. We get sick. We encounter injustice. When we understand where we're going, our mentality about this suffering changes from surviving to serving our purpose.

This view of earthly life as a mere staging ground for our real lives will sound radical to some American Christians. It *is* radical. We get to this way of thinking, one day at a time, by praying, "Our Father, today we want to seek first Your kingdom. Today, we want to serve the purposes for which You created us"—that is, "Your kingdom come, Your will be done, on earth as it is in heaven."[8]

AN EXAMPLE FROM RECENT HISTORY:
CORRIE TEN BOOM

We find the ultimate inspiring example of this in the life of Jesus. And we can also draw courage and inspiration from other Christian heroes who have lived this way in the face of unthinkable evil. Among those heroes, Corrie ten Boom tops my list of favorites. Corrie's many books offer real-life stories to prove that Christians in our era can choose to believe they are spiritually invincible—even in the face of murderous and dehumanizing evil.

Corrie was a Dutch Christian in Nazi-occupied territory during World War II. Corrie's father, Casper, was a watchmaker who had many Jewish friends. When the Nazis started to track down and kill the Jews in the town where Corrie lived, she broke the law and started hiding Jews in her house.

Corrie and her friends built secret rooms and passageways where the Jewish people could hide in their homes. In time, Corrie got caught and was sent to Ravensbrück—a Nazi concentration camp for women prisoners—as punishment for her good works. Ravensbrück was a horrific concentration camp where many of the women were experimented on for medical purposes. It had a crematorium and a gas chamber, and many of the women died from the cold, malnutrition, and deadly conditions.

Listen to Corrie's perspective as she and her sister Betsie (also called Bep by her family) were lying one night in the reeking, frigid, and lice-infested barracks of the concentration camp:

> The silence of night had fallen on seven hundred women, lying tightly packed together, asleep in the barracks of a concentration camp.
>
> Bep, my sister, awakened me and repeated to me in a whisper what God had told her about the work that would be waiting for us after our release.

"We must open a home for people who have suffered so much . . . But the most important part of our task will be to tell everyone who will listen that Jesus is the only answer to the problems that are disturbing the hearts of men and of nations. We shall have the right to speak because we can tell from our experience that His light is more powerful than the deepest darkness. Surely, nothing could be darker than our experiences here. I keep telling myself, 'Things cannot possibly grow worse,' but every day we see that misery only deepens. How wonderful that the reality of His presence is greater than the reality of the hell about us! . . . God will provide everything we need . . . All of our efforts must go into bringing the gospel, for we shall have many opportunities."[9]

Corrie continues, "Bep's eyes did not see the dirty throng around us. She was gazing into the future, and a glow of happiness brightened her emaciated face. Three days later, she passed away, and ten days later, just one week before all women of my age were killed, I was released from the concentration camp."

Corrie ten Boom suffered horrific pain, but just as her sister predicted, God had a plan for that pain. In God's plan, Corrie's sister Betsie was delivered out of the pain. When Betsie died, Corrie knew she was not just in a better place; she had moved to a place where there are no concentration camps and no death.

And the vision that God had given came true. Corrie ten Boom did travel the world after World War II, and she did tell millions of people about Jesus. She did minister to Germans, including some of the very soldiers who had beaten and imprisoned her. **God used Corrie as an agent of redemption within the chaos of evil.**

And God did so, not because Corrie was perfectly courageous in her own disposition, but because she chose to believe that God had a redeeming purpose for her placement within the evil.

Corrie could never have had her monumental ministry of eternal impact had she not gone through persecution in a concentration camp. Like Esther and like Jesus in His earthly life, Corrie lived with the mentality that "I'm not here to survive; I'm here to serve God's purposes." Because of that mentality, Corrie had a supernatural joy of the Lord. Even in the midst of suffering, she could say, "The joy of the Lord is my strength."[10] Even as a Nazi guard would be jamming a gun into her back, Corrie would be thinking, *You don't have authority over Jesus. You don't have authority over me. I'm being allowed to go through this so that I can serve God better.*

Corrie is living proof that Esther's faith and courage can be lived out in our modern era. Corrie followed God in this way less than eighty years ago. And we can resolve to follow God in this way in our own time. **And so we resolve that we are here not just to survive; we are here to serve our purpose.**

We choose to believe that God is the One who meets our needs, not our employers, not our investments, and not any government. It is God who provides for us. And it is God who protects us from danger, suffering, and death. As we stay true to Him, He will meet our needs so that we can fulfill our mission here, just as Corrie did. **We will be invincible until we serve God's purposes for us.**

Jesus spoke, thought, and behaved this way. When Pilate and Herod interrogated Jesus, they threatened Jesus with the prospect of death, but He calmly reminded them that they had no power to prevent God's plan from ultimately developing.

Jesus said things like, "No one takes [my life] from me, but I lay it down of my own accord."[11] When a world leader threatened Him with death, Jesus looked that leader in the eyes and declared, "You would have no power over me if it were not given to you from above."[12]

The same invincibility applies to every follower of Christ today. No nation or person or army has any power against us to do anything that will not eventually further God's kingdom. We resolve to start living with this kind of boldness.

With these things in mind, we pray:

Father, You have not given us a spirit of fear but of power and love and self-control. Lord, we feel fear in our human emotions, but You've given us a faith that overcomes fear. Jesus, You say You are the author and the perfecter of our faith. So, Lord, where our faith is weak, will You perfect it? Where our faith is weak, we remind ourselves that You birthed that faith in us, and You will perfect it through us as we choose You in difficulty and in persecution.

Lord, will You use us for such a time as this? Use us in businesses and in government, in nations, in homes, in lives to rescue the lost, to preserve Your people, to serve our purpose on earth.

We surrender ourselves. Give us the faith to walk boldly for You. Help us to choose You in crisis—as Esther chose You. We pray it in Jesus' name.

Believing that the words and promises of God are true, we resolve:

In a world where we are discriminated against, prejudged, and even persecuted, **we will be invincible** as we serve God's purposes for which we are placed here, now.

Watch the full explanation of Esther's story, as well as a video interview with Pariya from Iran, and find more inspiration toward this posture at:

www.HopeOfNations.net/POST-LIBERTY

Chapter 20

FEARLESS IN A POST-PEACE ERA

"Do not call conspiracy
     everything this people calls a conspiracy;
do not fear what they fear,
     and do not dread it.
The Lord Almighty is the one you are to regard as holy,
     he is the one you are to fear,
     he is the one you are to dread,
He will be a holy place."

ISAIAH 8:12–14, EMPHASIS ADDED

In a world divided by violence, terrorism, and war, **we will be fearless**.

It is only human to be afraid when we hear the blasting of bombs, when we see the spilling of blood, when the threat of violent death or pain moves from distant and hypothetical to near and actual.

If or when such realities become overwhelming to us, we will remind ourselves that God has steadied His people in times of war, violence, attack, and persecution for thousands of years. When evil shouts that it is the most powerful force in the universe, we will remind ourselves that it is not. We will be aware of evil—knowing it may prove impossible at times to walk through a day and not see evil as it marches across the nations. But we will not fear what our neighbors fear. This is because we see reality as it is—that there stands a Ruler greater than any president, dictator, or nation; a Power greater than any atomic bomb; an Army of justice greater than any earthly army or law or force of hatred.

Because Christ has defeated sin and death at the cross, we know He will chain all death and destruction and throw them into the lake of fire.[1] And so every suffering here is temporary. Every seeming victory for hell is temporary. But every future victory for Christ and His people will be eternal. We remind ourselves that evil has its limits. Evil is not an infinite power. Evil will start, and it will spill out to a certain degree, but God will always prevail over evil in the end.

If we are not intentional in remembering this, we can tend toward one of two emotional extremes: (1) living in ignorance, pretending that evil does not exist, or (2) acknowledging evil and then being so overcome by dread that we forget that evil's power is limited.

Instead, we will choose to revere and fear our God and Father as the mightiest force in the universe. We will remind ourselves that the strongest Player in the universal struggle is on our side, is for us, is protecting us, and is preparing a place for us.

We live in a violent, fear-inducing time. Routinely, we see shaky cell phone footage of bloody terrorist attacks or violent riots. We see great Western cities turned into war zones. Women and children screaming, running for their lives. Men huddling together next to cars and behind trees. A succession of gunshots echoing between the skyscrapers. San Bernardino. Orlando. Paris. London. Las Vegas. Dallas. Sutherland Springs. Parkland. Those are cities where violent evil has exploded as I write this. No doubt there are other cities to add to this list as you read this.

We live in fearful times. We live in divisive times. We live in times when hatred seems to rule the day. In response, we will live knowing that God has called us to fight for justice. We resolve to stand up for the least of these. We will draw from heaven the courage necessary to fight for justice the way Christ calls us to.

When God's people are rightly related to him, we have a spiritual steel in our backbones that gives us a courage and a confidence grown not from our human personalities, but from the supernatural power of the Holy Spirit.

When we focus on what is uncertain, it breeds fear in our minds. Yet our God has not created us to live under a cloud of fear. He has given us "a spirit not of fear but of power and love and self-control."[2] This doesn't mean we will never *feel* fear or *feel* afraid. We can acknowledge that there is a difference between feeling fear and being paralyzed by fear. By the power of God within us, we aim to never be controlled or paralyzed by fear—even when we feel it. We will not be slaves to fear.

When we have a sense of fear, we will declare that such a spirit is not from God. We will in those times fix our eyes and hearts on what is unchanging—our Father, His Word, the future victory of Christ, and the indwelling of the Holy Spirit, who is our source of power and fearlessness.

Understanding evicts fear. Understanding God's love and His plan extinguishes fear, for "perfect love drives out fear."[3] Love is the nature of God. When we rightly know who God is and that we are rightly related to Him through our relationship to Jesus, then we have that understanding. We will focus on God's future and present love, and it will evict fear from our hearts and minds.

God spoke to a prophet named Isaiah and told him why he could be unafraid, even as the world around him unraveled: "Do not call conspiracy everything this people calls a conspiracy."[4] Now, were people of power conspiring in Isaiah's time? Absolutely. God isn't saying that people never conspire. What He is saying is essentially,

"Do not draw your security and your hope from the earthly authorities in your life. Don't draw your security and strength from the society around you." In other words, "Do not fear what the people around you fear, and do not dread it."

Why do we not fear what our unbelieving neighbors fear? Because our neighbors can only find their security and their strength from the outside in. For our neighbors, if the Dow Jones Industrial Average is doing great, if society is stable, if all the economic and government indicators are good, then they are fearless. But as soon as those things start to shake, they become fearful.

God says to us, "It's different for you. You don't get your fearlessness, your stability, your courage, from the outside in. As a follower of Christ, you get your fearlessness from the inside out. You focus on what you do know, the God you know, rather than on all the uncertainties."

The prophetic word from Isaiah continues with this reminder: "The LORD Almighty . . . is the one you are to fear, he is the one you are to dread. He will be a holy place."[5] The Lord Almighty is the One we are to revere as holy, set apart, powerful.

We remind ourselves that God is more powerful than the European Union. He is more powerful than Iran. He is more powerful than ISIS or China or Russia or the United States. He is more powerful than racial hatred. He is more powerful than the American economy. He is more powerful than Islam, communism, Hinduism, and Post-Truth thinking. And when I see my God for how big He is, that's where I get my fearlessness.

WE BECOME FEARLESS WHEN WE UNDERSTAND WHAT IS HAPPENING

From Genesis to Revelation, God reveals a consistent cycle of humanity that I call the "blessing-judgment" cycle. A biblical understanding of this cycle can help Western Christians understand what may happen in Western society in the coming decades.

The blessing-judgment cycle goes like this:

1. People turn to God, and receive blessing as a result.
2. This blessing leads to prosperity materially and relationally.
3. Inheritor generations inherit the prosperity but begin turning away from God.
4. Eventually, a generation fully turns away from God, replacing Him with luxury and idols.
5. God patiently makes appeals through prophets and messengers for those people to turn back to Him.
   a. If the people turn back to God (see Nineveh in the book of Jonah), then they skip the judgment and return to a lifestyle of general blessing.
   b. If the people refuse to turn back to God (see Noah's neighbors, Sodom, and Romans 1), then judgment falls on those people. This judgment can materialize in the form of natural consequences from their godless choices, or it can be divine judgment, such as the flood in Noah's day or Sodom's fire from heaven. I refer to these as "natural judgment" and "divine judgment." Getting divorced by a spouse after choosing to have an affair (natural consequences) is a good example of natural judgment. Noah and the flood is a good example of divine judgment.

I theorize that God builds cycles within cycles. That is, God created the solar system so that we have a twenty-four-hour-day cycle, as well as monthly cycles and annual cycles. Our bodies have similar cycles, from the cellular level to the digestive system, with the wake-sleep cycle and subcycles within each of these, such as the various stages of sleep.

The narrative arc from Genesis to Revelation can be viewed as one massive blessing-judgment cycle, beginning in Eden with "blessing" and ending in Revelation with "judgment" for those who turn away. This includes redeemed "blessing" for those who repent and inherit the coming kingdom. Within that massive cycle, we find thousands of smaller cycles for individuals, families, nations, and eras. Israel's well-documented blessing-judgment cycles in the Old Testament are probably the best-known of these.[6]

While we should exercise caution about comparing the West or America to Israel, the reality is that the blessing-judgment cycle principle applied to humanity before Israel existed (see Noah) and to nations other than Israel (see Nineveh), and it applies to all of humanity (see Romans 1) in Scripture.

In this sense, I believe the blessing-judgment cycle can be cautiously applied to the Western nations that did seek God. Imperfect as they were, these nations sought God consistently enough to receive His blessing, and the inheritors are now completing their full turn away from God and His truth.

I do not claim to be a prophet from God, but based on my best understanding of this cycle in Scripture—and the telltale signs of a culture ripe to reap its own judgment—I will not be surprised if the Western nations that are intentionally completing the turn away from God bring on themselves a natural judgment that in time will result in their idols toppled, their prosperity lost, and their freedom pillaged.

Individuals and groups go through this cycle, and when we understand it, we understand that all humanity is on a conveyer belt of sorts that is moving toward the end, the culmination of the ultimate, macro, cosmic blessing-judgment of all humanity as recorded in Revelation and involving the formal "judgment seats."

Jesus said, "As it was in the days of Noah, so it will be at the coming of the Son of Man."[7] When He returns at the end of human history, He will not return as a gentle baby in a manger; He will return as a Warrior-Judge. He will have a sword protruding from his mouth and fire in his eyes. He will be riding on a white horse, and with Him in the clouds will be supernatural armies of angels.[8] He will come to judge the murderers, the haters, all who have turned from God. This will be the ultimate and final judgment.

As God describes it in the Bible, it is going to be fierce,[9] but the message is simple: "Trust in Christ for your forgiveness, and you will be spared from that."

Jesus predicted this in Matthew 24:6: "You will hear of wars and rumors of wars, but see to it that you are not alarmed." Even when there are wars and rumors of wars, we can be fearless. Why? Because we know that our judgment has already been absorbed at the cross. The coming judgment is not pointed at believers. Like Noah, we may witness the rising waters, but God will ultimately deliver us from them.

"Such things must happen," Jesus explained, "but the end is still to come. Nation will rise against nation, and kingdom against kingdom. There will be famines and earthquakes in various places. All these are the beginning of birth pains."[10] All these are signs that Jesus' return is getting closer.

WE BECOME FEARLESS WHEN WE UNDERSTAND WHO WILL PREVAIL

We choose a spiritual understanding that evicts fear. We remind ourselves what is happening in the world. Any convulsions we witness simply mean we are one day closer to Christ's return. Understanding evicts fear when we understand Who will prevail. That is, we become fearless when we understand Who is going to win at the end of all this.

The apostle Paul reminds us of what God has done for us to take away our fear:

> You see, at just the right time, when we were still powerless, Christ died for the ungodly . . . God demonstrates his own love for us in this: While we were still sinners, Christ died for us.
>
> *Since we have now been justified by his blood, how much more shall we be saved from God's wrath through him! . . .*

We also boast in God through our Lord Jesus Christ, through whom we have now received reconciliation.

ROMANS 5:6, 8–9, 11, EMPHASIS ADDED

GOD PROVIDES DELIVERANCE TO THOSE WHO SEEK HIM

God always looks out for the righteous. In his second letter, the apostle Peter describes how Noah and Lot lived in unrighteous cultures. God provided a way out for Noah and for Lot, who lived in unrighteous Sodom. What Peter said about that day is also true for us today: "The Lord knows how to rescue the godly from trials."[11] Aware of this, we will not be shaken.

We understand that things may get worse if our society continues resisting God's truth and welcoming a judgment phase. We will not be shocked or shaken by any downturn, earthquake, war, or unrest. We resolve to fix our hope on Christ's return. We will be faithful, no matter the cost. We resolve that if society does shake, we will not despair, knowing it leads one step closer to Christ's return.

We resolve to walk confidently, knowing we will be preserved so we can rescue others and knowing we will be delivered so we can enjoy eternal life in the kingdom. We will not cower, with our heads down, shaking and afraid. We will walk with a supernatural confidence, knowing this: We are still here to help rescue others. That's why God has planted us here in these times.

You may remember September 11, 2001, when the twin towers of the World Trade Center were collapsing, when the smoke was billowing out, when the steel was melting into giant fireballs. You may remember the stories of the heroic firefighters and police officers running up the stairs while everyone else was running down. They were going up the stairs because there were still more people who were bloodied and bruised and wounded, people who needed to be dragged out and saved before the collapse.

The spiritual reality in our lifetime is that all of humanity is a smoldering tower that is collapsing upon itself. And God has placed us here, not so we can criticize it, not so we can barricade ourselves, but so we can run *up* the stairs into the smoke to find "the least of these brothers and sisters" of Jesus[12]—the hurting, the bloodied, and the bruised—and drag them to salvation and Jesus Christ.

And so together, we join in this prayer:

Father, our hope is in You. And Lord, we are moving our eyes. We are moving the dial of our thoughts and our emotions away from circumstances and society and onto the Creator and the Sustainer. You breathe life. You give hope. You are salvation. You desire that all people would turn to You. You desire that no one would perish.

Father, will You fortify within us a spiritual spinal column of steel? Lord, may we be fearless and courageous in the face of suffering, in the face of unrest, in the face of hatred, and even death, because we know who we are, and we know Whose we are.

Lord, You have placed us here, not to worry about our own survival, but to run into the smoke and rescue those who are lost in sin.

Father, will You build in our lives this bedrock foundation, that we would see reality as it is? Will You empower us to live fearlessly for You?

Together, then, we resolve:

In a world divided by violence, terrorism, and war, **we will be fearless**.

Watch a detailed explanation of the blessing-judgment cycle and more free videos explaining why we can be fearless in times of violence, terrorism, and war at:

www.HopeOfNations.net/PEACE

CONCLUSION

In the buildup to World War II, British prime minister Winston Churchill and US president Franklin Delano Roosevelt (FDR) saw an undeniable evil in their day. The evils of Nazi fascism and Japanese imperialism were rising with a power that appeared to be invincible. Churchill and FDR encountered frightening military, ideological, and national strength. They each endured private moments when all hope seemed lost. They struggled not only to understand a formidable enemy, but also to stir an apathetic and exhausted people toward action.

Churchill and FDR saw coming events with unusual clarity. They were true leaders in this sense. They saw the ramifications of evil earlier than many of their peers in their own governments—and long before the masses of smaller-minded people with their heads buried in ignorant optimism that Hitler would not act on his frightening claims. Churchill and FDR saw evil. They acknowledged its severity. And then they resolved that they would overcome evil with good.

When they could have been paralyzed in fear, they instead launched into action. When they could have been overcome with hopelessness, they instead led, leveraged, and inspired others to join them.

Some historians point to one specific radio address from FDR as the turning point in World War II—and, as a result, the turning point in world history. It was a nationwide radio fireside chat titled

"The Arsenal of Democracy." At the time, the United States had not yet entered the war.

In his chat, FDR cast the vision that the United States could turn the course of a world war. At the time, most Americans were opposed to any involvement in the war. The nation had not yet recovered from the Great Depression. Many still lived without limbs or without loved ones because of World War I. Public sentiment could not have been more opposed to entering another war in Europe with Germany.

And yet, despite an overwhelming sea of fear and small-mindedness, FDR cast a compelling vision that the United States must turn the course of world history by leveraging its unique asset—industrial manufacturing—to become the world's "arsenal of democracy." He raised the eyes of the people to see reality as it was:

> But all our present efforts are not enough. We must have more ships, more guns, more planes—more of everything. This can only be accomplished if we discard the notion of "business as usual" . . .
>
> I want to make it clear that it is the purpose of the nation to build now with all possible speed every machine, every arsenal, every factory that we need to manufacture our defense material. We have the men, the skill, the wealth, and above all, the will.[1]

FDR correctly identified that right would only prevail if a great army of American men and women committed their lives and resources to turn the course of history.

It is a fact of history that the planes that flew above Germany and the Pacific, the tanks that would prevail in Normandy and Berlin—each began not as bolts or even as Pennsylvania steel, but each began as words in the mouth of a leader who understood ideology, who understood evil, and who gave his very health and well-being to overcome evil at any cost. In that December address nearly one year before the attack on Pearl Harbor, FDR convinced others to join his ideology.

I appeal to the owners of plants, to the managers, to the workers, to our own Government employees, to put every ounce of effort into producing these munitions swiftly and without stint. With this appeal I give you the pledge that all of us who are officers of your Government will devote ourselves to the same whole-hearted extent to the great task that lies ahead . . .

We must be the great arsenal of democracy. For us this is an emergency as serious as war itself. We must apply ourselves to our task with the same resolution, the same sense of urgency, the same spirit of patriotism and sacrifice as we would show were we at war.[2]

Following FDR's speech, the presidents and CEOs of Ford, Chrysler, Packard, and General Motors all committed to retool their automotive factories in Detroit. Soon, Cadillac was building aircraft engines, Chrysler was building tanks, and Ford was building B-24 bombers at its Willow Run plant in Michigan.

The largest industrial war machine in history had been awoken—by a leader who had vision, commitment, perseverance, and perspective. FDR cast this ideological vision nearly one full year before the crisis physically struck American soil at Pearl Harbor.

When we consider the end of Western civilization as documented in this book, we have moments of clarity in which we see the spiritual realm with an emotional chill. Like FDR, we must turn this emotion into motivation, direction, commitment, and a call to faith-filled action from our churches, from our Christian communities, from our families, and from ourselves. As we carry this understanding into our daily lives, we will battle the fatigue and apathy of our peers, much like Churchill and FDR did.

It takes a great exertion of moral energy to see reality as it is— particularly in an era of deceit, mindless entertainment, and lazy thinking. Like FDR, we strain to see not only through the fog of opinions, but also into the actual cogs that move nations and people in our time—and beneath it to the undergirding principles of Scripture that reveal where all of these things are leading.

Like FDR, then, we must resolve to give our lives and fortunes in an even higher pursuit of justice, truth, freedom, and righteousness. We must see that the stakes are higher than our neighbors realize. We must see that the consequences of our own action or inaction will affect our children, our grandchildren, our families, our nations, and even world history.

Inspired by FDR's call to become "the arsenal of democracy," that small group of automotive executives in Detroit went all-in. Some worked for $1 per year until the war ended. They gave all they had—every ounce of energy and production capacity and leadership—and together they changed the course of world history. In a sense, that small group of executives turned the tide of World War II. Their factories built the tanks, planes, and munitions that emptied the concentration camps and freed the world.

We in the American church find ourselves at the beginning of a similar global crisis of culture, ideology, and spirituality. We may feel powerless to do anything, but the reality is that we in the West are still the richest church in world history. We have more resources, tools, and money than any other church in history—if only we will unite and use those tools with urgency in Christ's mission.

We still live in unprecedented freedom. We have a closing window of world peace during which we can share Christ with the nations. And we have global communication tools that no other church in history has had. We can prepare our churches now to be lighthouses of stability as the world around grows darker and darker—so that our neighbors can find Christ in the crisis.

If we will go all-in, as FDR did, as those American automotive executives did, then we have the potential to turn the tide spiritually. Our devotion to Christ's cause can inspire others to join us in going all-in for Christ's kingdom now. Whether this will happen begins with you and me.

So what will we do?

- We will resolve to live as though we are engaged in a spiritual war for the souls and minds of humanity.
- We will claim that our victory is sure in Christ, but also that the time is now to give ourselves and our resources in this battle for His kingdom.
- We will recognize that the Post-Truth deceit of the West has been engineered by our adversary for more than two hundred years, and that what is now budding into cultural chaos is the fruit of a society that has turned away from Christian truth.
- We will recognize that there is no simple, immediate panacea for America or the West to be found in any one political party or act of law.
- We will recognize that there is only *one* simple Panacea for all of humanity, which is found in the work of Jesus Christ on the cross, and that our greatest call and highest commitment is to do anything and everything to declare this Good News as the only true Hope of Nations.
- We will embrace God's plan to change the nations through His Good News of salvation in Christ alone.
- We will commit to use Christ's means and methods for changing societies and souls.
- We will be ambassadors to those lost in the dark.
- We will educate our children and grandchildren to be true warriors of grace and truth, to know the Hope of Nations. We will train them in the Christian Scriptures so that they might become the next generation of John Harvards, John Adamses, Reverend Martin Luther King Juniors, Harriet Tubmans, and William Wilberforces.
- We will fortify our Christian churches, schools, and institutions to stand unashamed on the truth of God's Word.
- We will give our fortunes, our skills, our trusts, our wills, our talents, and our lives to join this effort.

■ Like Winston Churchill and Franklin Delano Roosevelt, we
will use our influence to convince other believers to move from
the sidelines of comfort into the fray and battle of this global
spiritual struggle.

It is a struggle for the nations. And the nations can only be
brought to peace by Christ, the true Hope of Nations.

And so together we resolve:

I: We will remain rooted to the Christian Scriptures.

In a world where truth is feelings-based, **we will
remain rooted to the Christian Scriptures** and their
life-giving direction.

II: We will train our young.

In a society of educated ignorance and blindness,
we will train our young in the freedom, knowledge,
and power of Christian truth.

III: We will be known for doing good.

In a world where Christians are labeled as bigots or
backward, **we will be known for doing good**, serving
the least of these and loving our neighbors.

IV: We will dignify all people as image bearers of God.

In a world where people are treated as commodities
or as opponents, **we will dignify all people as image
bearers of God**.

V: We will be ambassadors.

In a post-Christian world, **we will be ambassadors**
to foreign tribes, behaving diplomatically toward neighbors who have been told the worst about Christianity.

VI: We will love our persecutors.

In a world where opponents are vilified and crucified, **we will love our persecutors**.

VII: We will remain calm.

In a world competing for limited resources, driven by fear, unrest, and scarcity, **we will remain calm**, confident that our Father provides our daily bread.

VIII: We will be invincible.

In a world where we are discriminated against, prejudged, and even persecuted, **we will be invincible** as we serve God's purposes for which we are placed here, now.

IX: We will be fearless.

In a world divided by violence, terrorism, and war, **we will be fearless**.

These brief manifestos are seeds. Let us plant them in faith, water them by the Word of God, and bathe them in the warm light of prayer. Let us inhale these ideals as dreams, asking the Spirit to breathe them into our spirits.

May these simple biblical concepts take deep root in our lives and in the lives of our children, our families, our churches, our communities, and our ministries—that we may together be an army of light, having "put on the armor of light."[3]

My prayer for you is not just that God will grow these seeds in your thinking, but equally that God will grow these seeds in your life, that you and I will bear much fruit during our remaining time on earth.

God longs to have us join in His mission to "proclaim justice to the nations." Even now, He is continuing the work He has begun—a work that goes on "till he has brought justice through to victory." This victory is found in Christ alone: "In his name the nations will put their hope."[4]

Now as you go to share the Hope of Nations,

May the God of hope fill you with all joy and peace as you trust in him, so that you may overflow with hope by the power of the Holy Spirit.

ROMANS 15:13

ACKNOWLEDGMENTS

The people of Venture Christian Church in Los Gatos, California, made it possible for me to invest the hours necessary to research and write this book. Thank you to my good friend Chip Ingram for reaching out to me, inviting me into the ministry at Venture, encouraging me as a voice in my generation, and teaching me invaluable life lessons about how to join God's work and how to teach His Word. So many brothers and sisters from Venture encouraged me during the writing of this book, including close friends like Tom and Deb Steipp, Chi-Hua, Ken, Russ, and so many others. So many others spoke words of encouragement to me as I test-taught this material. They affirmed, shaped, and improved both the message and the messenger.

I prayed for an editor who could take my work and make it far better than I ever could; God answered that prayer in a living legend, John Sloan.

I prayed for an agent who would possess the heart of Christ; God answered that prayer in Wes Yoder.

I prayed for a publisher that would connect these truths to tens of thousands of people; God answered that prayer in the gifted team at Zondervan, including David Morris, Dirk Buursma, Tom Dean, and the entire team.

I prayed for partners to help steward the momentum this book will create; God answered that prayer in Giles, Alison, and the team at the Hope of Nations nonprofit.

I prayed for a team to help me in the next season of service; God answered that prayer in Craig Hanson, Greg Moore, Laura Basso, Brad, Denise, Brooke, Mike, Jen, and the entire elder team, staff, and body at Connection Pointe Christian Church.

To everyone above, I say thank you for investing your significant gifts and your valuable time into this work, past, present, and future.

More than anyone else, thank you to my confidante, partner, and best friend, Melanie. Thank you for believing in me and in the message I am called to carry. Thank you for your many sacrifices and your relentless love.

ABOUT THE AUTHOR

John S. Dickerson is a nationally awarded journalist, a bestselling author, and Lead Pastor of Connection Pointe Christian Church in the Indianapolis area.

Receive free updates from the author
by sending a blank email to:

Friend@IAmStrongBook.com

Find John's other books and video studies at:

www.JohnSDickerson.com.

_____

If you wish to support the vision and mission of this book, you may contribute a tax-deductible gift to the Hope of Nations nonprofit by visiting:

www.HopeOfNations.net/Foundation

_____

If you wish to be part of a church that understands the times and is committed to Christ's "grace and truth," join John and his congregation online at:

www.ConnectionPointe.org.

NOTES

Introduction: Understanding Our New Reality

1. William Love, "Folsom: A Perfect Place for Kids?" *East Bay Times*, September 29, 2005, www.eastbaytimes.com/2005/09/29/folsom-a -perfect-place-for-kids.

2. The Oxford linguists defined *Post-Truth* as "relating to or denoting circumstances in which objective facts are less influential in shaping public opinion than appeals to emotion and personal belief," https:// en.oxforddictionaries.com/word-of-the-year/word-of-the-year-2016.

3. That this observation comes from Oxford is more than a little ironic. Oxford, founded around AD 1100, is considered by many to be a father of the modern university, and its founding marks well the beginning of an era defined by "the pursuit of knowledge." The Latin word for *truth*—*veritas*—is embedded in the crests and mottos of many of the influential universities that have shaped Western culture, including Harvard and Johns Hopkins, among others. Truth was often symbolized as "light" in the Bible (see Psalm 119, among many other instances). For this reason, many of the most influential seed universities such as Oxford refer to truth in their founding mottos or crests by referring to light. Oxford's motto, *Dominus illuminatio mea*, is a direct quote from Scripture: "The LORD is my light." As Solomon wrote in Proverbs 9:10, "The fear of the LORD is the beginning of wisdom." An awareness and pursuit of this was present in the imperfect but upward era of Christianized Western civilization, stretching from Oxford's founding until our day.

4. Rodney Stark summarizes this cultural moment well. Dating the gestation of this movement between AD 1000 and 1200, he writes, "The most fundamental key to the rise of Western

civilization has been the dedication of so many of its most brilliant minds to the pursuit of knowledge. Not to illumination. Not to enlightenment. Not to wisdom. But to *knowledge.* And the basis for this commitment to knowledge was the Christian commitment to *theology*" (*How the West Won: The Neglected Story of the Triumph of Modernity* [Wilmington, DE: Intercollegiate Studies Institute, 2014], 159, emphasis original).

Chapter 1: My Hope for the Nations

1. These were once so well undisputed that they did not need compiling in place. The evidence on any individual claim is overwhelming. Because the claim is becoming controversial in my generation, I am compiling hundreds of pieces of primary evidence that prove this claim in my forthcoming book *Jesus Skeptic: A Journalist Investigates Christianity for a New Generation.* Send an email to Friend@ IAmStrongBook.com, and I'll notify you when *Jesus Skeptic* has released.
2. When I refer to Christianized Western civilization in the US and Europe as a "grand society," I do not mean that it was ever perfect. Its history is marred with slavery and injustice, just as every other major civilization in history has been. What I do mean is that despite these deep flaws, it has also been the only society to double life expectancy, spread literacy around the globe, eradicate open slavery, and continue moving toward more freedom and equality for more people.
3. Nicholas Kristof, "A Little Respect for Dr. Foster," *New York Times,* March 29, 2015, www.nytimes.com/2015/03/29/opinion/sunday/ nicholas-kristof-a-little-respect-for-dr-foster.html.
4. "Megan Fox: Biography," *IMDb,* www.imdb.com/name/nm1083271 /bio.
5. George Yancey, *So Many Christians, So Few Lions: Is There Christianophobia in the United States?* (Lanham, MD: Rowman & Littlefield, 2014).
6. George Yancey, *Hostile Environment: Understanding and Responding to Anti-Christian Bias* (Downers Grove, IL: InterVarsity, 2015), 9.
7. Yancey, *So Many Christians,* 61–87, 129–42.
8. Gary A. Tobin and Aryeh K. Weinberg, "Religious Beliefs & Behavior of College Faculty," vol. 2 in *Profiles of the American University* (San Francisco: Institute for Jewish & Community Research, 2007), 2, 12, www.jewishresearch.org/PDFs2/FacultyReligion07.pdf.

9. Peter Wood, "Preferred Colleagues," *Chronicle of Higher Education*, April 6, 2011, www.chronicle.com/blogs/innovations/preferred-colleagues/29160.

10. Ian Johnson, "In China, Unregistered Churches Are Driving a Religious Revolution," *The Atlantic*, April 23, 2017, www.theatlantic.com/international/archive/2017/04/china-unregistered-churches-driving-religious-revolution/521544/.

11. Revelation 7:9.

12. See 1 Thessalonians 4:13.

13. See 1 John 4:4.

14. See John 10:10.

Chapter 2: What Is Happening?

1. Corrie ten Boom, *The Hiding Place*, 35th anniv. ed. (1971; repr., Grand Rapids: Chosen, 2006), 29.

2. Ten Boom, *The Hiding Place*, 31.

3. Some recent studies suggest this figure may be as high as 20 million, but 6 million is the figure presently provided by the United States Holocaust Memorial Museum ("Documenting Numbers of Victims of the Holocaust and Nazi Persecution," *Holocaust Encyclopedia*, www.ushmm.org/wlc/en/article.php?ModuleId=10008193).

4. "Population by Religious Denomination (1910–1939)," in *Sozialgeschichtliches Arbeitsbuch*, vol. 3, *Materialien zur Statistik des Deutschen Reiches 1914–1945*, ed. Dietmar Petzina, Werner Abelshauser, and Anselm Faust, trans. Fred Reuss (Munich: Verlag C.H. Beck, 1978), 31, http://germanhistorydocs.ghi-dc.org/pdf/eng/JEW_RELIGIONZUGEHTABELLE_ENG.pdf.

5. See 2 Timothy 3:5.

6. This is well documented by multiple sociologists, including Dr. Christian Smith. I have aggregated much of that research in my book *The Great Evangelical Recession* (Grand Rapids: Baker, 2013), 21–35.

7. This is summarized well by a 1938 quote from Adolf Hitler: "These boys and girls enter our organizations [at] ten years of age, and often for the first time get a little fresh air; after four years of the Young Folk they go on to the Hitler Youth, where we have them for another four years . . . And even if they are still not complete National Socialists, they go to Labor Service and are smoothed out there for another six, seven months . . . And whatever class consciousness or

social status might still be left . . . the Wehrmacht [German armed
forces] will take care of that" (United States Holocaust Memorial
Museum, "Indoctrinating Youth," *Holocaust Encyclopedia*, www
.ushmm.org/wlc/en/article.php?ModuleId=10007820).

8. Describing the post-Christian academic tone in the universities in
the late 1800s, historian Mark A. Noll writes that Ernest Renan's
Life of Jesus "in 1863 presented Jesus as a simple Galilean preacher
who would have been flabbergasted at what later generations
said about his supposedly supernatural origins and powers." This
captures well the present academic mood regarding Jesus in many
American universities (Mark A. Noll, *Turning Points: Decisive
Moments in the History of Christianity*, 3rd ed. [Grand Rapids: Baker
Academic, 2012], 249).

9. In fact, when it comes to Christianity, many American university
curriculums today rely on the exact same German scholars from that
era in the late 1800s.

10. George M. Marsden, *The Soul of the American University: From
Protestant Establishment to Established Nonbelief* (Oxford: Oxford
University Press, 1994), 173–74, 206–7, 212–13.

11. Princeton has been the most theologically conservative of these
universities within the last century. But Princeton, like the others,
is no longer a safe environment for actual Christian ideas. In 2017,
pastor Timothy Keller had been chosen to receive a prestigious award
from Princeton. However, once it was noted that Keller interprets
sexuality as the Bible does and not as the Post-Truth culture does,
that award was revoked. That this happened at Princeton—the
last of the Ivies to stay true to its Christian roots—was a symbolic
moment. Ironically, in post-Christian fashion, the award is named
"The Kuyper Prize for Excellence in Reformed Theology and Public
Witness." But the most well-known Reformed Christian with the
most excellent record of public witness is not eligible. Why not?
Because he actually takes the truth claims of the Bible seriously. See
David Gibson, "Princeton Theological Seminary Reverses Decision
to Honor Redeemer's Tim Keller," *Religion News Service*, March 22,
2017, http://religionnews.com/2017/03/22/princeton-theological
-seminary-reverses-decision-to-honor-redeemers-tim-keller.

12. Primary evidence is available to substantiate this claim. I compile
this evidence in my forthcoming book *Jesus Skeptic*. Send an email to

Friend@IAmStrongBook.com, and I'll shoot you a heads-up when *Jesus Skeptic* releases. See also Marsden, *Soul of the American University*.

13. On this point, see particularly the chapter, "The German Connection," in Allan Bloom, *The Closing of the American Mind* (New York: Simon & Schuster, 1987), 141–56.

14. Bloom, *Closing of the American Mind*, 26; see 47–61. Reprinted with the permission of Simon & Schuster, Inc. All rights reserved.

15. Within these post-Christian "Christian" schools, Stalin was heavily influenced by a young thinker who had recently imported Marx's German ideas into the post-Christian seminary. The aim of this was "helping the dark masses see the light about social injustice and a purported all-purpose remedy" outside of Christianity (Stephen Kotkin, *Stalin: Paradoxes of Power: 1872–1928*, vol. 1 [New York: Penguin, 2015], 30).

16. Max Ehrenfreund, "A Majority of Millennials Now Reject Capitalism, Poll Shows," *Washington Post*, April 26, 2016, www.washingtonpost.com/news/wonk/wp/2016/04/26/a-majority-of-millennials-now-reject-capitalism-poll-shows.

17. Roberto Stefan Foa and Yascha Mounk, "The Danger of Deconsolidation: The Democratic Disconnect," *Journal of Democracy* 27, no. 3 (July 2016): 7–8, © 2016 National Endowment for Democracy and Johns Hopkins University Press. Reprinted with permission of Johns Hopkins University Press.

18. Richard Fry, "Millennials Match Baby Boomers as Largest Generation in U.S. Electorate, but Will They Vote?" *Pew Research Center: Fact Tank*, May 16, 2016, www.pewresearch.org/fact-tank/2016/05/16/millennials-match-baby-boomers-as-largest-generation-in-u-s-electorate-but-will-they-vote.

19. Si Yang, "Poll Finds Young Americans More Open to Socialist Ideas," *Voice of America*, October 23, 2016, www.voanews.com/a/young-americans-seen-less-opposed-to-socialist-ideas/3562681.html.

20. Aaron Blake, "More Young People Voted for Bernie Sanders Than Trump and Clinton Combined—by a Lot" *Washington Post*, June 20, 2016, www.washingtonpost.com/news/the-fix/wp/2016/06/20/more-young-people-voted-for-bernie-sanders-than-trump-and-clinton-combined-by-a-lot.

21. Claim based on life expectancy of the baby boomer generation, who are not all Truth-Based but who represent the largest remaining bloc of Truth-Based Americans.

22. I use this phrase "hybrid communism" because what exists in China today is not a pure expression of Marxism. It is an authoritarian, state-controlled hybrid of capitalist benefits and communist controls. It combines state monopoly power with capitalism and some other non-Marxist ideas. In this book, I'll use the term "hybrid communism" to summarize all of this. As much as China today is no pure Marxist expression, those of us living outside of China would do well to remember that the Communist Party is alive and well, that it controls every major industry, and that it can revoke the possessions or freedoms of individuals and businesses at any time it wishes.

23. PricewaterhouseCoopers, "The World in 2050, The Long View: How Will the Global Economic Order Change by 2050?" *PwC: Global,* February 2017, www.pwc.com/gx/en/issues/economy/the -world-in-2050.html.

24. Americans will remain deeply divided on ideology for at least another fifteen years, as long as the baby boomers are among us. We will see the generational data suggesting this in future chapters.

25. PricewaterhouseCoopers, "The World in 2050, The Long View."

26. Note that Islam is already the dominant religion in the world's fourth most populous nation, Indonesia, and sociologists expect India to be home to the world's largest Muslim population (by nation) by 2050. These two nations are projected to rank as #2 and #4 in the world economy in 2050. As such, the growth of Islam will not only be in population but also in economic influence.

27. Graham Allison, *Destined for War: Can America and China Escape Thucydides's Trap?* (New York: Houghton Mifflin Harcourt, 2017), vii–viii.

28. Jon Emont, "Jakarta's Christian Governor Sentenced to Prison in Blasphemy Case," *Washington Post,* May 9, 2017, www.washing tonpost.com/news/worldviews/wp/2017/05/09/jakartas-christian -governor-sentenced-to-prison-in-blasphemy-case.

29. "The Future of World Religions: Population Growth Projections, 2010–2050," Pew Research Center Religion & Public Life, April 2, 2015, www.pewforum.org/2015/04/02/religious-projections-2010-2050/. Note: All graphs and quotations from the Pew Research Center are Copyright © by the Pew Research Center and are reprinted with permission. The presence of such graphs and quotations within this book does not imply that the Pew Research

Center agrees with or endorses the thesis or conclusions of this book or its author. The Pew Research Center strives to be an objective third-party researcher, and as such the citations of Pew Research findings herein do not suggest or otherwise attribute any particular policy or lobbying objective or opinion to Pew Research, nor should the presence of such material be interpreted or inferred as a Pew Research endorsement of any cause, candidate, issue, party, product, business, organization, religion, or viewpoint.

30. "The Changing Global Religious Landscape," Pew Research Center, April 5, 2017, http://assets.pewresearch.org/wp-content/uploads/ sites/11/2017/04/07092755/FULL-REPORT-WITH-APPENDIXES -A-AND-B-APRIL-3.pdf.

31. Unless otherwise specified, in this book the term *Christian* includes Catholic, Orthodox, Protestant, and nondenominational combined—because that's the category used by the sociologists whose work I'm aggregating here. If you'd like a focused look at evangelical Protestant Christians in America, check out my book *The Great Evangelical Recession*.

32. Shan Juan, "Second-Child Policy Increases Births by 7.9 Percent," *China Daily*, January 23, 2017, www.chinadaily.com.cn/china/2017 -01/23/content_28029004.htm.

33. "The Future of World Religions: Population Growth Projections, 2010–2050."

34. Calculation included the UK population as it was formulated pre-Brexit.

35. Compared to a current US population of about 320 million (2017) and a Russian population of 143 million, consider the number of Muslims projected to live in the following five nations about thirty years from now in 2050: (1) India will be home to 311 million Muslims; (2) Pakistan will be home to 273 million Muslims; (3) Indonesia will be home to 257 million Muslims; (4) Nigeria will be home to 231 million Muslims; (5) Bangladesh will be home to 182 million Muslims. Combined, these five nations will be home to more than 1.25 billion Muslims—more than the combined 2050 populations of the US (projected to be about 425 million) and the European Union (projected to be about 526 million). For the Muslim population figures, see "The Future of World Religions: Population Growth Projections, 2010–2050"; for the EU population figure, see "People in the EU—Population Projections," *Eurostat*,

June 2015, http://ec.europa.eu/eurostat/statistics-explained/
index.php/People_in_the_%20EU_%E2%80%93_population_
projections; for the US population figure, see "Population
Projections," United States Census Bureau, www.census.gov/
programs-surveys/popproj/data/tables.html.

36. Of course, a lot of other factors can change in thirty years, or in five.
These are trajectories based on today's trends.

37. "The Future of World Religions: Population Growth Projections,
2010–2050."

38. "The Future of World Religions: Population Growth Projections,
2010–2050."

39. "The Future of World Religions: Population Growth Projections,
2010–2050."

40. "The Future of World Religions: Population Growth Projections,
2010–2050." These projections are unable to account for Christians
in China, as government policies there prohibit the full gathering of
information on China's Christians. For a good look into the church
in China, I recommend Ian Johnson, *The Souls of China: The Return
of Religion after Mao* (New York: Pantheon, 2017).

41. "The Future of World Religions: Population Growth Projections,
2010–2050." Globally, these nonreligiously "unaffiliated" will
actually decline as a percentage between now and 2050, according to
Pew Research projections. This is largely because they do not have as
many children as religious people do.

42. To support this claim, see the late Cornell professor Allan Bloom's
book *The Closing of the American Mind*, which I'll quote from
frequently in later chapters. For this claim, see pages 19–132
in particular. I'll also support this claim with sociological data,
including a report in which a majority of younger Americans believe
the definitions of "right" and "wrong" are determined by the culture
one lives in, not by an objective outside standard (see Bloom, *Closing
of the American Mind*, 132).

43. Some observers cite *Roe v. Wade* and the acceptance of abortion as
the beginning of the Post-Truth cultural turn (see Francis Schaeffer,
*How Should We Then Live? The Rise and Decline of Western Thought
and Culture*, 50th anniv. ed. [Wheaton, IL: Crossway, 2005]).
I prefer to place the beginning of America's Post-Truth turn a bit
earlier, in the late 1800s and early 1900s, when the last of the

original American seminaries (Harvard, Yale, Princeton) abandoned their belief in the authority of the Christian Scriptures. Within the large scope of history, this is all within the same era.

44. Kenneth M. Johnson, Layton M. Field, and Dudley L. Poston Jr., "More Deaths Than Births: Subnational Natural Decrease in Europe and the United States," *Population and Development Review* 41, no. 4, December 15, 2015.

45. Incidentally, the nations that will overtake the US and Western Europe economically are all the largest nations in the world. These are the nations that have not implemented abortion as the West has. Why will these nations become the world's largest economies? Because of basic economics: output = population x productivity. The populations of the dechristianized nations are largely going to overwhelm the productivity gains of the West.

46. Geoff Colvin, "Study: China Will Overtake the U.S. as World's Largest Economy Before 2030," *Fortune*, February 9, 2017, http://fortune.com/2017/02/09/study-china-will-overtake-the-u-s-as-worlds-largest-economy-before-2030.

47. For more detail on the important but often overlooked conflict between Shia Muslims (about 13 percent of the world's Muslims, mostly in Iran, Iraq, India, and Pakistan) and Sunni Muslims (about 87 percent of the world's Muslims, everywhere else, including Turkey, within ISIS, Saudi Arabia, and Indonesia), see these two helpful overviews: Joseph Liu, "Mapping the Global Muslim Population," *Pew Research Center's Religion & Public Life Project*, October 7, 2009, Pew Research Center, www.pewforum.org/2009/10/07/mapping-the-global-muslim-population; "The Sunni-Shia Divide," *Council on Foreign Relations*, February 2016, www.cfr.org/interactives/sunni-shia-divide#!/sunni-shia-divide.

48. The Catholic nations here (France, Italy, Spain) played different roles than the Protestant nations (UK, Germany, etc.), but we will use the term *Western civilization* to refer to that large scope of combined influence. While some Protestants may want to extricate Catholic influence from this, I don't think doing so is fair to history. The Reformation was a reforming of something, and it was the Catholics who gave the Protestants so many Scripture texts, universities, seminaries, monasteries, etc. Of course, France and Italy both experienced violent dechristianization in the eras of Napoleon and Mussolini.

49. I will build the case for this dramatic claim in future chapters and sections.

50. Peter Wood, "The Curriculum of Forgetting," National Association of Scholars, November 28, 2011, www.nas.org/articles/ the_curriculum_of_forgetting; Kevin Kiley, "Decline of 'Western Civ'?" *Inside Higher Ed*, May 19, 2011, www.insidehighered.com/ news/2011/05/19/national_association_of_scholars_report_finds_ no_mandatory_western_civilization_courses_at_top_universities; "The Case for a Western Civilization Requirement at Stanford," *Stanford Review*, February 20, 2016, https://stanfordreview.org/the -case-for-a-western-civilization-requirement-at-stanford.

Chapter 3: Pre-Tremors

1. Amy Graff, "Tips on Taking Kids to San Francisco's Gay Pride Parade," *SFGate*, June 25, 2016, www.sfgate.com/news/article/Is-the -Pride-Parade-appropriate-for-kids-Yes-8324556.php#photo-1879247.

2. William Love, "Folsom: A Perfect Place for Kids?" *East Bay Times*, September 29, 2005, www.eastbaytimes.com/2005/09/29/folsom-a -perfect-place-for-kids.

3. Love, "Folsom: A Perfect Place for Kids?" One online dictionary (yourdictionary.com) defines S&M as "sadism and masochism which is a practice of taking or causing abuse during sex. An example of S&M is one partner whipping another during intercourse."

4. Love, "Folsom: A Perfect Place for Kids?"

5. Love, "Folsom: A Perfect Place for Kids?"

6. Dianne de Guzman, "Nudists March in San Francisco Streets for Valentine's Parade," *SFGate*, February 12, 2017, www.sfgate.com/ bayarea/article/Nudists-march-on-San-Francisco-streets-as-part-of -10927342.php.

7. Sponsors of the San Francisco Pride parade are listed in the advertisement found at www.sfpride.org/sponsor.

8. Associated Press, "California Murder Convict Becomes First U.S. Inmate to Have State-Funded Sex Reassignment Surgery," *Los Angeles Times*, January 6, 2017, www.latimes.com/local/lanow/la-me -ln-inmate-sex-reassignment-20170106-story.html.

9. Associated Press, "California Murder Convict Becomes First U.S. Inmate to Have State-Funded Sex Reassignment Surgery."

10. Associated Press, "California Murder Convict Becomes First U.S. Inmate to Have State-Funded Sex Reassignment Surgery."

11. A related trait of the Post-Truth ideology is that certain classes of people are treated with special privilege, while other classes of people are treated with disdain because they are perceived as oppressors or bigots. The Post-Truth culture will frequently run roughshod over common sense and actual basic rights, as it attempts to secure rights and justice for the classes of people who deserve special privilege according to the Post-Truth moral scaffolding.

12. "Franklin D. Roosevelt: Joint Press Conference with Prime Minister Churchill at Casablanca, January 24, 1943," The American Presidency Project, www.presidency.ucsb.edu/ws/?pid=16408.

13. In chapter 5 I'll unpack the ideologies struggling for control of the world today. Interestingly, most of the growing ideologies in the world today aspire to conquest and subjugation.

14. This claim about the status of America's most educated people does not originate in my opinion; it originates in the observations and writings of Allan Bloom (see, for example, his *The Closing of the American Mind* [New York: Simon & Schuster, 1987]).

15. Revelation 7:9.

16. Matthew Yglesias, "We Should be Taxing Churches," *Slate*, August 22, 2013, www.slate.com/blogs/moneybox/2013/08/22/churches_should _be_taxed_then_everyone_can_speak.html.

17. Lee Moran, "Bill Maher Breaks Down Why All Religious Institutions Should Be Properly Taxed," *Huffington Post*, April 16, 2016, www.huffingtonpost.com/entry/bill-maher-church-tax -religion_us_5711dd19e4b0018f9cba30a7.

18. Mark Oppenheimer, "Now's the Time to End Tax Exemptions for Religious Institutions," *Time*, June 28, 2015, http://time.com /3939143/nows-the-time-to-end-tax-exemptions-for-religious -institutions.

19. Oppenheimer, "Now's the Time to End Tax Exemptions."

20. Oppenheimer, "Now's the Time to End Tax Exemptions."

Chapter 4: Forces 1 and 2: Humans Are Sinning and Satan Is Scheming

1. See Genesis 3.

2. Romans 3:23.

3. Francis Schaeffer is often cited as having described the condition of human beings as "glorious ruins."

4. See Jeremiah 17:9.

5. See Romans 1:21; Ephesians 4:18.

6. "The Declaration of Independence: In Congress, July 4, 1776," www .ushistory.org/declaration/document.

7. Jeremiah 17:9.

8. See John 8:44; 2 Corinthians 10:4–6; 11:3, 13–15; 2 Thessalonians 2:9–10; Revelation 12:9.

9. See Genesis 3:5.

10. See Ephesians 2:2.

11. John 10:10.

12. See 2 Corinthians 4:4.

13. See Revelation 20:10.

14. 1 Peter 5:8.

15. Jesus Christ is the one exception.

16. 2 Corinthians 4:4.

17. Ephesians 2:2.

18. See Revelation 12:17.

19. See Matthew 16:18.

20. Indeed, while we can feel far removed from it, such persecution is underway in Syria, Iraq, North Africa, Libya, Afghanistan, Pakistan, North Korea, and many other parts of the world.

Chapter 5: Force 3: Ideologies Are Warring

1. Ironically, as history shaping as ideologies are, most humans are consumed daily with their food, mating, and biological instincts— that is, with their physical comfort. Few people within a culture think about where its ideology will ultimately lead. For most, if the present way of things leads to a path of personal comfort, there is no reason to challenge or even assess the status quo.

2. Andrew Sorokowski, "Russian Christianity and the Revolution: What Happened?" *Christian History* 18, www.christianitytoday. com/history/issues/issue-18/russian-christianity-and-revolution-what -happened.html.

3. Within these post-Christian "Christian" schools, Stalin was heavily influenced by a young thinker who had recently imported Marx's German ideas into the post-Christian seminary. The aim of this was

"helping the dark masses see the light about social injustice and a purported all-purpose remedy" apart from Christianity; see Stephen Kotkin, *Stalin: Paradoxes of Power, 1872–1928*, vol. 1 (New York: Penguin, 2015), 30.

4. "Religion in Russia," Embassy of the Russian Federation to the UK, www.rusemb.org.uk/religion.

5. Cited in "The Russian Orthodox Church," in *Russia: A Country Study*, ed. Glenn E. Curtis (Washington: GPO for the Library of Congress, 1996), http://countrystudies.us/russia/38.htm.

6. Aleksandr Solzhenitsyn, "'Men Have Forgotten God': The Templeton Address," http://orthochristian.com/47643.html.

7. This ideology says that instead of believing in evil and sin and all that kind of thing, we should just accept everyone and not say anything negative about anyone. The only dangerous people are the people who do not accept everyone. If we all accept each other, life will be just fine. Such an ideology may play out innocently in a closed system. But the reality is that the system is not closed. The United States makes up less than 5 percent of the global population, and many people in the other 95 percent of the world hold to ideologies of conquest and subjugation.

8. Read the words of the Bolsheviks from 1917, and they also sounded noble and humane.

9. To support this claim, consider the standard of living in France during the dechristianization of the French Revolution (1789–1799). Consider the move toward post-Christian Germany, documented by most historians as occurring during the 1800s (and then leading to Nazi fascism). Consider also the dechristianization of Russia and its consequences under Stalin.

10. Mussolini was an ardent socialist in his early political life.

11. In contrast, Christianity claims to be a war for the soul of humanity, but it leads to actual peace and love. While the destination of Christianity is eternal peace in a place free from war, the journey leads us through spiritual battles.

12. "The Global Religious Landscape," Pew Research Center: Religion & Public Life, December 18, 2012, www.pewforum.org/2012/12/18/global-religious-landscape-exec.

13. "Global Religious Landscape." The majority are in China.

14. "Global Religious Landscape."

15. "Global Religious Landscape."

16. One footnote on these figures is that large percentages of people
    in Europe and the United States still self-identify as "Christian,"
    even though they are truly post-Christian and Post-Truth in their
    ideology. Exact figures are not available, but the generational shift
    is evident in recent Pew surveys of the American public. They
    reveal each younger generation of Americans to be aggressively less
    Christian, aggressively more atheistic/agnostic, and aggressively
    less traditional in moral values. Young Americans who openly say,
    "I am not a Christian," including the new group classified as the
    "nones" (those who cite no religious affiliation), fall into the "other"
    group in this listing. However, it should be noted that many who
    claim Christianity are religiously nominal and Post-Truth in their
    worldview. Similarly, communism and Islam have adherents with
    differing levels of commitment. In every ideology, most conveniently
    adopt the ideology of their homeland. And in every ideology, some
    percentages are true party loyalists, fundamentalists, or fanatics of
    the ideology.

17. This figure is simply the addition of the groups above, with the
    sum total being subtracted from the global population, which was
    about 7.4 billion at the time of this writing; see "U.S. and World
    Population Clock," U.S. Census Bureau, www.census.gov/popclock.

18. Some Post-Truth Americans and Europeans still self-identify as
    "Christian," but fewer bother to do so. A consistent Post-Truth
    ideology, of course, contradicts serious Christianity, which is a set of
    doctrines held together by truth claims.

19. Allan Bloom, *The Closing of the American Mind* (New York: Simon
    & Schuster, 1987), 26. Reprinted with the permission of Simon &
    Schuster, Inc. All rights reserved.

20. Bloom, *Closing of the American Mind*, 25–26. Reprinted with the
    permission of Simon & Schuster, Inc. All rights reserved.

21. Rodney Stark, *How the West Won: The Neglected Story of the Triumph
    of Modernity* (Wilmington, DE: Intercollegiate Studies Institute
    Books, 2014), 1.

22. Thomas Sowell, "Wimps versus Barbarians," *Creators*, May 21,
    2013, www.creators.com/read/thomas-sowell/05/13/wimps-versus
    -barbarians.

23. This figure varies by source. Stanford historian Norman Naimark

concludes that Stalin's policy-induced famines killed between 6 and 10 million Soviets during the decade of the 1930s alone; see Ilya Somin, "Did Joseph Stalin Commit Genocide?" *The Volokh Conspiracy*, November 23, 2010, http://volokh.com/2010/11/23/ did-joseph-stalin-commit-genocide.

24. Frank Dikötter, "Looking Back on the Great Leap Forward," *History Today* 66, no. 8, August 8, 2016, www.historytoday.com/ frank-dik%C3%B6tter/looking-back-great-leap-forward.

25. It is no coincidence that each of these movements controlled information, and each had a definitive book encapsulating its core ideas, as does Islam and Christianity. Muscular ideas (whether evil, noble, or benign) travel well in written form.

26. See the 2017 protests against free speech at Berkeley as one example.

27. "Oxford Dictionaries Word of the Year 2016 Is . . . Post-Truth," *Oxford Dictionaries*, November 16, 2016, www.oxforddictionaries. com/press/news/2016/12/11/WOTY-16.

28. This has been true within the United States and the West during the last five hundred years.

29. Ironically, in my anecdotal experience, it seems most Americans are convinced that *Post-Truth* applies to other Americans but not to them.

30. Thomas Sowell, *Intellectuals and Society* (New York: Basic, 2010), 146.

31. Thomas Sowell, *Inside American Education: The Decline, The Deception, The Dogmas* (New York: Free Press, 1993), 4, emphasis original.

32. Bloom describes what I call here "Post-Truth" and "Truth-Based" without using the same terms coined for this book.

33. Bloom, *Closing of the American Mind*, 25–26. Reprinted with the permission of Simon & Schuster, Inc. All rights reserved.

34. Bloom, *Closing of the American Mind*, 26. Reprinted with the permission of Simon & Schuster, Inc. All rights reserved.

35. Bloom, *Closing of the American Mind*, 27. Reprinted with the permission of Simon & Schuster, Inc. All rights reserved.

36. George M. Marsden, *The Soul of the American University: From Protestant Establishment to Established Nonbelief* (New York: Oxford University Press, 1994).

37. Barna Group, "The End of Absolutes: America's New Moral Code," *Research Releases in Culture and Media*, May 25, 2016, www.barna .com/research/the-end-of-absolutes-americas-new-moral-code.

38. Barna Group, "The End of Absolutes."
39. Barna Group, "The End of Absolutes."
40. I highly recommend all of Kinnaman's books, including a book that sorts through this research in depth: David Kinnaman and Gabe Lyons, *Good Faith: Being a Christian When Society Thinks You're Irrelevant and Extreme* (Grand Rapids: Baker, 2016). This book is referenced in the Barna Group's "The End of Absolutes" report.
41. Anjem Choudary, "People Know the Consequences: Opposing View," *USA Today*, January 7, 2015, www.usatoday.com/story/opinion/2015/01/07/islam-allah-muslims-shariah-anjem-choudary-editorials-debates/21417461.
42. Choudary, "People Know the Consequences."
43. Richard Engel et al., "Manchester Bomb Suspect Said to Have Had Ties to al Qaeda, Terrorism Training Abroad," *NBCNews.com*, May 23, 2017, www.nbcnews.com/storyline/manchester-concert-explosion/manchester-bomb-suspect-said-have-had-ties-al-qaeda-terrorism-n763691.
44. Michele Gorman, "These European Countries Are in States of Emergency," *Newsweek*, May 23, 2017, www.newsweek.com/these-european-countries-are-state-emergency-614186.
45. Again, I'm coining this term for this commentary. These traits are my best attempt to describe how the Post-Truth ideology exhibits itself commonly.
46. Katie Mettler, "Portland Rose Parade Canceled after 'Antifascists' Threaten GOP Marchers," *Washington Post*, April 27, 2017, www.washingtonpost.com/news/morning-mix/wp/2017/04/27/portland-rose-parade-canceled-after-antifascists-threaten-gop-marchers/?utm_term=.cd187c44ee11.
47. This is a reporting of my own anecdotal experience.
48. I document two specific examples in my *The Great Evangelical Recession* (Grand Rapids: Baker, 2013), 37–61.
49. For more on this, see the chapter titled "Bleeding" in my *The Great Evangelical Recession*, 97–108.
50. Alan Noble, "Keeping Faith Without Hurting LGBT Students," *The Atlantic*, August 15, 2016, www.theatlantic.com/politics/archive/2016/08/christian-colleges-lgbt/495815/; Patrick McGreevy, "Faith-based Colleges Say Anti-discrimination Bill Would Infringe on Their Religious Freedom," *Los Angeles Times*, June 22,

2016, www.latimes.com/politics/la-pol-sac-religious-freedom-bill-20160622-snap-story.html.

51. See Psalm 119:105; see also Matthew 5:14–16.

52. See Rodney Stark, *For the Glory of God: How Monotheism Led to Reformations, Science, Witch-hunts, and the End of Slavery* (Princeton, NJ: Princeton University Press, 2004), 121–99.

53. In today's climate, I must clarify that the economic and human progress from these regions was not a result of any ethnic or national superiority. It was not the result of race or nationalism. Quite to the contrary, these gains were the result of ideology and thinking, and these gains can be gained by any people, nation, or race who willingly adopt the underlying ideology.

54. Max Roser and Esteban Ortiz-Ospina, "Literacy," https://ourworldindata.org/literacy/.

55. See Peter Easton, "Sustaining Literacy in Africa: Developing a Literate Environment," *Norrag*, October 6, 2014, www.norrag.org/sustaining-literacy-in-africa-developing-a-literate-environment; Martyn Lyons, *Books: A Living History*, 2nd ed. (Los Angeles: Getty Museum, 2011), 97.

56. See Max Roser and Esteban Ortiz-Ospina, "Literacy," https://our worldindata.org/literacy.

57. See Max Roser, "Life Expectancy," https://ourworldindata.org/life-expectancy/; see also James C. Riley, *Rising Life Expectancy: A Global History* (Cambridge: Cambridge University Press, 2001).

58. Nicholas Kristof, "A Little Respect for Dr. Foster," *New York Times*, March 29, 2015, www.nytimes.com/2015/03/29/opinion/sunday/nicholas-kristof-a-little-respect-for-dr-foster.html.

59. See Marsden, *Soul of the American University*.

60. Nicholas Kristof, "Evangelicals Without Blowhards," *New York Times*, July 30, 2011, www.nytimes.com/2011/07/31/opinion/sunday/kristof-evangelicals-without-blowhards.html.

61. Mary Pat Clark, "Little Change in Public's Response to 'Capitalism,' 'Socialism'," Pew Research Center, December 28, 2011, www.people-press.org/2011/12/28/little-change-in-publics-response-to-capitalism-socialism/?src=prc-number. In a 2016 Harvard survey of eighteen- to twenty-nine-year-olds, a majority of young Americans did not support capitalism, but more supported socialism; see Max Ehrenfreund, "A Majority of Millennials Now Reject Capitalism,

Poll Shows," *Washington Post*, April 26, 2016, www.washingtonpost .com/news/wonk/wp/2016/04/26/a-majority-of-millennials-now -reject-capitalism-poll-shows/?utm_term=.f285ef98e805.

62. Clark, "Little Change in Public's Response."

63. Anatoly Kurmanaev, "Many Poor Venezuelans Are Too Hungry to Join Antigovernment Protests," *Wall Street Journal*, April 20, 2017, www .wsj.com/articles/many-poor-venezuelans-are-too-hungry-to-join-anti government-protests-1492680607; Alejandro Cegarra, "Caracas by Day Torments and by Night Terrifies," *Washington Post*, January 9, 2017, www.washingtonpost.com/news/in-sight/wp/2017/01/09/caracas -by-day-torments-and-by-night-terrifies; Matt O'Brien, "Venezuela Is on the Brink of a Complete Economic Collapse," *Washington Post*, January 29, 2016, www.washingtonpost.com/news/wonk/wp/2016/ 01/29/venezuela-is-on-the-brink-of-a-complete-collapse/?utm_term= .e867f3adb907; Nick Miroff, "Venezuela Seizes a General Motors Plant amid Anti-Government Protests," *Washington Post*, April 20, 2017, www.washingtonpost.com/world/venezuela-seizes-a-gm-plant -amid-antigovernment-protests/2017/04/20/e58a229c-25c7-11e7 -928e-3624539060e8_story.html; "Venezuelans Struggling in U.S. as Their Country Implodes," *CBS Miami*, April 23, 2017, http://miami .cbslocal.com/2017/04/23/venezuelans-struggling-country-implodes.

64. Thomas Sowell, "The Lure of Socialism," *Townhall*, February 17, 2016, https://townhall.com/columnists/thomassowell/2016/02/17/ the-lure-of-socialism-n2120485.

65. Barbara Rangel, "The Infamous Firing Squads," *Real Cuba*, November 26, 2016, www.therealcuba.com/?page_id=55.

66. Che Guevara, "Speech Delivered at the Second Economic Seminar of Afro-Asian Solidarity," February 24, 1965, www.marxists.org/ archive/guevara/1965/02/24.htm, emphasis added.

67. Clark, "Little Change in Public's Response."

68. Richard Fry, "Millennials Match Baby Boomers as Largest Generation in U.S. Electorate, but Will They Vote?" Pew Research Center, May 16, 2016, www.pewresearch.org/fact-tank/2016/05/16/ millennials-match-baby-boomers-as-largest-generation-in-u-s -electorate-but-will-they-vote.

69. Sowell, "Lure of Socialism."

70. Roberto Stefan Foa and Yascha Mounk, "The Danger of Deconsoli- dation: The Democratic Disconnect," *Journal of Democracy* 27, no. 3

(July 2016): 7–8. © 2016 National Endowment for Democracy and Johns Hopkins University Press. Reprinted with permission of Johns Hopkins University Press.

71. Foa and Mounk, "Danger of Deconsolidation," 17.

72. Si Yang, "Poll Finds Young Americans More Open to Socialist Ideas," *Voice of America*, October 23, 2016, www.voanews.com/a/ young-americans-seen-less-opposed-to-socialist-ideas/3562681.html.

73. Aaron Blake, "More Young People Voted for Bernie Sanders than Trump and Clinton Combined—by a Lot," *Washington Post*, June 20, 2016, www.washingtonpost.com/news/the-fix/wp/2016/ 06/20/more-young-people-voted-for-bernie-sanders-than-trump-and -clinton-combined-by-a-lot.

74. Kei Kawashima-Ginsberg et al., "2016 Election: Donald Trump and Young Voters," June 2016, Center for Information & Research on Civil Learning & Engagement, Tufts University, p. 4, https:// civicyouth.org/wp-content/uploads/2016/06/Trump-and-Youth -Vote.pdf.

75. Chart re-created in black-and-white from original color chart. Used with permission. Kawashima-Ginsberg et al., "2016 Election: Donald Trump and Young Voters," June 2016, p. 4, https://civic youth.org/wp-content/uploads/2016/06/Trump-and-Youth-Vote.pdf.

76. Fry, "Millennials Match Baby Boomers."

77. See "Islamophobia," "Opposing Fascism in the Media," "Prayer Facilities for Evenings and Weekends," and "Why Is My Curriculum White?" City Students' Union, November 2016, www.citystudents .co.uk/student-voice/unionmeetings/annualgeneralmeeting2016/.

78. Madison Park and Kyung Lah, "Berkeley Protests of Yiannopoulos Caused $100,000 in Damage," *CNN*, February 2, 2017, www.cnn .com/2017/02/01/us/milo-yiannopoulos-berkeley.

79. Thomas Fuller, "Berkeley Cancels Ann Coulter Speech over Safety Fears," *New York Times*, April 19, 2017, www.nytimes.com/2017/ 04/19/us/berkeley-ann-coulter-speech-canceled.html.

80. As the sea changes, some Americans, having been raised within this shifting mosaic, hold to a mixture of parts from the two competing ideologies without holding exclusively to either side.

81. See 2 Corinthians 4:4; 10:4; Ephesians 2:2; 6:12, among others.

82. John 14:6.

83. John 18:37.

84. Revelation 12:7, 9–11, emphasis added.
85. Ephesians 6:12 ESV.
86. 2 Corinthians 10:4–5 ESV, emphasis added.
87. See Marsden, *Soul of the American University*, 87.
88. Of course, the idea that ideas don't matter is in itself an idea that leads to death and bondage rather than life and freedom.
89. While many who hold the Post-Truth ideology do not realize it, even the Post-Truth ideology claims (indirectly) to be superior to other ideologies—particularly, Post-Truth claims that it is superior to the Christian or Truth-Based ideology. But as Allan Bloom describes well, today's academic environment refuses to wrestle with the obvious contradiction and inconsistency of such a position. To do so would require handling facts.

Chapter 6: Force 4: Western Civilization Is Unraveling

1. I document the overwhelmingly Christian foundings of each Ivy university in my forthcoming book *Jesus Skeptic*. The evidence is irrefutable and available to anyone who honestly seeks it out, for example, in Yale's founding charter, Harvard's founders, and so forth; see George M. Marsden, *The Soul of the American University: From Protestant Establishment to Established Nonbelief* (Oxford: Oxford University Press, 1994).
2. In such a scenario, one who is aware of basic, evidentiary facts of history might ask who the "ignorant" party actually is, but that is not my point here.
3. Joshua 24:13.
4. Abraham Lincoln, "The Perpetuation of Our Political Institutions: Address Before the Young Men's Lyceum of Springfield, Illinois, January 27, 1838," www.abrahamlincolnonline.org/lincoln/speeches/lyceum.htm.
5. This claim of fact can be measured and tested, as sociologist Rodney Stark has done and as my forthcoming book *Jesus Skeptic* does. I recommend all of Rodney Stark's works. Chief among them are his *How the West Won: The Neglected Story of the Triumph of Modernity* (Wilmington, DE: Intercollegiate Studies Institute Books, 2014).
6. My book *The Great Evangelical Recession* compiled research about the declining influence of Christianity in the US. In the introduction, I wrote, "I hope I'm wrong about all of this." Sadly, national events

following that book's publication in 2013 have proven its forecast accurate. Now, regarding this present book's broader assessment of Western civilization, I again write of this research and its conclusions: *I hope I'm wrong about all of this.* I hope that I look back in twenty-five years from a nation that is cohesive, comfortable, and prosperous and conclude that I was wrong. For more on this, see the chapter titled "Bleeding" in *The Great Evangelical Recession* (Grand Rapids: Baker, 2013).

7. See Elijah Morgan, *The Economic Pendulum: A Disastrous Global Swing* (Chambersburg, PA: eGenCo, 2014).

8. Allan Bloom, *The Closing of the American Mind* (New York: Simon & Schuster, 1987), 239. Reprinted with the permission of Simon & Schuster, Inc. All rights reserved.

9. Davide Castelvecchi, "Dark Matter Mapped at Cosmic Scale" *Nature*, April 13, 2015, www.nature.com/news/dark-matter-mapped -at-cosmic-scale-1.17311.

10. In addition to the force of gravity and perhaps other forces we do not yet fully understand.

11. Eric Hand, "Cameras to Focus on Dark Energy," *Nature*, September 12, 2012, www.nature.com/news/cameras-to-focus-on-dark-energy -1.11391. This discovery reminds me of Colossians 1:17, where Paul speaks of Jesus Christ: "In him all things hold together."

12. Castelvecchi, "Dark Matter Mapped at Cosmic Scale."

13. McCloskey's entire *Bourgeois* trilogy expands on this concept; see Deirdre N. McCloskey, *Bourgeois Equality: How Ideas, Not Capital or Institutions, Enriched the World* (Chicago: University of Chicago Press, 2016). A full list of McCloskey's work is available at www .deirdremccloskey.com/books.

14. McCloskey, *Bourgeois Equality*, xii.

15. Vishal Mangalwadi, in the foreword in Morgan, *Economic Pendulum*, 13.

16. See George M. Marsden, *The Soul of the American University: From Protestant Establishment to Established Nonbelief* (Oxford: Oxford University Press, 1994).

17. This is not my claim, but that of Allan Bloom. In his *The Closing of the American Mind*, see the chapters titled "The German Connection" and "The Nietzscheanization of the Left or Vice Versa."

18. Bloom, *Closing of the American Mind*, 147. Reprinted with the permission of Simon & Schuster, Inc. All rights reserved.

19. Bloom, *Closing of the American Mind*, 141. Reprinted with the permission of Simon & Schuster, Inc. All rights reserved.

20. Gallup, Inc., "Religion," www.gallup.com/poll/1690/religion.aspx.

21. Bloom, *Closing of the American Mind*, 56–58, emphasis added. Reprinted with the permission of Simon & Schuster, Inc. All rights reserved.

22. Francis A. Schaeffer, *How Should We Then Live? The Rise and Decline of Western Thought and Culture*, 50th anniv. ed. (Wheaton, IL: Crossway, 2005), 105, 110, 116, 128, 204, 217, 223, 252–53.

23. Francis A. Schaeffer, *The Great Evangelical Disaster* (Wheaton, IL: Crossway, 1984).

24. American Psychological Association, "Recent Generations Focus More on Fame, Money Than Giving Back," March 15, 2012, www.apa.org/news/press/releases/2012/03/fame-giving.aspx; see Jean M. Twenge, W. Keith Campbell, and Elise C. Freeman, "Generational Differences in Young Adults' Life Goals, Concern for Others, and Civic Orientation, 1966–2009," *Journal of Personality and Social Psychology* 102, no. 5, March 15, 2012, www.apa.org/pubs/journals/releases/psp-102-5-1045.pdf.

25. Megan McArdle, "Millennials Totally Not into Meaning, or Any of That Other Hippie Junk," March 16, 2012, www.theatlantic.com/business/archive/2012/03/millennials-totally-not-into-meaning-or-any-of-that-other-hippie-junk/254583.

26. Peter Y. Hong, "Money Top Goal of College Freshmen," *Los Angeles Times*, January 26, 2004, http://articles.latimes.com/2004/jan/26/local/me-survey26.

27. Jean M. Twenge and Joshua D. Foster, "Birth Cohort Increases in Narcissistic Personality Traits Among American College Students, 1982–2009," *Social Psychological and Personality Science* 1, no. 1, January 2010, http://journals.sagepub.com/doi/abs/10.1177/1948550609355719?journalCode=sppa.

28. William Kremer, "Does Confidence Really Breed Success?" *BBC News*, January 4, 2013, www.bbc.com/news/magazine-20756247.

29. Quoted in Kremer, "Does Confidence Really Breed Success?"

30. See Twenge, Campbell, and Freeman, "Generational Differences in Young Adults' Life Goals."

31. Os Guinness, *A Free People's Suicide: Sustainable Freedom and the American Future* (Downers Grove, IL: InterVarsity, 2012), 29.

32. Jean M. Twenge et al., "Generational and Time Period Differences in American Adolescents' Religious Orientation, 1966–2014," *PLoS One* 10, no. 5, May 11, 2015, www.ncbi.nlm.nih.gov/pmc/articles/PMC4427319.

33. Jean M. Twenge et al., "Generational and Time Period Differences."

34. The percentage of Americans who identify as Christian continues to decline every year, as groups like Pew continue to find. Some hopeful observers opine that this is merely Americans' being comfortable telling the truth and admitting they no longer have to "pretend" to be Christian. These optimists argue that the number of actual practicing committed Christians is not decreasing. While that *may* be true in some contexts, it is important to note that this optimistic explanation is not true or accurate regarding the data I've cited above—because that data is the percentage of each generation who are active in Christian activities such as prayer and Bible reading; that figure is decreasing, not merely those who self-identify as Christian.

35. I document this trend in depth in chapters 1, 5, and 6 of my book *The Great Evangelical Recession*.

36. Isayavech (Aleksandr) Solzhenitsyn, "I Am a Critic of the Weakening of the West," BBC Interview, March 1, 1976, in *The West's Betrayal of Civilisation* (Flesherton, Ontario: Canadian League of Rights, 1978), https://alor.org/Library/Solzhenitsyn%20I%20-%20Wests%20Betrayal%20of%20Civilisation.htm.

37. Solzhenitsyn, "All of Us Are Standing on the Brink of a Great Historical Cataclysm," BBC Address, March 26, 1976, in *The West's Betrayal of Civilisation*, https://alor.org/Library/Solzhenitsyn%20I%20-%20Wests%20Betrayal%20of%20Civilisation.htm.

38. Geoffrey Barlow, ed., *Vintage Muggeridge: Religion and Society* (Grand Rapids: Eerdmans, 1985), 104.

39. See Conway Center for Family Business, "Family Business Facts," www.familybusinesscenter.com/resources/family-business-facts; for more on this, visit the Family Business Alliance website at www.fbagr.org.

40. Roberto Stefan Foa and Yascha Mounk, "The Danger of Deconsolidation: The Democratic Disconnect," *Journal of Democracy* 27, no. 3 (July 2016): 7–8. © 2016 National Endowment for Democracy and Johns Hopkins University Press. Reprinted with permission of Johns Hopkins University Press.

41. Foa and Mounk, "Danger of Deconsolidation," 7.

42. Foa and Mounk, "Danger of Deconsolidation," 7–8.

43. I recommend *Good Faith* (Grand Rapids: Baker, 2016) and *UnChristian* (Grand Rapids: Baker, 2012) by David Kinnaman and Gabe Lyons, as well as my book *The Great Evangelical Recession*.

44. See Shiva Maniam and Samantha Smith, "A Wider Partisan and Ideological Gap between Younger, Older Generations," Pew Research Center, March 20, 2017, www.pewresearch.org/fact-tank/2017/03/20/a-wider-partisan-and-ideological-gap-between-younger-older-generations; "The Future of World Religions: Population Growth Projections, 2010–2050," April 2, 2015, Pew Research Center, www.pewforum.org/2015/04/02/religious-projections-2010-2050; Richard Fry, "This May Be the Last Presidential Election Dominated by Boomers and Prior Generations," August 29, 2016, Pew Research Center, www.pewresearch.org/fact-tank/2016/08/29/this-may-be-the-last-presidential-election-dominated-by-boomers-and-prior-generations.

45. Morley Winograd and Michael Hais, "How Millennials Could Upend Wall Street and Corporate America," May 2014, Governance Studies at Brookings, www.brookings.edu/wp-content/uploads/2016/06/Brookings_Winogradfinal.pdf.

46. See Paul Ratner, "How Many People Have Ever Lived on Planet Earth?" Big Think, http://bigthink.com/paul-ratner/how-many-people-have-ever-lived-on-planet-earth.

47. See Rodney Stark, *How the West Won: The Neglected Story of the Triumph of Modernity* (Wilmington, DE: Intercollegiate Studies Institute Books, 2014), chapters 1–3.

48. In my forthcoming book *Jesus Skeptic*, I answer these questions for a new generation by compiling hundreds of photos and other visual primary evidence to demonstrate that it was Christians in Christianized societies who planted these trees; shoot an email to Friend@IAmStrongBook.com to get a free preview sample of *Jesus Skeptic*.

49. See Bloom, *Closing of the American Mind*, 54, 56–58, 60, 62, 65–66, 252, 374–75.

50. Max Fennell-Chametzky, "At Co-op, Scholar Says Christian Fundamentalism More Dangerous than Islamic Terrorism," *Chicago Maroon*, October 20, 2016, www.chicagomaroon.com/article/2016/10/21/co-op-scholar-says-christian-fundamentalism-danger/.

51. Mark A. Noll, *Turning Points: Decisive Moments in the History of Christianity* (Grand Rapids: Baker Academic, 2012), 240.
52. Alexis de Tocqueville, *The Old Regime and the French Revolution*, trans. Stuart Gilbert (1856; repr., Garden City, NY: Doubleday, 1955), 149.
53. Stark, *How the West Won*, 159.
54. Bloom, *Closing of the American Mind*, 239–40. Reprinted by permission of Simon & Schuster, Inc. All rights reserved.
55. See George M. Marsden, *The Soul of the American University: From Protestant Establishment to Established Nonbelief* (Oxford: Oxford University Press, 1994).
56. Francis Schaeffer, *The Great Evangelical Disaster* (Wheaton, IL: Crossway, 1984), 43–44.

Chapter 7: Force 5: Christ and His People Are Prevailing

1. James 1:17.
2. See Revelation 3:14–22; 2:8–11.
3. See Matthew 24.
4. John 16:33.
5. See Philippians 2:10–11.
6. See Philippians 2.
7. They could never touch a Christian's soul, as Jesus once said: "Do not be afraid of those who kill the body but cannot kill the soul. Rather, be afraid of the One who can destroy both soul and body in hell" (Matthew 10:28).
8. Matthew 11:28.
9. Acts 1:8.
10. John 19:30.
11. See Romans 8:17; Philippians 3:10; 1 Peter 4:13.
12. Matthew 16:18 ESV, emphasis added.
13. For example, Saint Maurice (also known as Morris) of Switzerland.
14. Hebrews 12:28.
15. Philippians 3:20.

Chapter 8: What Can and Cannot Happen

1. See "Kindergarten in Palestine Teaches Children How to Kidnap and Kill Jews," YouTube, December 8, 2016, www.youtube.com/watch?v=_sVJE-BLxTU; Mark Banham, "Palestinian Children Taught 'How to Stab a Jew' Says Israeli UN Ambassador Danon,"

International Business Times, October 17, 2015, www.ibtimes
.co.uk/palestinian-children-taught-how-stab-jew-says-israeli-un
--ambassador-danon-1524470; Ali Waked, "Gaza Kids 'Training to
Kill Jews,'" *Ynetnews*, August 31, 2008, www.ynetnews.com/articles/
0,7340,L-3589842,00.html; Steven Emerson, "Palestinian Children
Kill Israelis in Hamas 'Play' (Video)," April 28, 2016, *Algemeiner*,
www.algemeiner.com/2016/04/28/palestinian-children-kill
-israelis-in-hamas-play-video; Abigail R. Esman, "Guest Column:
Palestinian TV Teaches Kids The Way to 'Jihad Street," *Investigative
Project on Terrorism*, May 20, 2014, www.investigativeproject.
org/4394/guest-column-palestinian-tv-teaches-kids-the-way#.

2. See Russell Goldman, "Chinese Police Dynamite Christian
Megachurch," *New York Times*, January 12, 2018, www.nytimes
.com/2018/01/12/world/asia/china-church-dynamite.html.

3. Graham Allison, *Destined for War: Can America and China Escape
Thucydides's Trap?* (New York: Houghton Mifflin Harcourt, 2017).

4. See John 6:66–70.

5. Titus 2:13.

6. These conclusions are based on a Western society that will continue
its present ideological trajectory. We can and should pray for a
spiritual revival that will change the trajectory for the better.

7. Geoff Colvin, "China Will Overtake the U.S. as World's Largest
Economy before 2030," *Fortune*, February 9, 2017, http://fortune.
com/2017/02/09/study-china-will-overtake-the-u-s-as-worlds-largest
-economy-before-2030. One expert estimates that China's economy
could be three times the size of the US economy by 2040; see Allison,
Destined for War, 216.

Chapter 10: What We Can and Cannot Control

1. Henry Cloud, *Necessary Endings: The Employees, Businesses, and
Relationships That All of Us Have to Give Up in Order to Move
Forward* (New York: HarperBusiness, 2010), 73–90.

2. Cloud, *Necessary Endings*, 56, emphasis original.

3. Cloud, *Necessary Endings*, 56, emphasis original.

Chapter 12: Rooted to Scripture in a Post-Truth Era

1. See John 1:1.

2. John 18:37.

3. 2 Corinthians 10:4–5 ESV.

4. 2 Timothy 3:1–5, emphasis added.

Chapter 13: Training Our Young in a Post-Knowledge Era

1. See John S. Dickerson, *The Great Evangelical Recession* (Grand Rapids: Baker, 2013), 97–108.

2. I attempt to do this in my forthcoming book, *Jesus Skeptic*. Sign up to receive it by sending an email to Friend@IAmStrongBook.com.

3. Proverbs 30:5.

4. Luke 12:48.

5. 2 Timothy 2:2.

6. Philippians 1:23.

Chapter 14: Known for Doing Good in a Post-Church Era

1. John S. Dickerson, *The Great Evangelical Recession* (Grand Rapids: Baker, 2013), 137–39. Used by permission.

Chapter 15: Dignifying All People in a Post-Human Era

1. Matthew 22:40.

2. John 1:14.

3. See Galatians 5:22–23 ESV.

4. Luke 23:34.

Chapter 16: Ambassadors in a Post-Christian Era

1. Romans 1:21.

2. 1 Peter 2:11.

3. Philippians 3:20.

4. See Ephesians 2:10.

5. 1 John 4:18.

6. James 1:19.

Chapter 17: Loving Our Persecutors in a Post-Decency Era

1. Matthew 5:44.

2. John 3:16.

3. Ephesians 5:18; Exodus 20:17.

4. See Acts 22:22–23:11.

5. Galatians 5:22–23 ESV.

6. Matthew 5:44.

7. Luke 10:27.
8. See Romans 9:3.
9. Corrie ten Boom, *The Hiding Place*, 35th anniv. ed. (1971; repr. Grand Rapids: Chosen, 2005). I recommend reading or listening to everything Corrie ten Boom wrote. She experienced more severe persecution than we likely ever will, and she proves that the Christlike view can be held supernaturally during the most evil and inhumane of persecutions against Christians.
10. See Matthew 10:16.

Chapter 19: Invincible in a Post-Liberty Era

1. Matthew 10:28.
2. Esther 4:16.
3. See Genesis 50:20.
4. See Luke 2:49; John 4:34; 5:30, 36; 6:38; 8:29; 17:4; 19:28, 30.
5. John 4:34.
6. John 17:4.
7. 2 Timothy 4:7–8.
8. Matthew 6:10.
9. Corrie ten Boom, *Amazing Love* (1953; repr., Fort Washington, PA: CLC Publications, 2018), 11.
10. See Nehemiah 8:10.
11. John 10:18.
12. John 19:11.

Chapter 20: Fearless in a Post-Peace Era

1. See Revelation 20:10.
2. 2 Timothy 1:7 ESV.
3. 1 John 4:18.
4. Isaiah 8:12.
5. Isaiah 8:13–14.
6. See the book of Judges.
7. Matthew 24:37.
8. See Revelation 19:12–15.
9. See Ezekiel 38; Daniel 12; Revelation 20.
10. Matthew 24:6–8.
11. 2 Peter 2:9.
12. Matthew 25:40.

Conclusion

1. Franklin D. Roosevelt, "Fireside Chat," December 29, 1940, online by Gerhard Peters and John T. Woolley, The American Presidency Project, www.presidency.ucsb.edu/ws/index.php?pid=15917.
2. Roosevelt, "Fireside Chat," December 29, 1940.
3. Romans 13:12.
4. Matthew 12:18, 20–21.

I Am Strong

Finding God's Peace and Strength in Life's Darkest Moments

John S. Dickerson

For many, the Christian life looks like this: I call out to God. My problems get worse. I suffer and wait. **Nothing changes.** Author John S. Dickerson knows the feeling. His own health problems drove him to examine the Bible's claim that "when I am weak, then I am strong." What he discovered compelled him to write this book—to give understanding, hope, and strength to the hurting.

In its chapters, *I Am Strong* equips you to

- understand how a loving God will resolve your pain
- understand why your suffering does not mean God is punishing you
- overcome life's circumstances as Jesus and Paul did
- discover the life-changing power of God's strength in your weakness

I Am Strong is a gift to anyone who is hurting. It's a word of encouragement in the grief of unexpected tragedy, in the daily pain of chronic illness, in the lifelong struggle of making your way through the sharp edges of this broken world. Much more, *I Am Strong* offers daily practices and a lifelong vision for an unshakable life of meaning and peace.

Available in stores and online!